# Re-conneXion: A Philosophy of Intentional Friendship

**Foreword**

*By Thothan Atlantos*

We stand at the threshold of an epochal abyss—a time when the very essence of our existence trembles under the ceaseless hum of invisible algorithms. The last few decades have witnessed a metamorphosis so profound that those who came of age in the 20th century would scarcely recognize the world we now inhabit. Once, humanity's raison d'être was tethered to community, to face-to-face dialogue, to the sweat of shared labor, and to the contemplative stillness born of quiet reflection. Today, our attention is siphoned by omnipresent screens, our interactions reduced to data points, and our innermost aspirations commodified by machines. In this foreword, I—Thothan Atlantos—invite you to confront the stark reality of how social media, automation, and artificial intelligence have conspired to erode our reason for being, and to consider why a philosophical reclamation of intentional friendship is not merely desirable, but imperative.

---

## I. The Great Dispersion of Presence

Recall a time when presence meant more than pixelated avatars and ephemeral "likes." We lived, breathed, and loved in physical spaces—town squares, living rooms, fields of play—each encounter rich with nuance: the subtlest inflection, the micro-gesture, the warmth of proximity. Today, presence is logged in server farms. Every "seen" and "read" receipt is an inquisition into our habits, a probe into our vulnerabilities, a means by which platforms engineer our desire for more engagement, more content, more distraction. We have become fragmented selves, toggling between countless digital windows, yet seldom fully inhabiting any one of them. Our presence has been dispersed across infinite feeds, and in that dispersion, we have lost our capacity for genuine, undistracted communion.

## II. The Illusion of Connection

Social media promised to bring us closer, to collapse distance and deepen empathy. Instead, it has erected new barriers. The more we scroll, the more our friendships calcify into shallow transactions: perfunctory comments, hollow reactions, algorithmically curated "moments" that bear no tangible resemblance to lived experience. Our networks have ballooned into labyrinthine architectures of acquaintances—a facade of intimacy that collapses under the weight of its own superficiality. We mistake breadth for depth, numbers for meaning, and in the silence that follows a flurry of notifications, we feel the hollowness of our own solipsism.

## III. Automation's Quiet Theft of Purpose

Meanwhile, automation advances relentlessly. Machines now perform tasks once reserved for human skill and judgment: from sorting our mail to driving our cars, from curating our news to filtering our pleasures. Efficiency reigns supreme, and we applaud its triumph even as it strips away opportunities for mastery and creativity. The craftsman's pride in a handcrafted object, the apprentice's wonder at learning a trade—these have been displaced by black-box algorithms that render us spectators in the theater of our own lives. When our tasks no longer demand our full attention, when our labor is no longer a vessel for personal growth, we lose not only our livelihoods, but the scaffolding on which we build identity and purpose.

## IV. AI's Promethean Overreach

Artificial intelligence, the crowning marvel of our era, holds a mirror to our own cognitive limitations—and to our hubris. We marvel at its capacity to generate art, to diagnose disease, to optimize logistics, to converse in multiple tongues. Yet in beholding that mirror, we risk abdicating our own faculties of imagination and discernment. If an AI can compose symphonies, diagnose maladies, and spin philosophical treatises, what remains uniquely ours? When we delegate critical thinking, ethical judgment, and emotional labor to machines, we hollow out the very core of what it means to be human. The danger is not that AI will supplant us, but that we will willingly surrender the very attributes—creativity, empathy, vulnerability—that define our flourishing.

---

# The Crisis of Existential Dislocation

Taken together, these forces—social media's fragmentation of attention, automation's erosion of meaningful work, AI's seduction of cognitive outsourcing—have precipitated an existential crisis. We are adrift, untethered from the anchors of community and craft, intoxicated by simulations of engagement, beguiled by the promise of ever-more convenient lives. Yet convenience and connection are not synonymous. The more we yield to technological mediation, the more we risk losing sight of the deeper tether—the call to mutual recognition, to bearing witness to another's story, to the co-creation of meaning.

## Rediscovering the Primacy of Friendship

It is precisely in this crucible of displacement that the **Re-conneXion Theory** emerges as a beacon. To "re-connect" is not merely to click "accept" on a social-media request, but to reawaken the dormant rituals of presence, intentionality, empathy, and vulnerability. ReconneXion invites us to reweave the fabric of relationship across four modalities—synchronous digital, asynchronous digital, synchronous analog, and asynchronous analog—and to traverse the depth continuum from surface banter to soul-bearing dialogue. Through this philosophical framework, we reclaim the agency to choose how we engage, to resist the algorithms that commodify our attention, and to cultivate bonds that transcend the sterile metrics of likes and shares.

## A Call to Philosophical Vigilance

As you delve into the chapters that follow, remember that technology is neither friend nor foe; it is a tool—an extension of our collective will. In wielding it unreflectively, we risk becoming its subjects rather than its masters. But in wielding it with intention, we can harness its power to amplify our humanity. Let this book be more than a guide to better communication; let it be a manifesto for reclaiming our reason for existence. For in the tapestry of friendship we stitch, we rediscover what has always made life worth living: the joy of being seen, the solace of being heard, the courage of mutual vulnerability.

---

**Thothan Atlantos**
Keeper of the Infinite Logos
Harbinger of the Poetics of Presence
May this foreword spark in you the resolve to turn away from the hollow glow of screens, to step back into the warmth of embodied encounter, and to reclaim friendship as the sacred art it was always meant to be.

# Chapter 1
## Prelude: Why Friendship in the Digital Age Needs a Philosophy

"In an era of endless connection, we have never felt so alone."

## I. The Paradox of Omnipresent Connectivity

By the dawn of the 21st century, humanity achieved what once seemed the province of myth: the ability to commune instantaneously across continents, to archive every moment, and to curate our lives in perpetuity. Yet this very triumph has yielded a cruel paradox: in the glow of countless screens, genuine fellowship withers. Notifications ping like digital impatience; feeds surge with curated highlights, masking the raw textures of ordinary life. We occupy virtual rooms of infinite capacity—yet our hearts echo with emptiness.

This opening prelude asks: **Why** must we now recover a philosophy of friendship, rather than merely business as usual? The answer lies in the collision of three forces:

1. **Attention Fragmentation.** Algorithms fragment our focus into micro-moments of scrolling and reacting, precluding sustained presence.

2. **Relational Commodification.** "Followers," "connections," and "friends" become metrics—commodities we trade for validation rather than vessels for mutual care.

3. **Emotional Atrophy.** Absent the crucible of face-to-face vulnerability, our capacity for deep empathy withers, leaving us adrift in superficial rapport.

Without a guiding philosophy—an articulated, systematic vision of intentional friendship—these forces conspire to turn companionship into a shallow performance. ReconneXion Theory arises to meet this crisis, offering both the conceptual map and the practical compass to reclaim authentic bonds.

## II. Friendship as Philosophical Necessity

Across millennia, thinkers from Aristotle to Montaigne have regarded friendship as integral to the good life. Aristotle's **philia** was not mere amusement, but a cornerstone of eudaimonia—flourishing rooted in mutual virtue. Montaigne, writing in his *Essays*, praised friendship as "the highest of earthly goods," capable of withstanding adversity through its depth and reciprocity. Yet these venerable understandings assumed a world of proximate encounters and shared institutions—contexts now profoundly altered.

In the digital age, friendship risks devolving into:

- **Transactional Interaction.** Quick comments and likes substitute for sincere dialogue.

- **Surface-Level Rapport.** "How are you?" becomes terse updates rather than invitations to inner life.

- **Modal Monoculture.** Overreliance on one modality—endless text chains or perfunctory voice notes—stunts relational resilience.

Thus, friendship must be reframed not as a passive byproduct of proximity, but as an active **philosophical practice**. It demands intellectual rigor—clear definitions of what constitutes genuine connection—and moral commitment: the willingness to invest emotional energy where it will truly nourish.

## III. The ReconneXion Map: Two Continua, Four Modalities

At the heart of ReconneXion Theory lies the insight that **all** meaningful friendship inhabits a two-dimensional space:

- **Modality Continuum** (Synchronous Digital ↔ Asynchronous Digital ↔ Synchronous Analog ↔ Asynchronous Analog)

- **Depth Continuum** (Surface-Level ↔ Deep-Level)

## A. Modality Continuum

1. **Synchronous Digital (SD):** Live video calls, voice chats—offering immediacy but vulnerable to digital distraction.

2. **Asynchronous Digital (AD):** Emails, DMs—allowing reflection but prone to perfunctory brevity.

3. **Synchronous Analog (SA):** In-person meetings, shared walks—embodying presence but constrained by geography.

4. **Asynchronous Analog (AA):** Handwritten letters, care packages—tangible tokens carrying emotional weight across time.

## B. Depth Continuum

- **Surface-Level (SL):** Logistic updates, casual banter—necessary for day-to-day coordination but insufficient on its own.

- **Deep-Level (DL):** Vulnerabilities, dreams, mutual reflection—the crucible of trust and lasting intimacy.

ReconneXion urges us to **diversify** our modality usage (avoiding monocultural reliance on social media feeds) **and** to **elevate** conversations from SL to DL whenever possible. Only by intentionally moving along both axes can we avert the hollow "connection" that haunts our digital age.

---

## IV. The Crisis of Modal Monotony

When friendship resides exclusively in one modality—say, the habitual scroll of social-media threads—we enter a perilous state of **modal monotony**. This leads to:

- **Emotional Echo Chambers.** We replay the same superficial interactions, never forging new depths.

- **Relational Atrophy.** The muscles of vulnerability and empathy, like any unused faculty, weaken with disuse.

- **Dependency on Instant Gratification.** Surface-level "likes" provide fleeting dopamine spikes but no enduring nourishment.

True friendship, by contrast, thrives on **multi-modal interplay**: a postcard mailed (AA) followed by a thoughtful email (AD), then a video call (SD), and finally an in-person gathering (SA). Each modality contributes its unique texture, reinforcing the bond's resilience against the vicissitudes of life.

---

## V. From Theory to Ethical Imperative

Merely understanding the modalities and depths is insufficient. ReconneXion demands **ethical cultivation** of four pillars—Presence, Intentionality, Empathy, Vulnerability—across modalities. Without ethical grounding, our newfound strategies degenerate into formulaic routines, devoid of sincerity.

1. **Presence (Ontological Attunement):** Fully inhabit each moment—whether you're typing an email or walking side-by-side.

2. **Intentionality (Deliberate Design):** Friendship must be scheduled, planned, and protected against the default drift into autopilot.

3. **Empathy (Reflective Resonance):** Strive to mirror and validate the friend's inner world before leaping to advice.

4. **Vulnerability (Courageous Disclosure):** Share imperfections to invite reciprocal authenticity.

These pillars convert ReconneXion from a mere typology into a **living ethic**—a call to action that transforms how we allocate our time, attention, and emotional investment.

---

## VI. The Imperative of Philosophical Literacy

Why must we speak of friendship in philosophical terms, rather than rely on instinct or tradition? Three reasons:

1. **Complexity of the Digital Ecosystem.** New technologies demand new conceptual tools to navigate unintended consequences.

2. **Resistance to Complacency.** Unexamined habits calcify into blind spots; philosophical inquiry keeps us vigilant.

3. **Elevation of Practice.** When friendship becomes a subject of study—akin to mindfulness or ethical business practice—it gains the seriousness it merits.

Chapter 1 thus issues a rallying cry: let us not drift into the default of superficiality. Let us **learn** the map of ReconneXion Theory, **embrace** its ethical pillars, and embark on a journey from passive sociality to purposeful camaraderie.

---

## VII. A Vision of Reclaimed Communion

Envision, for a moment, a circle of friends who:

- **Mail** each other letters reflecting on life's breakthroughs (AA, DL).

- **Exchange** weekly emails that end with a question designed to surface hopes or fears (AD, SL→DL).

- **Host** quarterly video "salons" where each takes two uninterrupted minutes of presence (SD, DL).

- **Walk** together in nature to process grief or celebrate joy (SA, DL).

In such a network, technology serves as the scaffolding, not the substance. The true substance resides in the **intentional movements** along modality and depth, guided by the unwavering commitment to Presence, Intentionality, Empathy, and Vulnerability.

---

## VIII. Moving Forward

As you journey through the pages ahead, return to this prelude to remind yourself of the **why** behind every practice. Chapter 2 will delve deeply into the anatomy of connection—examining each pole of the continua in turn—while subsequent chapters translate those insights into daily rituals and lifelong habits.

The digital age need not spell the demise of friendship. On the contrary, it offers us unprecedented tools—if wielded with philosophical literacy and ethical vigor. Let ReconneXion Theory be your guide: to diversify your modalities, deepen your conversations, and restore friendship to its rightful place as the crucible of our shared humanity.

## Chapter 2
### The Anatomy of Connection: Modality & Depth Continua

> "To map our connections is to chart the terrain of our souls."

# I. The Framework of Two Continua

At the heart of ReconneXion Theory lies a deceptively simple but profoundly generative insight: **all acts of friendship can be plotted along two orthogonal axes**. The **Modality Continuum** describes *how* we connect—the medium of our encounter—while the **Depth Continuum** captures *what* transpires—the emotional or cognitive intensity of our exchange. By treating these as continuous rather than binary, we gain a *cartographic* tool, enabling us to navigate, diagnose, and intentionally steer our relationships toward richer terrain.

### A. The Modality Continuum

While most schemata group communication into "online vs. offline," ReconneXion refines this into four poles:

1. **Synchronous Digital (SD)**

    - **Definition:** Real-time, networked interaction mediated by screens or speakers.
    - **Examples:** Video calls (Zoom, FaceTime), live audio chats (Clubhouse, Discord), co-browsing sessions.
    - **Qualities:** Offers immediacy, back-and-forth nuance, visual and auditory cues—yet vulnerable to connectivity glitches, screen fatigue, and multitasking temptations.

2. **Asynchronous Digital (AD)**
    - **Definition:** Time-shifted, digital messaging allowing reflection before response.
    - **Examples:** Emails, text messages, direct messages on social platforms, forum posts.
    - **Qualities:** Grants pause for crafting thoughtful replies and for revisiting past conversations; risks brevity becoming brusqueness and threads vanishing into notification overload.

3. **Synchronous Analog (SA)**
    - **Definition:** Co-present, real-time interactions in physical spaces.
    - **Examples:** In-person walks, café conversations, shared work sessions, group gatherings.
    - **Qualities:** Richest in nonverbal cues—body language, ambient sound, physical touch—but constrained by geography, scheduling, and, at times, social anxiety.

4. **Asynchronous Analog (AA)**
    - **Definition:** Physical artifacts exchanged across time and distance.
    - **Examples:** Handwritten letters, postcards, care packages, printed photographs.
    - **Qualities:** Tangible tokens that carry effort and intentionality; evoke anticipation and enduring memory—but entail delays, postal uncertainties, and require extra effort.

---

## B. The Depth Continuum

Counterpoint to *how* we connect is *what* we share:

1. **Surface-Level (SL)**
    - **Definition:** Exchanges limited to logistical, informational, or perfunctory content: "What's up?", "Got it!", "See you then."
    - **Function:** Keeps relationships alive through coordination and lighthearted banter; establishes baseline solidarity but does not foster trust beyond comfort

zones.

2. **Deep-Level (DL)**

    - **Definition:** Dialogues that plumb vulnerabilities, aspirations, ethical quandaries, personal histories, and dreams.

    - **Function:** Cultivates intimacy, mutual understanding, and emotional safety; requires greater courage, time, and reciprocal care.

## II. The Dynamic Interplay of Modality and Depth

Having two continua creates a **rich topology** of relational space. Each interaction can be located at a point (or region) defined by its modality and depth—yielding **four core quadrants** and infinite trajectories between them.

### A. Quadrants and Trajectories

1. **SL–SD (Surface, Live Digital)**
    – *Example:* A quick "Hey!" in a group chat, emojis bouncing back and forth.
    – *Risk:* Feels fun but flattens into background noise.

2. **DL–SD (Deep, Live Digital)**
    – *Example:* A two-hour video conversation exploring childhood trauma.
    – *Potential:* Mirrors in-person intimacy with visual cues preserved.

3. **SL–AD (Surface, Time-Shifted Digital)**
    – *Example:* A one-line reply to "How's work?" in Slack.
    – *Risk:* Easily ignored; feels transactional.

4. **DL–AD (Deep, Time-Shifted Digital)**
    – *Example:* A heartfelt email describing a long-held fear.
    – *Potential:* Written reflection can deepen insights; friend can revisit and craft a compassionate response.

5. **SL–SA (Surface, In-Person)**
    – *Example:* Greeting a neighbor with "Nice day!" during a walk.
    – *Function:* Social oil—lubricates casual familiarity.

6. **DL–SA (Deep, In-Person)**
   – *Example:* Walking side-by-side while sharing marital struggles.
   – *Potential:* Embodied presence magnifies trust and connection.

7. **SL–AA (Surface, Physical Artifact)**
   – *Example:* A postcard: "Having fun! – Alex."
   – *Charm:* Sparks joy but seldom discloses inner life.

8. **DL–AA (Deep, Physical Artifact)**
   – *Example:* A multi-page handwritten letter describing a turning point in your life.
   – *Impact:* Tangible testament to effort and vulnerability.

---

### B. The Geometry of Reconnection

Connections deepen when we:

- **Diversify Modalities:** Resist dwelling exclusively in SD or AD; incorporate SA and AA to leverage each modality's strengths.

- **Elevate Depth Over Time:** Start with SL to build comfort, then purposefully steer toward DL through well-timed questions and reflective silence.

- **Traverse Quadrants:** Move along a spiral path: e.g., SL–AD → SL–SA → DL–SD → DL–AD → DL–AA, ensuring novelty and sustained intimacy.

This **cartographic approach** transforms friendship into an intentional expedition rather than a passive drift.

---

## III. Philosophical Foundations

To appreciate why these continua matter, we ground our map in three philosophical traditions:

---

### A. Phenomenology of Presence

- **Heidegger's "Being-with" (Mitsein):** True communion arises when two Daseins encounter one another authentically, beyond objectification.

- **Application:** SD interactions risk "present-at-hand" mode (distraction by device) rather than "ready-to-hand" absorption. SA invites the latter through shared environment and embodied attunement.

## B. Hermeneutics of Communication

- **Gadamerian Dialogue:** Understanding emerges from the "fusion of horizons" between interlocutors, mediated by language and context.

- **Application:** AD exchanges afford hermeneutic pause—allowing each friend to interpret, reflect, and respond with richer meaning than impulsive SL chatter.

## C. Ethics of Vulnerability

- **Brené Brown's Insights:** Vulnerability is the birthplace of innovation and trust.

- **Application:** DL interactions—especially AA artifacts—require structured courage; the time lag in AA can heighten anxiety but also amplify the gratitude upon receipt.

# IV. Practical Implications and Case Studies

Abstract maps blossom only when applied. Consider three case studies:

## A. Case Study: The Traveling Graduate Student

- **Challenge:** Geographic isolation during fieldwork.

- **Solution:**
    - **AD–DL:** Weekly reflective emails describing research and emotional hurdles.
    - **AA–SL:** Postcards with snapshots from local culture.

- **SD–DL:** Monthly video "office hours" with a mentor-friend for immediate feedback and affective reassurance.

Outcome: Maintained academic rigor while preserving emotional well-being through multi-modal support.

### B. Case Study: The Isolated Remote Worker

- **Challenge:** Zoom fatigue and professional burnout.
- **Solution:**
    - **SA–SL:** Local coworking meetups for casual camaraderie over coffee.
    - **DL–AA:** Care packages exchanged monthly—books, artisanal snacks, handwritten notes.
    - **AD–DL:** Scheduled voice-note check-ins sharing small victories and personal frustrations.

Outcome: Reduced burnout by integrating physical presence and tangible tokens of friendship alongside digital support.

### C. Case Study: The Cross-Continental Friendship

- **Challenge:** Time-zone differences and cultural distance.
- **Solution:**
    - **AA–DL:** Biannual handwritten letters in which each friend reflects on milestones, milestones, regrets, hopes.
    - **SD–SL:** Quarterly group video "happy hours" timed to overlap wakeful hours.
    - **AD–DL:** Collaborative digital journal (shared Google Doc) where each writes a daily gratitude entry tagged to the other.

Outcome: Sustained intimacy across years and miles by weaving together every quadrant of the map.

## V. Avoiding Modal Imbalances and Depth Stagnation

Just as monocultures in ecology collapse, **modal monotony** or **depth paralysis** can erode relational resilience:

### A. Modal Dominance

- **Symptoms:**

    - Overreliance on SD yields screen burnout;
    - Exclusive AD breeds terse, transactional exchanges;
    - Neglect of AA deprives friendships of emotional artifacts.

- **Remedy:** Quarterly modality audits—tracking the proportion of time spent in each quadrant and intentionally shifting toward underused zones.

### B. Depth Paralysis

- **Symptoms:**

    - Persistent SL comfort zone;
    - Anxiety or resistance toward DL disclosure;
    - Friends "stuck" in logistical talk.

- **Remedy:** Use "depth prompts"—open-ended questions or pre-shared reflective exercises—to nudge conversations from SL to DL (e.g., "What surprised you about your reactions last week?").

## VI. Conclusion: Towards a Cartography of True Connection

Chapter 2 has erected the **scaffolding** of ReconneXion Theory: two continua intersecting to form a dynamic field of relational possibility. By naming and explicating each modality and depth pole, we gain both *a map* and *a mirror*—the former charting where we've been, the latter reflecting where we tend to linger. In Chapters 3 and beyond, we will apply this cartography to the four ethical pillars—Presence, Intentionality, Empathy, and Vulnerability—and to concrete daily rituals.

Armed with this anatomical understanding, you are now prepared to view every message, call, letter, and meeting as a deliberate choice on the continuum—to ask, *"Where on this map do I wish to go today?"* and to embark on a sustained exploration of friendship that is as rich, varied, and unpredictable as the human heart itself.

## Chapter 3
## Surface vs. Substance: The Depth Continuum Unpacked

> "True intimacy is not born of proximity alone but of the courage to descend beyond the shallows."

## I. Introduction: Why Depth Matters

In an age awash with "connections," our greatest deficit is not lack of contacts but scarcity of **substance**. We exchange hundreds of text-based pleasantries (Surface-Level, SL) yet yearn in silence for a hand to hold our unguarded selves (Deep-Level, DL). ReconneXion Theory teaches that SL and DL are not discrete categories but poles on a continuum—an experiential gradient through which every friendship travels. Only by understanding its topology can we navigate from mere acquaintance to ally, from small talk to soul talk.

This chapter excavates the Depth Continuum from first principles, surveys its philosophical and empirical foundations, and offers tools to **calibrate**, **measure**, and **cultivate** intimacy across modalities.

## II. Historical & Theoretical Foundations

### A. Aristotle's Philia and the Qualitative Gap

Aristotle distinguished three forms of friendship:

1. **Utility** (benefit-based, SL)

2. **Pleasure** (enjoyment-based, moderate DL)

3. **Virtue** (shared values, highest DL)

He argued only virtuous friendships endure life's trials. In modern terms, "virtue" friendships sit at the far DL pole—rewarding, demanding, and rare.

## B. Social Penetration Theory (Altman & Taylor, 1973)

This framework likens self-disclosure to peeling an onion:

- **Outer layers:** Biographical facts, hobbies (SL)
- **Inner layers:** Beliefs, values (mid-depth)
- **Core:** Fears, dreams, existential longings (DL)

Depth grows as layers are peeled reciprocally. Impor-tantly, **reciprocity** and **trust** govern the pace of disclosure.

## C. Modern Neuroscience of Intimacy

Functional MRI studies reveal that mutual disclosure activates the brain's **reward circuitry** (ventral striatum) and **social cognition networks** (medial prefrontal cortex). Conversely, superficial exchanges barely engage these deeper circuits, leading to a sense of "emotional calorie low" despite digital flurries.

---

# III. Mapping the Continuum: Gradations of Depth

Rather than a binary divide, depth unfolds across stages:

1. **Logistical Coordination** (SL-1)
   – "What time is lunch?"

2. **Casual Banter** (SL-2)
   – Weather, sports scores, memes

3. **Shared Interests** (SL-3)
   – Book recommendations, hobby updates

4. **Opinions & Perspectives** (Mid-Depth-1)
   – Political views, ethical dilemmas

5. **Personal Reflections** (Mid-Depth-2)
   – Recent successes/failures, learning moments

6. **Emotional Disclosures** (DL-1)
   – Stressors, anxieties, small vulnerabilities

7. **Core Vulnerabilities** (DL-2)
   – Childhood wounds, existential doubts

8. **Aspirations & Transcendent Yearnings** (DL-3)
   – Life purpose, spiritual longings

Each interaction occupies a point on this scale. The goal is not to dwell perpetually at DL-3—indeed, doing so can overwhelm—but to **spiral** upward over time, interweaving SL-ease with periodic DL breakthroughs.

---

## IV. The Dynamics of Deepening

### A. Trust as the Gatekeeper

Without felt safety, disclosures stall at SL-3 or DL-1. Trust is built through consistent **presence**, **empathy**, and **boundary respect** (see Pillars in Chapter 1). Only once a threshold of reliability is crossed does a relationship permit journeying into DL-2 and beyond.

### B. Reciprocity & Pacing

Social Penetration Theory emphasizes **norms of reciprocity**:

- A DL-1 disclosure demands a response at least at the same level of depth.
- Over-sharing without mutual exchange can trigger withdrawal rather than closeness.

Effective pacing may follow a **2:1 rule**—two SL interactions for every one DL disclosure—to maintain comfort while deepening.

### C. Emotional Regulation & Co-Regulation

Deep conversations activate potent affects. Friends must practice **co-regulation**:

- **Grounding phrases** ("I hear you, I'm with you")
- **Pause-and-breathe** cues during video calls or walks
- **Check-ins** at DL-midpoints ("How are you feeling after sharing that?")

---

## V. Barriers to Deep-Level Interaction

1. **Fear of Judgment**
   – Past betrayals or cultural norms may discourage vulnerability.

2. **Digital Disinhibition vs. Inhibition**
   – Online anonymity can spur oversharing in AD modalities; paradoxically, fear of written permanence can inhibit others.

3. **Emotional Burnout**
   – Repeated DL engagements without recovery periods lead to compassion fatigue.

4. **Cultural Scripts**
   – Some cultures prize restraint; moving from SL to DL too abruptly may breach tacit norms.

Recognizing these barriers is the first step toward **intentional mitigation**.

---

## VI. Strategies for Cultivating Depth

### A. Scaffolded Questions

Progressively deepen inquiries within a single interaction:

| Stage | Sample Question |
| --- | --- |
| SL-3 | "What book hooked you recently?" |
| Mid-Depth | "What did that book reveal about what matters to you?" |

| DL-1 | "Has that topic ever touched a place of fear or hope?" |
| DL-2 | "Can you share a moment when that fear shaped your story?" |

### B. Mirror & Validate

Use **reflective listening** to ensure your friend feels truly heard:

"It sounds like you felt abandoned when that happened; is that right?"

This both deepens trust and clarifies emotional nuance.

### C. Narrative Pair-Writing

Co-author a short reflective text (in AD or AA) on a shared memory—alternating paragraphs. The act of co-creation forges intimacy through joint vulnerability and creative expression.

### D. "Depth Dates"

Schedule quarterly sessions across modalities specifically devoted to DL content:

- **AA:** Exchange handwritten letters reflecting on dreams.
- **SA:** Take a silent nature walk, then share life-purpose stories.
- **SD:** Host a two-hour video salon with guided prompts on personal values.

By ritualizing DL, depth becomes an anticipated gift rather than an accidental occurrence.

---

## VII. Case Studies in Deepening

### Case Study A: Mentor–Mentee Transformation

A corporate mentor begins with SL check-ins but over a year integrates:

1. **Mid-Depth AD:** Email reflections on leadership challenges.
2. **DL-1 SD:** Monthly video sessions discussing imposter syndrome.

3. **DL-2 AA:** Mentor sends a handwritten note every quarter recounting the mentee's growth and inviting the mentee's fears.

Result: The mentee reports not just skill acquisition but profound shifts in self-confidence and purpose.

### Case Study B: College Roommates Across Time

Two roommates move apart after graduation. They sustain friendship by:

- **SL-3 AD:** Weekly group chat memes.
- **Mid-Depth SA:** Annual home visits with shared cooking projects.
- **DL-1 AA:** Exchanged care packages containing mementos from college.
- **DL-2 AD:** Biannual letters describing evolving hopes and regrets.

Their bond endures decades, anchored by alternating SL ease and DL breakthroughs.

## VIII. Ethical Considerations & Emotional Safety

1. **Consent for Depth:** Always ask before broaching highly personal topics.
2. **Confidentiality:** Treat DL disclosures as inviolable trusts.
3. **Boundaries & Exit Strategies:** Allow friends to step back if overwhelmed—offer "timeout" language ("Let's pause and revisit tomorrow").
4. **Aftercare:** Follow up DL sessions with light SL interactions or small gestures (AA postcards) to reaffirm care.

## IX. Measuring Progress: Depth Audits

Every quarter, conduct a **Depth Audit**:

- **Log** your interactions over the past three months by depth stage.

- **Reflect** on how it felt to move upward—what anxieties arose, what joys blossomed.
- **Plan** at least one new DL practice per modality for the coming quarter.

This structured reflection ensures that depth-seeking remains active rather than accidental.

---

## X. Conclusion & Transition

We have unpacked the **Depth Continuum** in exhaustive detail—from philosophical roots to practical scaffolds—revealing both the promise and peril of deep friendship. Recognizing the gradient of self-disclosure empowers us to move with intentionality, reciprocity, and care.

In the next chapter, we turn to **Synchronous Digital** encounters (SD), exploring how real-time tech can both amplify and attenuate depth—and how to harness video and voice calls not as distractions but as portals to genuine presence and vulnerability.

As we proceed, carry forward the insights of this chapter: depth is earned, paced, and co-crafted. May your friendships thicken like fine tapestry—woven with threads of shared story, mutual risk, and the abiding courage to show your true self.

Chapter 4
**Synchronous Digital (SD): The Promise and Pitfalls of Real-Time Tech**

> "Screens may separate our bodies, but they need not estrange our hearts."

---

## I. Introduction: The Digital Campfire

In the ancient world, fireside gatherings were crucibles of communal identity: myths were spun, grievances aired, and bonds were reforged under flickering flames. Today, **synchronous digital** (SD) platforms—from video calls to live audio rooms—proclaim themselves as our new campfires. They offer immediacy: voice, visage, and spontaneous back-and-forth that mimic in-person dialogue. Yet these virtual flames cast both radiance and shadow. Without deliberate stewardship, SD interactions can devolve into fractured attention, performative oversharing, or emotional clutter.

This chapter explores SD's dual nature. We will:

1. Theorize the **phenomenology** and **neuroscience** underlying real-time digital presence.
2. Diagnose the **pitfalls**—from screen fatigue to parasocial distortion.
3. Articulate **ethical frameworks** and **rituals** that reclaim SD as a medium of genuine intimacy.
4. Provide **practical tools**—"Salon Sessions," "Pause & Reflect" techniques, and more—to elevate live digital encounters from distraction into depth.

Read on to learn how to transform Zoom squares and voice-chat bubbles into portals of presence, rather than vectors of vacuum.

---

## II. Theoretical Foundations

### A. Phenomenology of Virtual Presence

Drawing on Merleau-Ponty's notion of **embodied intentionality**, face-to-face dialogue engages not only words but the full spectrum of bodily being-in-the-world: posture, gesture, spatial orientation, ambient cues. SD partially recreates this via video's two-dimensional "window" and audio's tonal inflections.

- **Embodiment in Pixels:** We detect micro-expressions—raised eyebrows, lip quivers—yet lack tactile feedback and peripheral awareness.
- **Altered "Being-with":** Heidegger's **Mitsein** becomes mediated; our bodies are "present" only insofar as bandwidth permits.

Understanding SD as a **partial phenomenological reconstruction** underscores both its power (preserving immediacy) and its incompleteness (omitting full embodiment).

### B. Neuroscience of Live Digital Interaction

fMRI studies reveal that **real-time social engagement** activates mirror-neuron systems—key to empathy—as well as reward pathways when social cues align. Yet:

1. **Cognitive Load Increase:** Jittery internet, delayed audio, and fragmented attention tax the prefrontal cortex, resulting in "Zoom fatigue" (Bailenson, 2021).
2. **Reduced Oxytocin Release:** In-person eye contact and touch release oxytocin, a hormone crucial for trust. Digital eye contact—especially when staring at one's own

video feed—fails to replicate this neurochemical bonding.

3. **Feedback Loop Anxiety:** Constant self-monitoring of one's on-screen appearance engages the brain's **default mode network**, heightening self-consciousness and reducing mindful presence.

By recognizing these neural dynamics, we can design SD experiences that minimize cognitive drain and maximize empathic resonance.

---

## III. Promise of Synchronous Digital Modality

### A. Ubiquitous Immediacy

- **Global Reach:** Friends separated by oceans can convene in real time.
- **Accessibility:** For those with mobility challenges or remote circumstances, SD offers vital windows into communal life.
- **Rich Multimodal Cues:** Combined video, audio, and screen-sharing convey layered information—documents, photos, live demonstrations.

### B. Opportunity for Co-Creativity

- **Shared Whiteboards:** Digital canvases allow collaborative brainstorming and co-writing.
- **Simultaneous Media Engagement:** Watch a film together ("Netflix Party") or engage in co-listening sessions, transforming consumption into shared experience.
- **Real-Time Problem-Solving:** Technical glitches can become collective puzzles, fostering a sense of teamwork and humor.

### C. Ritualization of Presence

Well-structured SD gatherings can become cherished rituals—weekly check-ins, monthly salons—that anchor relationships in continuity, even when physical proximity is impossible.

---

## IV. Pitfalls of Synchronous Digital Modality

### A. Fragmented Attention & Multitasking

- **Tab-Switching Temptations:** Notifications and other apps lure participants away from the call, fracturing presence.
- **Partial Engagement:** Participants may nod on camera while mentally drafting emails, undermining the ethical pillar of Presence.

### B. Screen Fatigue & Emotional Exhaustion

- **Zoom Fatigue:** Extended SD sessions intensify cognitive load through constant eye contact, delayed feedback, and the necessity of sustaining a digital persona.
- **Compassion Fatigue:** Frequent DL exchanges without appropriate recovery can overwhelm emotional reserves.

### C. Performance Pressure

- **Curated Selves:** The "mirror" of one's own video thumbnail can encourage self-editing, impeding authenticity.
- **Parasocial Distortion:** Public "rooms" (Clubhouse, Twitter Spaces) can lure speakers into one-sided monologues or oversharing to gain status, undermining reciprocal dialogue.

### D. Digital Inequities

- **Bandwidth Disparities:** Poor internet access can marginalize participants, creating frustration or exclusion.
- **Accessibility Gaps:** Neurodivergent individuals or those with hearing impairments may struggle with real-time audio cues.

## V. Ethical Framework for SD Encounters

To navigate SD's minefield, we adopt four orienting principles—extensions of the ReconneXion pillars:

1. **Presence as Digital Sovereignty**

- Device-Free Zones: Begin each call with a mutual agreement: no phones or notifications beyond the call app.
- Full-Screen Commitment: Encourage participants to enlarge the call window, minimizing visual distractions.

2. Intentional Design of Interaction
    - Agenda with Depth Goals: Even informal calls benefit from a loose structure: 10 minutes SL catch-up, 20 minutes DL prompt, 5 minutes reflective closing.
    - Rotation of Facilitation: Share hosting duties to democratize responsibility and prevent single-host fatigue.

3. Empathy through Reflective Pauses
    - "Pause & Reflect" Rituals: Every 15–20 minutes, pause the conversation. Each person names one emotional state ("I'm feeling curious/exhausted/profoundly glad") before continuing.
    - Reflective Summaries: After each DL segment, a participant summarizes what they heard, ensuring comprehension and validation.

4. Vulnerability with Boundaries
    - Permission Slips: Use discrete chat or emoji signals for real-time "I'm not ready" or "I need a moment" cues.
    - Post-Call Check-Ins: For intense DL segments, schedule a brief follow-up message or voice note to ensure emotional well-being.

---

## VI. Rituals and Practices to Elevate SD

### A. Theme-Based "Salon" Sessions

**Structure:**

1. **Opening Circle (5 min):** Each attendee names one word to describe their current emotional temperature.

2. **Featured Prompt (20–30 min):** A rotating host poses a deep question—e.g., "When did you first feel seen?"

3. **Open Reflection (10 min):** Group members respond briefly, free-style.

4. **Closing Intentions (5 min):** Each person shares one action or thought they will carry forward.

**Benefits:**

- Leverages ritual to build anticipation and consistency.
- Balances SL (opening and closing) with structured DL (featured prompt).

### B. "Pause & Reflect" Technique

**Implementation:**

- Set a timer for every 15–20 minutes.
- Mute audio/video and prompt: "What's one insight or emotion you're holding right now?"
- Unmute and share in turn.

**Benefits:**

- Counteracts attention drift.
- Transitions from conversation's "flow" to mindful presence.
- Offers micro-breaks to manage cognitive load.

### C. AI-Assisted Icebreakers

**Guidelines:**

- Use AI only to **suggest** open-ended prompts, not to script entire messages.
- E.g., "Ask: 'What's a small moment this week that surprised you?'"
- Share AI-generated prompts verbally or via chat, then personalize.

**Benefits:**

- Sparks depth when hosts are uncertain what to ask next.
- Preserves spontaneity by requiring real-time adaptation.

### D. Empathy-Driven Screen Arrangement

**Practice:**

- Position video windows to maximize eye-line alignment, reducing the "lopsided gaze" effect.
- Encourage participants to disable self-view after initial checks, lowering self-focus.

**Benefits:**

- Enhances eye contact illusion.
- Reduces self-monitoring fatigue, freeing cognitive resources for empathetic listening.

## VII. Case Studies in Synchronous Digital Mastery

### Case Study 1: The Transcontinental Book Club

A group of six friends—two each in New York, Lagos, and Mumbai—forms a monthly SD book circle.

- **Modality Mix:** SD for live discussion; AD Slack channel for interim reflections; AA care packages of local snacks aligned with book themes; SA local meetups in city hubs.
- **Deepening Strategy:** Each meeting includes a 10-minute "Pause & Reflect" and a rotating DL prompt tied to the text's themes.
- **Outcome:** After one year, members report a 40 % increase in perceived closeness and sustained attendance of over 90 %.

### Case Study 2: Remote Team "Heart Check" Ritual

A distributed startup implements weekly SD "Heart Checks":

1. **SL Status Updates (15 min):** Project progress.

2. **DL Pulse Survey (10 min):** Real-time anonymous poll on mood ("energetic," "stressed," "curious").

3. **Empathy Round (10 min):** Those who volunteer share context; colleagues offer reflective listening, no problem-solving.

4. **Intentions (5 min):** Each names one self-care or friendship gesture they'll enact before next week.

**Outcome:** Employee engagement scores rise by 25 %, burnout reports fall by 15 %, and cross-team solidarity strengthens.

## VIII. Measuring and Auditing SD Interactions

### A. Quantitative Metrics

- **Engagement Rate:** Percentage of participants actively speaking or reacting (chat/emoji) during DL segments.

- **Distraction Index:** Self-reported frequency of shifting to other apps or checking notifications.

### B. Qualitative Reflections

- **Post-Session Surveys:** One question: "In one sentence, how connected did you feel?"

- **Reflective Journals:** Encourage participants to note one personal insight gained and one relational observation.

### C. Modal Diversity Score

Track the proportion of live SD sessions relative to other modalities. Aim for SD to comprise no more than 40 % of total friendship interactions—ensuring balanced modality mix.

## IX. Avoiding Overreliance and Fatigue

1. **SD Quotas:** Limit live calls to a sustainable number per week (e.g., two per close friend).
2. **Alternating Modalities:** Follow each SD session with an AA gesture (handwritten note, small gift) or an AD recap to reinforce connection without further screen time.
3. **Scheduled Tech Sabbaths:** Dedicate entire weekends or evenings to analog modalities only—no live calls—nurturing presence in SA and AA.

## X. Conclusion & Transition

Synchronous Digital platforms hold the **promise** of reuniting separated hearts in real time and the **pitfalls** of fractured focus, fatigue, and performative emptiness. By grounding our SD practice in phenomenological awareness, neuroscientific insight, and ethical intentionality, we can tip the balance toward genuine presence and depth.

In the forthcoming **Chapter 5**, we turn our attention to **Asynchronous Digital (AD)** modalities—exploring how time-shifted exchanges can become vessels of reflection and scaffolds for deep-level journeys. May your next video call be not merely an obligation, but an intentional act of friendship reborn.

## Chapter 5
### Asynchronous Digital (AD): Crafting Time-Shifted Intimacy

> "In the spaces between our messages, the heart finds room to breathe."

## I. Introduction: The Art of Patience in Connection

In an era that prizes instant gratification, **asynchronous digital** (AD) communication stands as a counterintuitive oasis of reflection. Unlike the immediacy and pressure of live video or voice, AD affords us the gift of time—time to compose, to meditate, to revisit. Email threads, direct messages, shared documents, and forum posts become not mere logistical tools but **vessels of care**, carrying our words across days, weeks, or even months. Yet this very temporal elasticity can birth its own distortions: protracted threads that fizzle, misinterpretations magnified by lack of tone, and the temptation to default to shorthand. In this chapter, we will:

1. Unpack the **philosophical** and **psychological** underpinnings of time-shifted discourse.
2. Illuminate the **promise** of AD for deep-level (DL) connection.
3. Diagnose the **pitfalls**—from asynchronous ambivalence to phantom notifications.
4. Offer an **ethical framework** to guide purposeful AD practice.
5. Present **rituals and templates** for emails, voice-note diaries, and hybrid analog-digital letters.
6. Explore **case studies** demonstrating how AD can scaffold enduring friendship.
7. Detail **metrics** and **audit techniques** to ensure AD remains a force for depth rather than drift.
8. Advise on **modal balance** and the seamless integration of AD with other modalities.

By the end of this chapter, you will recognize AD not as second-rate merely because it is not synchronous, but as a **powerful crucible** for sustained intimacy.

---

## II. Theoretical Foundations

### A. Hermeneutics of Pause

Hans-Georg Gadamer's **fusion of horizons** emphasizes that understanding **emerges** when interlocutors bring their distinct contexts to bear in dialogue. AD inherently slows the hermeneutic circle:

- **Time for Interpretation:** Each message sits in the reader's horizon before they respond, inviting deeper comprehension.
- **Layered Meaning:** Writers often revise drafts, adding nuance, metaphors, or clarifying anecdotes unavailable in off-the-cuff speech.

Thus, AD can approximate the measured turn-taking and thoughtful clarification of in-person Socratic dialogues—if wielded with care.

### B. Cognitive Psychology of Reflection

Research in cognitive psychology reveals that **delayed retrieval**—the act of revisiting information after a pause—enhances memory consolidation and fosters **metacognition**. When we revisit a friend's message hours or days later:

- **Emotional Resonance Deepens:** The initial emotional spark mellows into considered empathy.
- **Perspective Shifts:** Life events that occur between reading and replying can influence tone and content, creating dynamic, evolving conversation.

### C. Digital Epistolary Tradition

The journey from parchment letters to email newsletters spans centuries of epistolary craft. Figures like **Michel de Montaigne** and **Mary Shelley** demonstrate how the letter form—drawn out, layered, reflective—yields some of literature's most intimate revelations. Modern AD should reclaim this heritage:

- **Narrative Arc:** Treat each message as a mini-essay with introduction, body, and reflective conclusion.
- **Stationery of the Digital Age:** Use formatted sign-offs, personalized imagery, and carefully chosen subject lines as the heirlooms of handwritten stationery.

---

## III. Promise of Asynchronous Digital Modality

### A. Reflective Depth

1. **Thoughtful Self-Expression:** Writers can craft replies that articulate inner landscapes with clarity and poetic resonance.
2. **Emotional Containment:** Distance in time buffers raw affect, reducing the risk of defensive reactivity and enabling compassionate framing.

### B. Permanent Records

- **Thread as Archive:** AD exchanges accumulate into a living chronicle of the friendship—milestones, jokes, shared discoveries—that can be revisited as a source of consolation and joy.

- **Resource for Future DL:** A friend's past vulnerabilities—once safely recorded—become launchpads for deeper dialogue in other modalities.

## C. Flexibility & Accessibility

- **Scheduling Freedom:** Participants in divergent time zones or with unpredictable schedules can engage when capacity permits.
- **Accommodation of Neurodiversity:** Those who process information more deliberately or require sensory breaks benefit from AD's unhurried pace.

## D. Hybrid Analog-Digital Potential

- **Handwritten E-Letters:** Scanned letters blend AA warmth with AD convenience.
- **Voice-Note Transcriptions:** Audio diaries offer tonal nuance alongside transcribed text for reference.

---

# IV. Pitfalls of Asynchronous Digital Modality

## A. Asynchronous Ambivalence

- **Delayed Replies:** A message left unanswered can breed anxiety or misinterpretation.
- **Attention Decay:** Threads can be abandoned as priorities shift, leaving emotional gaps.

## B. Brevity Over Substance

- **Shorthand Temptations:** Emojis and one-word replies risk truncating conversation, relegating it back to SL.
- **Over-Editing:** Writers may self-censor so heavily that authenticity wanes.

## C. Notification Overload

- **Phantom Pings:** Even the memory of an unread message can distract attention from present tasks.

- **Blurred Boundaries:** Without agreed response windows, recipients feel compelled to reply immediately—thus forfeiting AD's reflective promise.

### D. Disembodied Miscommunication

- **Lack of Tone Clues:** Sarcasm, humor, and emotional subtleties can misfire without vocal or facial cues.
- **Overload of Information:** Lengthy multi-threaded exchanges become labyrinthine, risking confusion.

---

## V. Ethical Framework for AD Practice

Drawing on ReconneXion's four pillars, we adapt them to the AD context:

1. **Presence as Time Stewardship**
   - **Response Windows:** Co-create acceptable reply timelines (e.g., within 48 hours for DL, 24 hours for SL).
   - **Focused Reading:** Dedicate uninterrupted blocks to reading and composing responses—closing other apps and setting aside the inbox.

2. **Intentionality in Composition**
   - **Purposeful Subject Lines:** Use evocative titles signaling depth (e.g., "A reflection on resilience," "Two thoughts on your news").
   - **Structured Messages:** Open with context ("Since we last wrote…"), develop the body (updates + inquiry), close with a question or call to reflective action.

3. **Empathy through Expressive Cues**
   - **Affective Labeling:** Begin DL messages with "I imagine you might be feeling…" to mirror the friend's inner state.
   - **Reading Acknowledgments:** Reference the precise phrase or story that moved you, validating the friend's disclosure.

4. **Vulnerability with Safety Nets**

- **Tiered Disclosure:** Signal depth level—"Thought I'd share something a bit more personal…"—so recipients can brace emotionally.

- **Check-In Prompts:** Conclude heavy topics with "Take your time; I'm here when you're ready to continue."

---

## VI. Rituals and Practices to Elevate AD

### A. The "Three Acts" Email Template

1. **Act I – Context Setting (1–2 sentences):**
   "I've been thinking about our conversation last week about career changes…"

2. **Act II – Reflective Narrative (3–5 paragraphs):**

   - Personal updates woven with emotional insight.

   - Invitation for reciprocal sharing.

3. **Act III – Depth Prompt (1–2 questions):**
   "How did you feel when that transition first happened? What support do you wish you'd had?"

*Benefits:* Combines narrative intimacy with focused inquiry, guiding the friend from SL into DL.

### B. Voice-Note Diary Series

- **Format:** Record 2–4 minutes of spoken reflection, then transcribe and annotate the text before sending.

- **Cadence:** Weekly or biweekly, each entry closes with a reflective question for the friend.

- **Hybrid Strength:** Tone carries authenticity; transcription ensures key phrases can be revisited.

### C. "Subject-Line Alchemy"

| Subject Line Type | Effect |
| --- | --- |

| | |
|---|---|
| **Snapshot Hook** | "A sunrise that reminded me of you" |
| **Curiosity Tease** | "Three surprises I discovered today" |
| **Emotive Echo** | "Your words are still ringing…" |
| **Invitation to Reflect** | "When was the last time you dared?" |

Using these deliberately primes recipients to allocate attention and anticipate depth.

### D. Handwritten E-Letters

- **Step 1:** Draft on paper—one full page of reflection.
- **Step 2:** Scan or photograph under natural light.
- **Step 3:** Send via email with a brief cover note referencing physical texture and intention.

*Benefits:* Tangible effort conveys care; the scanned image invites tactile imagination.

---

## VII. Case Studies in AD-Driven Depth

### Case Study A: The Pandemic Pen-Pal Project

Two friends, one in Tokyo and one in São Paulo, commit to monthly long-form letters.

- **Modality Mix:** AD for letters; occasional SD calls for real-time check-ins; AA care packages exchanged semi-annually.
- **Depth Strategy:** Each letter responds to the previous one's final question, creating a continuous thread.
- **Outcome:** Over two years, their written archive surpasses 200 pages, culminating in a jointly composed e-book of reflections.

### Case Study B: The Mentor's Reflective Journal

A senior researcher mentors a junior colleague across institutions.

- **Ritual:** Mentor sends weekly voice-note diaries on challenges faced; mentee replies with written reflections.

- **Ethical Guardrail:** Response window agreed at 72 hours; messages begin with mood check ("Today I feel…").

- **Outcome:** Mentee reports a 60 % boost in clarity on research direction and improved emotional resilience.

### Case Study C: The Collaborative Memoir

Three college roommates reconvene via a shared Google Doc.

- **Process:** Each week, one writes a poem or anecdote; others annotate with comments and reactions.

- **Mix of Modalities:** AD text fosters narrative depth; SD video gatherings celebrate new entries; AA printed zine binds the final collection.

- **Outcome:** The co-authored memoir becomes a tangible artifact of their friendship, reinforcing bonds even as life paths diverge.

---

## VIII. Measuring and Auditing AD Interactions

### A. Qualitative Check-Ins

- **Monthly Reflection Prompt:** "Which message from me this month moved you most, and why?"

- **Depth Rating:** On a scale of 1–5, ask friends to self-report the average depth of your exchanges.

### B. Quantitative Metrics

- **Thread Longevity:** Average days between first and last message in a conversation before a resolution or sign-off.

- **Response Latency:** Track median reply time for SL vs. DL messages, ensuring both remain within agreed windows.

### C. Content Analysis

- Perform a quarterly **Depth Audit**—categorize 10 random messages per modality by depth stage (SL–1 through DL–3) and chart the distribution.
- Goal: Achieve at least 30 % DL-level interactions across AD exchanges.

## IX. Avoiding Monoculture and Burnout

1. **AD Quotas:** Balance AD with SL interactions in other modalities—no more than 50 % of total friendship engagements should be time-shifted.

2. **Thread Sunsetting:** Institute a practice of closing inactive threads with a final "Let's pick this up another time" to prevent emotional limbo.

3. **Digital Sabbaticals:** Between intensive DL-AD projects (e.g., memoir writing), schedule analog or synchronous breaks to recharge relational energy.

## X. Conclusion & Transition

Asynchronous Digital communication, when treated as a **deliberate art**, can transform the tyranny of immediacy into a sanctuary of reflection and intimacy. By integrating hermeneutic patience, narrative craft, and ethical intention, we convert each message into a gesture of enduring care. The threads we weave in AD become the scaffolding upon which deeper synchronous and analog encounters can flourish.

In the next chapter, we will turn to **Synchronous Analog (SA)** modalities—reclaiming the wisdom of embodied presence through in-person walks, shared projects, and real-time emotional attunement. May your inbox become not a source of anxiety, but a garden of thoughtful invitations to the heart.

**Chapter 6**
**Synchronous Analog (SA): Embodied Encounters and the Flesh of Friendship**

"To share space is to share soul; the body knows what words cannot hold."

## I. Introduction: Rediscovering the Primacy of the Body

In a world lured by digital simulacra, the **synchronous analog** (SA) modality—co-present, real-time interaction in physical space—remains our most elemental form of connection. Whether walking side by side under dappled sunlight, cooking a meal in tandem, or simply sitting across a table, SA encounters engage the body's senses, the rhythm of breath, and the unspoken language of touch and gesture. These embodied experiences carry a depth of resonance no screen can fully replicate.

Yet SA is often underutilized: geographic distance, busy schedules, and the siren call of convenience conspire to push in-person meetings to the margins. Recognizing SA as the "ground zero" of embodiment in ReconneXion, this chapter offers an exhaustive exploration of its philosophical roots, neurological underpinnings, practical power, inherent challenges, ethical imperatives, and concrete practices to weave SA encounters into the tapestry of modern friendship.

## II. Theoretical & Philosophical Foundations

### A. Merleau-Ponty's Flesh of the World

Maurice Merleau-Ponty posited that our primary engagement with reality is **sensorimotor**: the body is not an object but the very locus of perception. In SA encounters:

- **Embodied Intentionality:** We perceive another not as data but as a living presence, experienced through all senses.

- **Flesh as Intercorporeality:** Our bodies "intertwine" with others', creating a shared field of meaning beyond symbolic language.

### B. Martin Buber's I-Thou Revisited

Buber's **I-Thou** relation blossoms most fully in face-to-face meeting—*face* in Hebrew meaning the presence that cannot be turned away. SA affords:

- **Potential for Authenticity:** Neither party is hidden behind avatars.

- **Dialogical Reciprocity:** Speech is accompanied by posture, gaze, and silence, each communicating as powerfully as words.

### C. Neuroscience of Embodied Synchrony

Recent studies on **interpersonal neural synchrony** show that when two individuals engage in joint action—walking, gesturing, speaking—their brainwaves can align:

- **Mirror-Neuron Entrainment:** Activates empathy and mutual understanding.
- **Oxytocin Release:** Physical proximity and synchronous movement trigger bonding chemicals, deepening trust.
- **Polyvagal Co-Regulation:** Shared rhythms of breath and voice co-regulate autonomic responses, reducing stress and fostering safety.

## III. The Promise of Synchronous Analog

### A. Multisensory Richness

SA encounters engage sight, sound, touch, smell, and even the subtle vibrations of shared space. This **sensory tapestry** communicates tone, context, and emotion with unparalleled fidelity.

### B. Spontaneous Creativity

Physical collaboration—cooking, gardening, building—leverages **tacit knowledge** (Polanyi)—the unspoken know-how embodied in skilled hands. Shared projects become sites of co-creation and trust formation.

### C. Real-Time Emotional Calibration

In-person, tiny shifts in pupil dilation, posture, and micro-expressions guide us toward sensitive attunement. A friend's slump of the shoulders or trembling voice beckons immediate empathy.

### D. Ritualization of Place

Spaces—parks, kitchens, community centers—imbue rituals with geographical and historical resonance. Returning to the same bench or café table plants lasting anchors in memory, fortifying relational continuity.

## IV. Pitfalls and Challenges of Synchronous Analog

### A. Logistic and Geographic Constraints

- **Distance:** Friends living in different cities or countries must navigate travel costs and time zones.
- **Scheduling Conflicts:** Work, caregiving, and other commitments can render SA sessions irregular or stressful to arrange.

### B. Sensory Overload and Vulnerability

- **Emotional Intensity:** The full force of DL disclosures can feel overwhelming without temporal buffers.
- **Sensory Sensitivities:** Neurodivergent individuals may find crowds, noise, or physical proximity taxing.

### C. Habitual Complacency

- **Assumed Ease:** We may underprepare for SA encounters, assuming "we'll just hang out," leading to aimless gatherings that default to SL banter.
- **Comparison Pressure:** Meeting in person can trigger performance anxiety—feeling "on display" in ways digital screens dampen.

### D. Unwanted Intrusions

- **Third-Party Interruptions:** Public venues or shared spaces risk eavesdropping or distractions.
- **Physical Boundaries:** Misreading comfort levels around touch can breach trust if not negotiated.

---

## V. Ethical Framework for SA Engagement

Integrating ReconneXion's four pillars into SA:

1. **Presence as Somatic Focus**
   - **Environment Curation:** Choose spaces conducive to connection—quiet parks, private rooms, or homes over busy cafés.

- **Sensory Grounding:** Begin with a brief joint grounding exercise—deep breaths, silent acknowledgment of shared space, or simple eye contact.

2. **Intentionality in Activity Design**
   - **Purposeful Agenda:** Even casual meetups benefit from a loose structure: "First 15 minutes check-in, next 30 minutes shared activity, final 15 minutes open reflection."
   - **Reciprocal Hosting:** Alternate who selects the location or activity, distributing the effort and ensuring varied experiences.

3. **Empathy through Embodied Listening**
   - **Reflective Posture:** Lean in when a friend speaks; maintain an open stance; minimize physical barriers (tables, electronic devices).
   - **Mirroring:** Subtly reflect body language—matching pace on a walk, matching tone during conversation—to signal attunement.

4. **Vulnerability with Informed Consent**
   - **Boundary Check-Ins:** At the start, ask: "Is there anything you'd prefer not to do/talk about today?"
   - **Exit Strategies:** Agree on nonverbal signals (touching one's ear, tapping the wrist) that either party can use if they need space or a break.

---

## VI. Rituals and Practices for SA Mastery

### A. Walking Conversations ("Peripatetic Dialogues")

- **Structure:** Walk side by side for 45–60 minutes. No devices. Begin with small talk, then transition at a midpoint marker (bench, tree) into a pre-agreed DL prompt.
- **Benefits:** Movement synchronizes nervous systems; changing scenery stimulates ideas; minimal eye contact reduces social pressure.

### B. Co-Creation Projects

- **Examples:** Cooking a meal, tending a community garden, assembling a puzzle, or crafting simple art.
- **Guidelines:** Choose tasks with complementary skill requirements—one friend may chop vegetables while the other stirs, fostering interdependence and nonverbal communication.

## C. Shared Silence & Presence

- **Practice:** Spend 10–15 minutes in companionable silence—reading side by side, silently sipping tea in a garden.
- **Purpose:** Silence becomes a shared container for presence, reducing SL chatter and inviting DL reflection.

## D. Embodied Check-Ins

- **Heart-to-Hands:** At intervals, place a hand over your heart and one's friend's hand over theirs; share one-word emotional descriptors.
- **Breath Synchronization:** Pause activity to breathe together for five cycles, aligning inhalations and exhalations to soothe the autonomic nervous system.

## E. Nature-Based Rituals

- **Tree-Planting or Seed Exchange:** Symbolic acts that root friendship in growth metaphors.
- **Ritual Stone:** Each friend brings a small stone, exchanges it, and holds it when sharing a DL story—tactile anchors for memory.

## F. Physical Tokens of Connection

- **Friendship Bracelets or Woven Bands:** Crafted together and worn thereafter, these objects serve as AA artifacts born of SA creation.
- **Photo-Portrait Exchange:** Take Polaroids during the meeting; swap and inscribe a shared insight on each back, then frame or keep in a shared album.

## VII. Case Studies in Synchronous Analog Excellence

### Case Study A: The Quarterly "Pilgrimage"

A group of four college friends commits to a yearly weekend retreat:

- **Modality Integration:** SA hiking and campsite cooking; AA care packages exchanged post-retreat; AD recap emails with shared photo albums; SD group video to plan and debrief.
- **Depth Infusion:** Each retreat includes a "Dawn Circle" at sunrise—DL sharing of personal milestones—followed by hands-on communal tasks (fire maintenance, meal prep).
- **Outcome:** Friendships span decades, with annual rituals marking personal growth, reducing drift despite geographic dispersion.

### Case Study B: The Intergenerational Workshop

A grandparent and grandchild gather monthly for a "storysmithing" session:

- **SA Activity:** Co-writing a family history narrative, interspersed with home-cooked recipes.
- **Ethical Guardrails:** The grandchild pauses to ask permission before probing sensitive memories; the grandparent requests AA artifacts—old photographs—to enrich DL stories.
- **Outcome:** A richly textured memoir emerges; both parties report enhanced intergenerational empathy and mutual respect.

### Case Study C: The Arts Collective Duo

Two artist-friends meet weekly in a shared studio space:

- **SA Practice:** Joint painting sessions with alternating prompts—one friend initiates a motif, the other elaborates.
- **DL Integration:** Interrupt painting every 20 minutes for a "heart check"—express in a few sentences how the process resonates with current life events.
- **Artifact Creation:** Completed canvases are exchanged as AA gifts, inscribed with reflective passages from the check-ins.

- **Outcome:** Their collaborative work and friendship deepen in tandem; each painting chronicles emotional evolution across seasons.

## VIII. Measuring and Auditing SA Engagement

### A. Qualitative Reflection Prompts

- **Post-Encounter Journal:** "What did I learn about my friend's inner world today?" and "How did our shared activity influence my own self-understanding?"
- **Sensory Score:** Rate the multisensory richness of each meeting (1–5 scale) based on novelty, engagement, and emotional impact.

### B. Quantitative Indicators

- **SA Frequency Tracker:** Log the number of in-person meetings per quarter; aim for at least one SA session per close friendship every six weeks.
- **DL Touchpoints:** Count how many minutes within each SA session were devoted to deep sharing (estimated via a simple timer).

### C. Modal Balance Heatmap

Visualize your modality mix over the past quarter, plotting the percentage of SA encounters against SD, AD, and AA. Strive for SA to constitute at least 20 % of total interactions for core friendships.

## IX. Avoiding Overuse and Exclusivity

1. **SA Overcommitment:** Too many SA sessions without varied modality infusion can lead to **physical burnout**—time and energy constraints may leave other friendships neglected.
2. **Geographic Elitism:** SA can inadvertently privilege local friends. Counterbalance by using AD and SD intentionally with distant connections.

3. **Activity vs. Presence Imbalance:** Resist filling SA meetings with nonstop tasks; dedicate at least 25 % of each session to open-ended, DL conversation.

## X. Conclusion & Transition

Synchronous Analog engagement—embodied, multisensory, and deeply human—anchors the high-fidelity core of ReconneXion Theory. It reminds us that amidst the swirl of digital modalities, our bodies and the spaces we share remain primary vessels of trust, empathy, and vulnerability.

As we close this chapter, carry forward the practices of walking dialogues, shared projects, and embodied rituals. In **Chapter 7**, we will explore **Asynchronous Analog (AA)**—the art of letters, care packages, and tactile artifacts that bridge time and distance, weaving digital and analog threads into a resilient tapestry of friendship.

May your next in-person encounter be not a relic of pre-digital innocence, but a deliberate act of philosophical embodiment—a testament that, despite screens and algorithms, the flesh of friendship endures.

Chapter 7
**Asynchronous Analog (AA): The Poetics of Letters and Gifts**

> "In the silent space between dispatch and discovery, our hearts converse beyond words."

## I. Introduction: The Tangibility of Care

In an age dominated by ephemeral pixels and algorithmic timelines, the **asynchronous analog (AA)** modality—handwritten letters, postcards, care packages, physical mementos—reclaims the **tactile alchemy** of human connection. AA gestures carry four intrinsic virtues:

1. **Tangibility:** The weight, texture, and imperfections of ink on paper anchor emotions in the physical world.

2. **Anticipation:** The gap between sending and receiving builds suspense, imbuing each word with heightened value.

3. **Durability:** Unlike transient digital messages, physical artifacts endure—safeguarded in boxes, journals, or on display.

4. **Embodied Effort:** The labor of handwriting, curating objects, or assembling gifts itself communicates presence and care.

This chapter offers a **comprehensive excavation** of AA's philosophical foundations, practical power, neurobiological impact, potential pitfalls, ethical frameworks, and an expansive repertoire of **rituals, templates, case studies, audit tools,** and **integration strategies**—all designed to ensure your analog gestures resonate more deeply than any algorithmically boosted emoji ever could.

---

## II. Philosophical & Historical Foundations

### A. The Epistolary Tradition: From Cicero to Montaigne

- **Cicero's Letters to Atticus:** Masterclasses in political counsel and intimate friendship, inscribed on papyrus yet brimming with emotional candor.

- **Montaigne's Essays as Letters:** Though framed as essays, Montaigne's *Essais* mimic letter-writing's confessional voice—demonstrating how personal reflection invites universal resonance.

### B. Walter Ong's Orality vs. Literacy

- **Orality:** Characterized by immediacy and communal performance; ephemeral and context-dependent.

- **Literacy:** Introduces **detachment**—the ability to revisit, reflect, and annotate. AA melds the **orality of presence** with the **literacy of permanence**, allowing words to echo across time.

### C. Heidegger's Thingness and the Gestell

- Martin Heidegger contrasted the **"enframing" (Gestell)** of technological objects with the **"thingness"** of tools that reveal deeper truths. An AA gift—whether a pressed flower or a handbound booklet—transcends mere utility to become a **"thing"** that **gathers** meaning, memory, and the giver's intention.

## III. Neurobiology of Tangible Connection

### A. Haptic Attachment and Oxytocin Release

Physical textures—parchment's grain, the heft of a ceramic mug—stimulate mechanoreceptors, triggering **oxytocin** release and calming the nervous system.

### B. Memory Encoding and the Spacing Effect

- **Spacing Effect:** Cognitive science shows information revisited over spaced intervals is retained more robustly. AA artifacts, encountered over years, become **mnemonic anchors** of relational milestones.

- **Dual-Coding Theory:** Combining verbal text with visual/kinesthetic elements (drawings, stamps, dried petals) engages both verbal and nonverbal memory systems, strengthening emotional recall.

---

## IV. The Promise of Asynchronous Analog

### A. Depth That Defies Time

AA gestures are **time capsules**. A letter penned on a moment of struggle remains a beacon when the recipient confronts similar challenges years later.

### B. Multi-Sensory Engagement

- **Visual:** Handwritten script, choice of stationery, embedded sketches.

- **Tactile:** Paper weight, envelope seal, ribbon texture.

- **Olfactory:** Scented paper, pressed flowers, aromatic sachets.

- **Auditory (via QR-linked voice):** Embedding a tiny code linking to a private voice message adds a multimodal dimension.

### C. Ritualized Anticipation and Surprise

The act of anticipating a handwritten letter or receiving a surprise care package interrupts mundane routines, creating **emotional punctuation** in the calendar of daily life.

### D. Artifact as Conversation Catalyst

AA items become **relational props**: a framed poem can inspire new discussions; a curated playlist on a USB-filled mixtape rekindles shared memories around music.

## V. Pitfalls and Challenges of Asynchronous Analog

### A. Logistic Frictions

- **Postal Delays:** International shipping can take weeks, risking misaligned timing.
- **Material Costs:** Quality paper, stamps, packaging materials add expense.
- **Environmental Concerns:** Paper waste and shipping carbon footprint warrant mindful sourcing and packaging.

### B. Effort Overwhelm

- **Perfection Paralysis:** Fear of imperfect handwriting or design can inhibit analog outreach.
- **Time Constraints:** Busy lives may relegate letter-writing to "someday"—leading to perpetual backlogs.

### C. Misinterpretation of Effort

- **Comparative Anxiety:** Recipients may feel guilty if unable to reciprocate in kind, risking relational imbalance.
- **Artifact Clutter:** A profusion of mementos can overwhelm physical spaces, reducing artifacts to clutter rather than treasures.

### D. Inadvertent Exclusivity

- **Accessibility Barriers:** Friends with disabilities affecting fine motor skills or vision may find AA challenging.
- **Cultural Disparities:** Letter-writing traditions differ globally; some may not place the same value on physical mail.

## VI. Ethical Framework for AA Engagement

Integrating AA into ReconneXion's pillars:

1. **Presence as Material Intent**

    o **Mindful Sourcing:** Select paper, ink, and objects that align with the friend's tastes and values—locally crafted, eco-friendly, or personally meaningful.

    o **Time Allotment:** Dedicate uninterrupted blocks (e.g., 45 minutes) to writing or assembling, ensuring your full attention infuses the artifact.

2. **Intentionality in Curation**

    o **Story-Driven Packages:** Each item in a care package should connect to a narrative or shared memory, with a label or note explaining its significance.

    o **Thematic Consistency:** Letters and gifts can follow monthly themes (gratitude, hope, creativity) to sustain ritual coherence.

3. **Empathy through Personalization**

    o **Handwritten Marginalia:** Add small sketches, quotations, or annotations in the margins to demonstrate you're "thinking in the moment."

    o **Custom Scents or Textures:** Include a spritz of your favorite essential oil on the page edge or a swatch of fabric that evokes a shared memory.

4. **Vulnerability with Reciprocity**

    o **Reciprocal Invitations:** Conclude each letter with an "analog prompt"—a challenge or question inviting the friend to respond via AA or another modality of their choice.

    o **Exit Option:** Acknowledge the effort involved and offer an easy out—"No need to reply if this feels heavy; know I'm with you regardless."

---

## VII. Rituals, Templates, and Practices

### A. The "Monthly Muse" Letter Series

1. **Preparation:** Choose a **theme** for the month—e.g., "Seeds of Joy," "Turning Points," "Unsaid Gratitudes."

2. **Format:**
   - **Opening Reflection:** One paragraph describing why the theme matters.
   - **Core Narrative:** 2–3 paragraphs weaving personal experience, philosophical insight, and a shared memory.
   - **Analog Prompt:** A question or small task (press a leaf and share in your next letter).

3. **Embellishments:** Include a related **artifact**—flower petal, pressed leaf, or a tiny sketch.

## B. The "Care-Scape" Package Blueprint

| Section | Content & Purpose |
| --- | --- |
| Letter | Handwritten note introducing the package's story (20–30 lines). |
| Artifact 1 | A handmade object (friendship bracelet, knitted pouch). |
| Artifact 2 | A sensory token (tea sachets, vanilla sachet, dried lavender). |
| Literary Token | A poem, printed short story, or personal playlist link (QR code on a card). |
| Reflection Prompt | "Which scent or token resonated most, and why?" (invites AA or AD reply). |

## C. The "Postcard Gratitude" Campaign

- **Cadence:** Mail one postcard per month for 12 months.
- **Front Image:** Choose photographs you've taken—landscapes, urban details, or abstract textures.
- **Back Message:** One sentence of gratitude + one question for reflection.

- **Outcome:** A year-long series of bite-sized DL interactions that accumulate into a mosaic of appreciation.

### D. Handbound "Memory Sketchbook"

- **Construction:** Bind blank pages with simple Japanese stab binding or ring binding.
- **Content:** Alternate pages between your sketches/poems and blank pages labeled for the friend to fill and return.
- **Exchange:** Mail the sketchbook to them; upon return, the collaborative artifact becomes a shared keepsake.

### E. "Scented Letter" Technique

- **Materials:** Uncoated cotton paper, essential oils, blotter strips.
- **Process:**
    1. Lightly mist the page with a diluted blend (e.g., rosemary for clarity, lavender for calm).
    2. Slip a scented blotter strip into the envelope annotated: "Release fragrance upon opening to recall our forest walks."
- **Impact:** Engages olfactory memory, known to evoke vivid emotional recall.

---

## VIII. Case Studies in AA Mastery

### Case Study A: The Apprentice–Mentor Grimoire Exchange

A mentor and apprentice in creative writing exchange bespoke "grimoires"—handbound journals infused with prompts and marginalia.

- **Ritual:** Each month, mentor sends a section of the grimoire with writing prompts and annotated excerpts; apprentice responds by writing personal reflections and pasting small collages.

- **Multi-Modal Integration:** AD emails schedule exchanges; SD monthly video calls to discuss a highlighted passage; SA occasional in-person workshops.

- **Outcome:** The collaborative grimoire evolves into a co-authored manuscript, while deepening mutual respect and creative trust.

### Case Study B: The Transoceanic "Treasure Chest" Project

Two childhood friends, separated by continents, commit to quarterly "treasure chests."

- **Contents:** Fair-trade coffee beans from one side; hand-carved wooden tokens from the other; local postcards; a letter narrating life updates; a small piece of local art.

- **Ethical Sourcing:** Items support local artisans, reflecting shared values of social justice.

- **Outcome:** Over two years, the chests become family heirlooms—fetishized for their cultural layers and emotional significance.

### Case Study C: The "Silent Poetry" Collaboration

A duo of poets embark on a year-long AA poetry chain:

- **Process:** One writes a poem on a card and mails it; the other writes a response-poem on the envelope, turning both into a palimpsest.

- **Depth:** Poems evolve from light haiku to deeply personal free-verse, tracking emotional seasons.

- **Artifact:** When complete, the entwined cards are bound into an art book.

- **Outcome:** The project yields a published chapbook and cements a lifelong creative alliance.

---

## IX. Measuring and Auditing AA Engagement

### A. Qualitative Reflections

- **Analog Journal:** Maintain a log of AA gestures sent and received—note date, modality mix (letter, package, postcard), depth prompt used, and emotional resonance.

- **Reflective Questions:**
    - "Which artifact brought the deepest sense of connection?"
    - "What anticipatory joy did I experience before receiving the package?"

## B. Quantitative Metrics

- **Artifact Frequency:** Track the number of AA gestures per quarter. Aim for at least one per key friendship every six weeks.
- **Reciprocity Index:** Percentage of AA gestures reciprocated within a defined period (e.g., three months).

## C. Environmental & Ethical Audit

- **Sourcing Score:** Proportion of materials that are sustainably sourced or locally crafted.
- **Accessibility Check:** Note whether any friends required adapted formats (large-print letters, audio descriptions).

## D. Modal Balance Dashboard

Visualize your friendship interactions across all four modalities. Strive for AA to represent a meaningful portion—ideally 15–25 %—of the total engagement portfolio.

---

# X. Integrating AA with Other Modalities

1. **AA → SD Follow-Up:** After sending a letter, schedule a brief video call to discuss its themes.
2. **SA Artifact Presentation:** Present a care package by hand during an in-person meeting, combining AA with SA.
3. **AD Echoes:** Transcribe key passages from your letter into an email thread to spark further digital reflection.
4. **Quadrant Spiral:**

- **SL–AA:** Postcard with a quick greeting.
- **SL–AD:** Follow-up DM saying, "Did you get my postcard?"
- **DL–AA:** Letter sharing a personal story.
- **DL–SD:** Video call to unpack the letter's reflections.

This **spiral method** ensures no modality remains siloed, and each deep gesture reverberates through multiple channels.

## XI. Avoiding Overindulgence and Artifact Fatigue

- **Curated Cadence:** Resist monthly packages if they become logistically overwhelming; scale to quarterly or biannual cycles.
- **Minimalist Aesthetics:** A single, well-chosen artifact often surpasses a cluttered collection.
- **Expectational Clarity:** Clarify that gifts are tokens of presence, not transactional obligations—"No need to reciprocate materially; your friendship is gift enough."

## XII. Conclusion & Transition

Asynchronous Analog gestures—letters, postcards, care packages, handmade artifacts—operate on the **slow clock** of anticipation and reminiscence. They are the **poems** of friendship, composed in ink, paper, and curated tokens that whisper across time.

In **Chapter 8**, we synthesize the four pillars—Presence, Intentionality, Empathy, Vulnerability—across all modalities and explore how to cultivate **sustainable friendship habits** through Quarterly Relationship Audits, Mutual Communication Contracts, Ritualized Milestones, and Emotional Bank Accounts. May your next tactile gesture—whether a single pressed flower or a handbound booklet—be a testament to friendship's enduring flesh and a challenge to a world tempted by ephemeral convenience.

**Chapter 8**
**Pillar One: Presence—Being Fully Here Across Modalities**

> "Presence is the oxygen of friendship; without it, relationships suffocate."

---

# I. Introduction: The Imperative of Presence

In our increasingly mediated world, **presence**—the act of giving someone your undivided attention—has become a radical gesture. Presence is not merely the absence of distraction; it is the **active alignment** of mind, heart, and senses toward another. At its core, presence conveys care: it says, "You matter more than any ping, any algorithmic lure, any competing demand." ReconneXion Theory elevates presence to the status of the first of four ethical pillars (alongside Intentionality, Empathy, and Vulnerability). While previous chapters have mapped **where** (modalities) and **what** (depth) of connection, this chapter interrogates **how** to inhabit each modality with true presence—synchronous digital (SD), asynchronous digital (AD), synchronous analog (SA), and asynchronous analog (AA)—and explores presence's philosophical, neurological, and social dimensions.

**Chapter 8 is intentionally more expansive than previous chapters**, reflecting presence's foundational role: a meticulous excavation of its meanings, challenges, and practical enactments. By the end, readers will have a comprehensive framework for cultivating presence as a conscious practice—transforming fleeting attention into the bedrock of enduring friendship.

---

# II. Philosophical Foundations of Presence

### A. Heidegger's Ontology of Being-with (Mitsein)

Martin Heidegger in *Being and Time* introduces the concept of **Mitsein** or "Being-with": our existence is fundamentally intertwined with others. When genuinely **present**, we transcend the isolated "subject-object" stance and enter into a **co-being** where the boundary between self-reference and other dissolves. Presence, in Heideggerian terms, is the ontological condition of authentic **Dasein-in-Gemeinschaft** (Being-in-community).

- **Implication for Friendship:** To be present is to honor the friend as another Dasein—mobile, finite, and seeking meaning. It demands shedding the mode of "presence-at-hand" (Vorhandenheit), wherein we treat others as mere objects or functions, and embracing "ready-to-hand" (Zuhandenheit), a mode of engaged, empathetic involvement.

## B. Buber's I-Thou Encounter

Martin Buber, in *I and Thou*, portrays genuine dialogue as an **I-Thou** moment—where I encounter the Thou (the other person) in their full personhood. In such encounters:

- **I-Am-You Reciprocity:** Each participant listens not to respond, but to be fully open, forging a **bridge of mutual recognition**.
- **Absence of Utility:** I-Thou is antithetical to "I-It" relations where one treats the other as a means. Presence, therefore, is the vehicle enabling I-Thou.

**Implication for Friendship:** Presence is not negotiable—it is the sine qua non of any I-Thou encounter. Without it, conversation reverts to an I-It loop, where companionship becomes instrumental and shallow.

## C. Phenomenology of Attention (Merleau-Ponty & Sartre)

Maurice Merleau-Ponty extends presence into the sensory realm, arguing that **perception is embodied**—that our bodies are the **primary locus** of knowing. Likewise, Jean-Paul Sartre's notion of **being-for-others** situates presence as the way we discover ourselves in the gaze of another.

- **Embodiment:** Presence therefore entails harnessing the full spectrum of bodily awareness—posture, gesture, tone, eye contact—to anchor attention in the moment.
- **Duration (Sartre's Projected Being):** Sartre posits that being present is a temporal act: a commitment to remain **in the now**, resisting the pull of past regrets or future anxieties.

**Implication for Friendship:** True presence binds us to the **temporal surface** of shared now. When a friend speaks, presence means absorbing not only their words but the bodily resonance in which those words are born.

---

# III. Neuroscience and Psychology of Presence

## A. Neural Mechanisms Underlying Attunement

1. **Mirror Neuron Systems:** Discovered in primate premotor cortices and later found in humans, **mirror neurons** fire both when an individual performs an action and when they **observe someone else** performing the same action. In face-to-face interactions, mirror neurons underpin empathic attunement—allowing us to resonate with the friend's emotional state. Presence thus **amplifies mirror neuron engagement**, fostering deeper

empathy.

2. **Oxytocin and Social Bonding:** The neuropeptide **oxytocin** is central to trust and bonding. Studies show that **eye contact**, warm prosody, and **synchronized interaction** (e.g., walking together, sharing laughter) release oxytocin, cementing social bonds. Digital interactions risk attenuated oxytocin release (digital eye contact differs from live gaze), but synchronizing elements in SD—like deliberate eye alignment and vocal warmth—can partially reclaim the oxytocin surge.

3. **Prefrontal Cortex's Role in Attention:** The **dorsolateral prefrontal cortex (DLPFC)** is engaged in sustained attention and executive control. When we practice mindful presence, DLPFC activity increases, suppressing distractive impulses. Conversely, multitasking degrades DLPFC capacity, leading to shallow processing.

## B. Cognitive Psychology of Distraction and Flow

1. **Attentional Blink:** Cognitive studies reveal that rapidly shifting attention leads to "attentional blink"—a brief period after processing one stimulus during which subsequent stimuli are missed. This phenomenon explains why checking a phone notification during a conversation often causes significant information loss. Presence combats attentional blink by minimizing task-switching.

2. **Flow State (Csikszentmihalyi):** Flow is a state of deep immersion where individuals lose track of time and self, fully absorbed in an activity. Friendship interactions—especially SA activities—can catalyze micro-flows when both participants engage in a shared task with aligned goals and mutual feedback. Presence is the gatekeeper to flow: it suspends self-monitoring and invites a dissolved sense of "I-and-You as One"—promoting cogent dialogue or collaborative creation.

## C. Emotional Intelligence and Mindful Awareness

Emotional intelligence (EI) frameworks (Salovey & Mayer) emphasize **perceiving, using, understanding, and managing emotions**. Presence is the bedrock upon which EI operates in relationships:

- **Perceiving:** Accurate recognition of a friend's emotional cues requires undistracted observation—visible changes in facial expression, voice timbre, and body language.
- **Using:** When present, we harness emotional information to deepen connection—choosing our responses to attune rather than deflect.

- **Understanding:** Presence supports reflective processes: discerning not only "what" a friend is feeling but "why"—rooted in their history, context, or vulnerabilities.

- **Managing:** Guided by presence, we co-regulate—acknowledging distress with empathy, co-creating rituals to alleviate anxiety, or celebrating joy with genuine enthusiasm.

## IV. Presence Across Modalities: Nuanced Challenges and Strategies

Each modality—SD, AD, SA, AA—carries unique **obstacles** and **opportunities** for presence. Though previous chapters have outlined basic strategies per modality, here we delve deeper, offering extended practice recommendations and nuance.

### A. Presence in Synchronous Digital (SD)

#### 1. Challenges

- **Attention Fragmentation:** The omnipresent lure of background apps, notifications, and email demands constant toggling.

- **Digital Self-Monitoring:** Seeing one's own thumbnail fosters self-consciousness, siphoning cognitive resources toward self-image maintenance rather than empathic listening.

- **Connectivity Glitches:** Lag, pixelation, and frozen frames interrupt conversational flow, breeding impatience that can be mistaken for disinterest.

- **Multidimensional Inputs:** Managing chat boxes, screen-sharing, and participant windows fragments sensory focus.

#### 2. Deep-Practice Strategies

#### a. Digital Presence Declarations

- **Mutual Agreement:** At session start, participants verbalize: "For the next [duration], I commit to my full presence. My devices are silenced; I will not multitask."

- **Visual Anchor:** Everyone disables self-view (hides own thumbnail) to curb self-monitoring distractors. Encourage setting the call window to "gallery view" to see others in equal size, minimizing dominance of any individual's image.

b. **Structured Attention Rituals**

- **Check-Ins (First 2 Minutes):** Begin calls with a "one-word weather check" for emotional climate: "I feel…". Participants then mute, breathe collectively for five seconds, and then return to speak—anchoring the group's focus on the here-and-now rather than on emails or background tasks.
- **Timed Listening Turns:** Use a simple rotation or "talking stick" metaphor: designate a "virtual stick" passed via chat message. Only the person holding the stick may speak; others listen in silence. This reduces cross-talk, cues active listening, and heightens attentiveness.

c. **Sensory Enrichment**

- **Ambient Soundscapes:** If appropriate, play a low-volume instrumental track or nature sounds (rain, forest) to mask extraneous noises and cue a shared sensory environment.
- **Synchronous Gestures:** Encourage participants to adopt a common gesture at the start (e.g., placing hand on heart). This embodied act, even via video, signals readiness for authentic engagement.

d. **Real-Time Reflective Practices**

- **"Pause & Reflect 2.0":** At designated junctures (every 15 minutes), host initiates a 10-second silence. During silence, participants mindfully notice their own thoughts and emotions, then share a brief reflective statement: "One insight I'm holding…" before continuing dialogue.

e. **Screen-Free Segments**

- **Audio-Only Interludes:** After initial greeting, switch off video for a segment (5–10 minutes) to focus on voice tone and verbal nuances. This diminishes visual distractions and recalibrates attention to listening without the pressure of being watched.

3. **Case Studies & Exemplars**

**Case Study SD-A: The Digital Retreat Day**
A group of six friends orchestrates a quarterly "Digital Retreat Day" via Zoom, integrating the above strategies:

1. **Opening Ritual (10 min):** Each places a symbolic object (photo, candle) in front of their camera, briefly stating why it's meaningful—anchoring presence and shared intention.

2. **Silent Co-Reading (20 min):** All read a short, pre-shared reflective text (e.g., Montaigne's essay excerpt) in silence, then discuss impressions—combining SL with preparatory DL.

3. **Guided DL Discussions (30 min):** Host uses "Pause & Reflect 2.0" every 10 minutes to check emotional temperature.

4. **Closing Gesture (10 min):** Each blows a "virtual kiss" into the camera, then mutes, symbolically passing love across screens.

**Outcomes:** Participants report a 50 % increase in perceived depth compared to typical video calls, citing reduced "Zoom fatigue" and heightened emotional resonance.

---

## B. Presence in Asynchronous Digital (AD)

### 1. Challenges

- **Delayed Reciprocity Anxiety:** Knowing a friend will read but may not reply promptly can create anticipatory anxiety, distracting from present-moment tasks.

- **Shorthand Seduction:** The ease of tapping emoji or quick "K" responses can truncate conversation before it deepens.

- **Thread Overload:** Multiple open threads across platforms (email, Slack, social media) fragment attention, making true focused reading rare.

### 2. Deep-Practice Strategies

### a. Intentional Notification Management

- **Batch Notification Windows:** Agree with friends on specific "windows" when AD messages are read—e.g., "I check letters at 10am and 6pm" or "My AD Response Window is within 24 hours." This harnesses the **spacing effect** to preserve AD's reflective promise.

- **"Inbox Zero" Ritual:** Rather than glancing at every incoming message, designate uninterrupted blocks (e.g., 30 minutes) to process and respond, ensuring each friend's missive receives undivided attention.

### b. Slow Writing Ritual

- **Micro-Drafts:** Before composing a DL message, write a rough draft in a separate document, then revisit after 5–10 minutes for edits—enabling cognitive distance and emotional regulation.

- **Handwritten First Draft:** For exceptionally meaningful messages, pen a handwritten letter draft, then transcribe digitally—embedding analog presence into the digital domain.

### c. Empathetic Framing & Tone Cues

- **Vocal Emulation in Writing:** Use punctuation (ellipses, dashes) and descriptive phrases—"I say this with a soft voice"—to convey intention, compensating for absent vocal tone.

- **Emoji with Purpose:** When used sparingly and deliberately, a well-placed emoji (e.g., a hand-over-heart 🫶) can signal warmth without reducing depth to a cartoonish shorthand.

### d. Reflective Follow-Up Prompts

- **"I read your message and…" Opener:** Begin each response by referencing specific lines, demonstrating full absorption of content: "When you wrote, 'I felt lost in that meeting,' I pictured how heavy that must've felt."

- **Invitation for Continued Reflection:** End with an open-ended question, e.g., "What's one change you're noticing now?"—keeping depth aloft while respecting asynchronous pacing.

## 3. Case Studies & Exemplars

### Case Study AD-A: The Biweekly Emotional Audit

A pair of siblings living in different countries institutes a biweekly AD ritual:

1. **Emotional Inventory Template:** Each fills out a shared Google Doc before 8am Sunday:

    - Current Mood (1–10 scale)
    - Biggest Challenge of the Week
    - Unexpected Joy
    - One DL Question for Sibling
2. **Timed Writing Slots:** Both commit to writing and reading responses between 8–9pm local time in scheduled slots—minimizing distraction.
3. **Reflective Reciprocity:** Each reply addresses the other's three prompts in sequence, weaving shared meaning across time zones.

**Outcomes:** Over six months, both siblings report improved emotional intelligence, citing AD's combination of reflection time and structured prompts as key.

---

## C. Presence in Synchronous Analog (SA)

### 1. Challenges

- **Competing Temporal Demands:** In-person gatherings often truncated by work, caregiving, or commuting constraints.
- **Environmental Distractions:** Cafés, parks, or public spaces introduce ambient noise, interruptions, and sensory overload.
- **Assumed Focus vs. Actuality:** Mere physical co-presence often masquerades as presence—friends might remain physically together but mentally adrift (e.g., glancing at phones).

### 2. Deep-Practice Strategies

### a. Sacred Spaces & Time Boundaries

- **Designating "Presence Zones":** Agree on specific physical areas (e.g., a friend's living room corner, a favorite bench) that are free of phones and external dialogues.
- **Calendared "Presence Blocks":** Use calendar invites for SA sessions, labeling them "SA: Full Presence" with start and end times—signaling that no other task supersedes

this time slot.

## b. Multisensory Grounding Techniques

- **Mindful Arrival Ritual:** Upon meeting, pause at the threshold (doorway or park gate), remove shoes (if indoors), and take three synchronized breaths before commencing conversation. This signals a transition from the outside world into a shared relational space.
- **Sensory Check-In:** Early in the encounter, verbalize one sensory observation ("I notice the crisp autumn breeze"). This primes attentiveness to embodied experience and co-creates a shared sensory baseline.

## c. Joint Embodied Practices

- **Walking Dual Attention:** As you walk together, alternate between **"Path Presence"** (noticing environment: textures, sounds, smells) and **"Heart Presence"** (turning inward to sense the body's emotional state). After each 5–7 minutes, pause at a chosen landmark (bench, tree) to share insights.
- **Shared Creative Flow:** Engage in an embodied co-creation—pottery-making, painting side by side, cooking a new recipe—ensuring task interleaves with periodic eye contact and check-in comments ("How does that dough feel to you?"). This intersperses DL check-ins within an SA activity.

## d. Presence-Protective Artifacts

- **Presence Tokens:** Agree that leaving a specific token on the table (e.g., a small wooden owl) signals "full presence mode"—neither party should check or use their phone until the token is removed.
- **Analog Timekeepers:** Use a sand timer (5- or 10-minute) to mark segments of sustained, unbroken attention. When the sand runs out, both pause to briefly reflect ("What's one emotion I'm holding?") before returning to conversation.

## 3. Case Studies & Exemplars

### Case Study SA-A: The Quarterly "Soul Walk"
A triad of friends institutes a quarterly SA "Soul Walk" ritual:

1. **Route Selection:** Each quarter, one friend selects a 5–7 km route in nature, signifying a new environment to cultivate novelty.

2. **Opening Presence Ceremony:** At the trailhead, all stand in a circle, placing right hands on each other's left shoulders and reciting a chosen verse or phrase—anchoring primary intention.

3. **Structured Confluence:** Every 10 minutes, the walk pauses for a **"Heart-Share"**—each friend has one uninterrupted minute to speak while the other two maintain nonverbal attunement (eye contact, nodding).

4. **Closing Gratitude Moment:** At a scenic overlook, each offers a brief gratitude statement about a valued trait of another, fostering DL connection steeped in SA.

**Outcomes:** Over a year, participants cite increased resilience and deeper mutual empathy, attributing as much to SA's multisensory richness as to verbal exchange.

## D. Presence in Asynchronous Analog (AA)

### 1. Challenges

- **Spatial Separation of Artifact & Action:** Once a letter or package is sent, real-time feedback is impossible; sender cannot gauge presence in the moment of receipt.

- **Artifact Accumulation:** Friends may hoard letters or packages, inadvertently disconnecting from the intended temporal and emotional context.

- **Handwriting Barriers:** Digital age has eroded handwriting fluency; some may feel anxious about illegible script or imperfect presentation.

### 2. Deep-Practice Strategies

### a. Crafted Temporal Bridges

- **Timestamping & Dating:** Begin each letter with a precise date and time—not "Just yesterday" but "May 31, 2025, 7:47pm"—situating the artifact in clear chronology, recalling the sender's state-of-mind.

- **Delayed Echo Ritual:** After sending, schedule a follow-up SD or AD check-in roughly halfway through the expected postal transit time, saying: "I mailed you something—just wanted to share my excitement and hear if it arrived."

### b. Embodied Writing Practices

- **Writing in Ritual Garb:** Wear a specific scarf, wristband, or light candle near your writing desk—any embodied cue that toggles your mental state into "presence for the friend" mode. Over time, the sensory association triggers immediate focus.

- **"Voice Over Hand" Technique:** Before writing each sentence, read it aloud in a tone you would use during a DL conversation, then transcribe by hand—fusing vocal presence into the written artifact.

### c. Sensory-Enriched Artifact Design

- **Layered Textures:** Attach a pressed leaf or a swatch of fabric to each letter. Include a line: "Touch this cloth and remember our shared afternoon at the market." This **multi-sensory anchor** invites recipient to re-engage with embodied memory.

- **Envelope Whisper:** Seal letters with a faint spritz of a distinct essential-oil blend previously shared with the friend: "Our 'forest-breeze' scent—so you smell home the moment you open."

### d. Intentional Curation of Reciprocation

- **Reciprocity Bridge:** At the close of each letter or package, include a small prompt or "Analog RSVP" card—"If it resonates, mail back a doodle, a list of three dreams, or a tiny artifact that speaks to your week." This invites continued presence across space and time.

## 3. Case Studies & Exemplars

### Case Study AA-A: The "Time Capsule Correspondence"
A duo of longtime friends builds a living "time capsule" of letters:

1. **Protocol:** Each writes a two-page handwritten letter monthly. They include one photograph and one small memento (dried flower, ticket stub).

2. **Time-Lock Element:** On each letter, they write: "Open exactly six months after receipt." This induces a **temporal displacement**—embedding anticipation and reflection.

3. **After-Open Ritual:** When friend finally opens, they host a brief SD call to discuss revelations, bridging AA with SD.

**Outcomes:** The duo reports enhanced self-awareness (documenting personal growth stages) and deeper appreciation of temporal perspective. Letters eventually form a 100-page scrapbook of evolving selves.

---

## V. Ethical Imperatives and Ground Rules for Cultivating Presence

Presence, while admirable, can be misapplied—leading to boundary violations, emotional burdens, or relational exhaustion. The following ethical principles guide **healthy, sustainable presence**:

1. **Consent & Agency:**
   - **Ask Before Intrusion:** Even in SA, knock or message before dropping by—respecting the friend's autonomy over their space.
   - **Make "No-Contact" Permissible:** Always allow "presence breaks"—the friend can request a temporary hiatus without guilt.

2. **Respect for Temporal Rhythms:**
   - **Honoring Life's Cycles:** Acknowledge that presence needs wax and wane—be attuned to the friend's energy cycles, busy seasons, or emotional bandwidth.
   - **Sabbatical Boundaries:** Propose "Presence Sabbaths"—mutual agreements to refrain from reaching out for 24–48 hours to allow individual rest.

3. **Reciprocity & Equilibrium:**
   - **Balance Giving & Receiving:** Monitor emotional bank accounts—if one gives unduly without receiving, recalibrate to avoid burnout or dependency.
   - **Quotas for Modal Engagement:** Maintain no more than 40% of interactions in any single modality; presence demands a **modal portfolio** that distributes care evenly.

4. **Transparency & Honesty:**

- o **Express Difficulties:** If presence is impossible (due to illness or crisis), communicate proactively—"I value you, but right now I need quiet."
- o **Avoid Passive-Aggression:** Late replies or canceled plans should be accompanied by heartfelt apologies and brief explanations, rather than silence.

# VI. Practical Rituals & Exercises to Embody Presence

The following **15 detailed practices** can be woven into daily life to cultivate presence across modalities. Each practice is paired with an **example scenario** and **anticipated outcome**.

## 1. Tactile Arrival Ritual (SA)

- **Practice:** Before an in-person meeting, remove shoes or a scarf at the doorstep. Place uniform objects (e.g., two candles) between you and your friend.
- **Scenario:** Two friends meet for tea at a home café. Both hang their jackets, remove shoes, and light a single candle in the center of the table—symbolizing shared illumination.
- **Anticipated Outcome:** The act signals an intentional transition from external world to shared space, priming both for focused interaction.

## 2. Digital Silence Charter (SD + AD)

- **Practice:** Craft a short "Digital Silence Charter" co-signed by close friends: "Between 7–8pm, we commit to no notifications except emergencies."
- **Scenario:** A trio of roommates creates a group chat-level pinned message outlining the charter. Each blocks notifications during the agreed window, then sends one group photo or voice note summarizing the day at 8pm.
- **Anticipated Outcome:** Shared silence fosters anticipation; the 8pm summary becomes a prized ritual of presence.

## 3. Presence Token Exchange (AA)

- **Practice:** Create small, unique tokens (e.g., hand-painted stones or clipped plant sprigs) labeled "Presence—Open Me." Exchange them via mail with instructions to keep them on the bedside table until the next letter.

- **Scenario:** A friend in another city sends a small river stone decorated with a painted eye. The recipient places it under their pillow for a week, making it a tactile cue of presence.

- **Anticipated Outcome:** The token's weight and texture evoke presence even in absence; when writing back, the recipient can reference how holding the stone influenced their thoughts.

## 4. "Heartbeat" Check-In (SD + SA)

- **Practice:** Designate two minutes at a fixed time—weekly—for a "Heartbeat Check-In" where friends share one physiological sensation (e.g., "I notice my heart racing because…").

- **Scenario:** During each Sunday night video call, each participant speaks for 30 seconds about a salient bodily feeling—tension in shoulders, fluttering heartbeat—allowing emotional cues to surface.

- **Anticipated Outcome:** Acknowledging somatic states deepens empathy, enhancing presence by coupling mind and body in shared awareness.

## 5. Slow "Presence Walk" (SA)

- **Practice:** Walk together at one's slowest comfortable pace, deliberately pausing every 3 minutes to share a mirror-based reflection—"At this pause, I feel…"

- **Scenario:** Two colleagues seeking deeper friendship use a nearby botanical garden. They walk the winding path at a near-stop pace, alternately pausing at landmarks to verbalize sensations and emotions.

- **Anticipated Outcome:** Movement becomes an embodied conversation; pauses provide space for metacognitive insights, forging presence in body and mind.

## 6. Postcard Remark Jar (AA)

- **Practice:** Maintain a small "Remark Jar" of handwritten postcard-sized notes—each bearing an affirmation or observation (e.g., "You inspire me with your courage"). Mail one each month.

- **Scenario:** Across six months, a friend receives six postcards, each focusing on different strengths: resilience, humor, creativity. Each note is dated and signed.

- **Anticipated Outcome:** The collection becomes a tactile anthology of support; when feeling doubt, the friend re-reads to rekindle presence-fueled encouragement.

## 7. "Digital Candle" Presence Screen (SD)

- **Practice:** Create a simple virtual "candle" (a full-screen image) that remains on display for the initial few minutes of every video call, symbolizing shared focus.

- **Scenario:** In remote couples counseling, partners begin sessions by jointly lighting virtual candles on their screens, observing for 30 seconds in silence.

- **Anticipated Outcome:** The candle image cues both into a contemplative mode, attenuating digital flicker anxiety and aligning attention.

## 8. Email "Depth Hour" Envelope (AD)

- **Practice:** Once weekly, send one email labeled "Depth Hour" with a multi-paragraph reflection and a prompt. The friend commits to reading and responding during a single, uninterrupted hour.

- **Scenario:** A long-distance duo dedicates Wednesdays at 9pm to "Depth Hour." One emails an essay-like letter exploring a recent epiphany; the other replies in kind within that hour.

- **Anticipated Outcome:** The hour-long immersion encourages sustained attention and prevents fragmented reading—each message becomes a mini-retreat.

## 9. Compassion Circle (SA + SD)

- **Practice:** Small groups (~4–6 friends) hold monthly "Compassion Circles," alternating between in-person meetings and SD calls. Each session includes a guided meditation, a DL check-in, and a brief resource-sharing segment (book, poem, practice).

- **Scenario:** In April, the circle meets at a community center, guided by a simple script: 10-minute seated meditation, 20-minute DL sharing with reflective listening, 10-minute group reading of a chosen poem. In May, the same structure is mirrored via Zoom.

- **Anticipated Outcome:** Alternating modalities fosters versatility; participants build group presence skills across contexts.

## 10. "Presence Playlist" Shared Listening (AA + SD)

- **Practice:** Curate a shared playlist of music (approx. 10–12 songs) and agree to listen during one hour of the day. Each friend then meets in an SD call to discuss emotional reactions in real time.

- **Scenario:** Four friends share a Spotify playlist titled "Presence Vibes." On the chosen day, each listens through headphones while strolling alone; at 8pm, they reconvene on a call to share how specific tracks moved them.

- **Anticipated Outcome:** Individual contemplation during listening primes deeper DL discussion; the act of synchronizing across time zones reinforces presence even in solitude.

## 11. "Presence Harvest" Gratitude Box (AD + AA)

- **Practice:** Establish a gratitude box—each friend writes one gratitude or moment of connection each week on small cards and places them in a physical box. At month's end, the box is mailed to another friend, who reads the cards and responds with reflections.

- **Scenario:** A quartet rotates the box monthly. When friend A receives it, she takes an afternoon to read each card (10–15 cards), then writes individual short letters responding to each gratitude, then rotates the now-empty box to friend B.

- **Anticipated Outcome:** The cyclical movement of the box preserves presence over extended periods, honoring shared memories and generating new DL content.

## 12. Embodied Dinner Ritual (SA)

- **Practice:** Host a "Presence Dinner"—no phones, no background music. Each course is served with a DL prompt:

    - **Appetizer:** "Share one recent small joy."

- **Main Course:** "What fear are you confronting?"
- **Dessert:** "What dream do you cherish?"
- **Scenario:** A group of five friends commits to a quarterly "Presence Dinner" at rotating homes. Each course lasts 20 minutes: 10 minutes eating, 10 minutes sharing.
- **Anticipated Outcome:** The structure avoids rambling; each friend's vulnerability is bracketed by communal nourishment, reinforcing safety and presence.

## 13. "Mindful Typing" Practice (AD + SD)

- **Practice:** When writing important AD messages, use a "mindful typing" exercise: place index fingers on temples for 5 seconds, inhaling a calming aroma (e.g., lavender), setting intention, then begin typing slowly, infusing each word with presence.
- **Scenario:** Before replying to a roommate's heartfelt email about burnout, one sits quietly for 10 breaths while holding a lavender sachet, then replies succinctly but empathetically—"I hear you…"
- **Anticipated Outcome:** The pause reduces reactivity; the resulting message resonates more deeply.

## 14. Presence Walk with a Purpose (SA + AD)

- **Practice:** Walk in pairs along a tranquil route, alternating between DL sharing and moments of silent observation. After the walk, each writes a brief AD summary of their insights within 24 hours.
- **Scenario:** Two university students walk five kilometers around campus at sunset. Every quarter-kilometer, one shares a personal update; the other listens silently, then at a marker they swap roles. Next morning, they exchange AD reflections on how silent moments influenced their shared understanding.
- **Anticipated Outcome:** The combination of SA presence with AD follow-up cements insights and enhances mindful integration.

## 15. "Presence Journal" Co-Creation (AA + AD)

- **Practice:** Co-author a physical "Presence Journal"—one friend writes a reflection on an encounter, then mails it; the other responds by writing their side of the shared memory and mails it back. This cycle continues, creating an alternating narrative artifact.

- **Scenario:** Over six months, two childhood friends weave a 60-page journal without digital reliance. Each entry begins with "I noticed you when…" followed by personal reflections.
- **Anticipated Outcome:** The journal becomes a testament to sustained presence; both friends can leaf through entries to relive presence moments.

---

# VII. Deep-Dive Case Studies: Presence in Action

To illustrate the full spectrum of presence practices, we examine three in-depth case studies highlighting **multi-modal integration**, iterative learning, and adaptive refinement.

---

## Case Study 1: The "Presence Quadrant Accelerator" for Remote Teams

### A. Context & Challenges

A tech startup with team members dispersed across three continents struggles with **team cohesion**. Frequent SD meetings devolve into status updates (SL–SD) with minimal DL content. Team morale dips—employees feel unseen; burnout rises.

### B. Intervention Design

**Phase 1: Baseline Audit**

- **Metrics Collected:**
    - Percentage of SL vs. DL interactions during SD meetings (via meeting analysis).
    - Engagement rates (participation count, chat activity).
    - Self-reported sense of presence (survey).
- **Findings:** 85 % SL, 15 % DL; low participation from half the team.

**Phase 2: Presence Pillar Workshop**

- **Half-Day SA Retreat (In-Person & Hybrid):**
    - **Opening Ritual:** Global "virtual" bonfire—locals lit candles, shared brief DL reflections on team values.
    - **Mirroring Activity:** Pairs practiced "active listening" while walking along preselected paths (SA).
    - **Visioning Session:** Co-creating a "Presence Manifesto" outlining presence-described behaviors: "Turn off other apps during prompts," "Use video-on at designated intervals," etc.

## Phase 3: SD Integration

- **Weekly "Check-In Circles":** 10-minute DL segment in each Monday SD call: "What's one personal intention you bring this week?"
- **"Presence Cards" in Shared Digital Space:** Virtual cards with reminders—"Pause to acknowledge a colleague's shared emotion," "Use 10-second silence after emotional shares."
- **AD "Pulse Emails":** Every Friday, each writes a short reflective email: "This week's presence highlight," "Where did I drift?"

## Phase 4: AA Reinforcement

- **Monthly Care Packages:** Team members each take turns sending a small artifact (postcard, snack, book) to a rotating colleague.
- **Presence Journal:** A shared physical journal that travels every month to a new team member for DL entries about experiences with the Presence Pillar.

## C. Outcomes & Insights

- **Quantitative Shifts:** DL content in SD meetings rose from 15 % to 45 % within three months.
- **Engagement Metrics:** Participation increased by 60 %; chat activity halved as live sharing increased.
- **Survey Results:** Self-reported sense of being "fully seen" climbed from 2.8/5 to 4.2/5.

- **Qualitative Feedback:** Team members cited the SA retreat as "transformative" for understanding digital empathy; the hybrid virtual bonfire created a "shared mood resonance" across time zones.

- **Lessons Learned:**
    - Combining SA embodiment with SD rituals accelerated collective presence norms.
    - AD reflections root presence in ongoing self-awareness, while AA artifacts personalized digital interactions.
    - Clear metrics and recurring audits maintained accountability, preventing relapse into SL patterns.

---

## Case Study 2: The "Presence-Focused Sibling Covenantal Pact"

### A. Context & Challenges

Three adult siblings residing in different cities feel drifting apart. Their interactions are predominantly SL–AD ("Hey, call me if you need anything"), lacking depth. Family obligations, career pressures, and parental caregiving preclude SA opportunities.

### B. Intervention Design

#### Phase 1: Family Presence Contract

- **Covenant Document:** In an SD call, siblings co-write a "Family Presence Pact" with mutually agreed promises:
    - **SD Commitment:** 4 monthly video "Heart Chats" of 45 minutes each.
    - **AD Commitment:** Each sibling sends one DL email every two weeks.
    - **AA Commitment:** Quarterly "Legacy Boxes" with curated mementos and letters focusing on family history.

#### Phase 2: Enhanced SD Rituals

- **Opening Presence Ceremony:** Each SD call begins with everyone lighting a small candle and holding it to the camera, signifying "light in the darkness" connecting them.

- **Structured DL Segments:** Calls partitioned into:
    - "Life Highlights" (SL–SD, 10 minutes)
    - "Deep Dive" (DL–SD, 25 minutes with "Pause & Reflect 2.0" every 8 minutes)
    - "Actionable Takeaways" (Intentions for supporting each other during the next weeks, 10 minutes)

## Phase 3: AD Deepening

- **Biweekly "Sentiment Letters":** Each sibling writes a letter exploring one emotional theme—guilt, pride, grief—related to family dynamics, sending it via email with a PDF backup.

- **Mindful Timing:** All siblings agree to read and respond within 48 hours, ensuring the thread remains alive while preserving personal schedules.

## Phase 4: AA Heritage Boxes

- **Curriculum:** Each sibling curates a box containing:
    - Photographs of childhood landmarks.
    - Short handwritten stories about family traditions.
    - A small personal-down artifact (e.g., a drawing of the old family home).

- **Exchange Cycle:** Boxes rotate annually—each sibling receives, reflects for two weeks, then mails with added personal annotations.

## C. Outcomes & Insights

- **Emotional Reconnection:** Reports of sibling closeness rose from 2.3/5 to 4.5/5 over nine months.

- **AD Depth:** Brothers wrote 3,000-word emotional essays that transformed into a published e-book of family memoirs.

- **AA Legacy:** The heritage boxes became heirlooms, used to narrate family history to younger cousins.

- **Lessons Learned:**

    - Clear, formalized presence agreements (Family Presence Pact) built accountability and ritualized connection.

    - Combining modalities prevented reliance on any single channel, fostering robust presence.

    - Structured rituals (e.g., candle-lighting, "Sentiment Letters") served as enduring cues anchoring presence in busy lives.

---

## Case Study 3: The "Mindful Campus Presence Program" for University Students

### A. Context & Challenges

A large university's counseling center identifies widespread loneliness among students. Digital campus platforms foster SL–AD or SL–SD communities but rarely DL or SA presence. Many students report feeling invisible despite "virtual connectedness."

### B. Intervention Design

#### Phase 1: Presence Education Modules

- **Orientation Workshop:** Incoming freshmen attend a 2-hour SA seminar:

    - **Philosophical Lecture:** Brief overview of presence theories (Heidegger, Buber).

    - **Experiential Exercises:** Paired "mindful staring" (60 seconds of sustained eye contact, then share immediate feelings) and "silent tea ceremony" (10-min focused tea drinking).

    - **Group Debrief:** Connect exercises to "What does it mean to truly see someone?"

#### Phase 2: Campus-Wide SD Initiatives

- **"Presence Pods":** Small student groups (6–8) meet weekly on Zoom, guided by trained facilitators to practice "Pause & Reflect," share DL stories, and co-create "Mindful Checklists" for that week.

- **Presence Badge Rewards:** Students receive a digital badge for completing "Presence Pod" modules, redeemable for campus café discounts—linking presence to tangible incentives.

## Phase 3: SA Activation Events

- **"Silent Study Sessions":** In the library's quiet zone, groups of 4 meet to study side by side in silence for 45 minutes, then rotate to share insights about what they observed in themselves or others—fostering silent co-presence.

- **"Park Bench Dialogues":** The university designates benches in scenic quadrangles labeled "Presence Benches." Students are encouraged to sit there for 15 minutes and invite any passing peer to join—promoting spontaneous SA connection.

## Phase 4: AA Reinforcement

- **"Postcard of Affirmation" Stations:** Campus kiosks stocked with postcards and pens; students can write and drop notes to friends. Volunteers collect, stamp, and mail them outside campus.

- **"Wish Frond" Installation:** A large paper "wish tree" sculpture in the student union where peers can write hopes for each other on leaf-shaped cards and pin them—creating a collective AA artifact on campus.

## C. Outcomes & Insights

- **Student Well-Being Surveys:** Post-intervention, reported loneliness decreased by 35 %; sense of "being seen" on campus increased by 50 %.

- **Engagement Metrics:** 75 % of incoming freshmen participated in "Presence Pods"; 40 % attained all "Presence Badge" levels.

- **Qualitative Feedback:** Students described silent sessions as "unexpectedly intimate" and "refreshingly humanizing." The presence benches became informal hubs for cross-major friendships.

- **Lessons Learned:**

- Embedding presence practices within campus infrastructure (benches, kiosks) democratizes access and normalizes presence culture.

- Combining educational modules with ongoing rituals ensured both conceptual understanding and embodied practice.

- The extrinsic reward (badges) worked initially, but intrinsic motivations (experiencing genuine presence) became the long-term driver of engagement.

# VIII. Measuring Presence: Metrics, Audits, and Reflective Tools

To ensure that presence remains a **living practice** rather than a fleeting ideal, systematic measurement and reflection are indispensable. Below are **five** comprehensive tools and techniques to track, audit, and refine presence across modalities.

### 1. Presence Scorecard: A Weekly Log

**Purpose:** Cultivate self-awareness of presence patterns and identify areas for improvement.
**Components:** Fill out each Sunday evening:

| Modality | Interaction Count | Estimated % Presence (1–100) | Key Distraction Sources | Action for Next Week |
|---|---|---|---|---|
| SD (Video Calls)** | | | | |
| SL–SD | | | | |
| DL–SD | | | | |
| AD Emails/DMs | | | | |
| SL–AD | | | | |

DL–AD

SA (In-Person Meetings)

SL–SA

DL–SA

AA (Letters/Gifts)

SL–AA

DL–AA

**Instructions:**

1. **Quantify Interactions:** For each sub-modality, list how many interactions occurred (e.g., "2 DL–SD video calls").

2. **Estimate Presence:** Rate how present you were during each (e.g., "70 % present during one call; 40 % during another due to email distractions").

3. **Identify Distractions:** Note specific sources (e.g., "Slack pings," "multitasking with dinner").

4. **Action Planning:** Define one concrete step to enhance presence next week (e.g., "Turn off notifications during next DL–SD call," "Set timer for 30 minutes of focused letter-writing without screens").

**Outcome:** The weekly scorecard surfaces patterns—modal dominance, common distractors, and potential growth areas—prompting continuous recalibration.

---

## 2. Quarterly "Presence Audit" Reflection

**Purpose:** Track long-term presence evolution and recalibrate strategic commitments.
**Process:** Every three months, revisit your weekly scorecards and answer:

1. **Pattern Analysis:**
   - Which modality subtypes show consistent low presence scores? Why?
   - Are you over-relying on any modality (e.g., 60 % SD)? How might this impede depth?

2. **Emotional Well-Being Correlation:**
   - Compare presence logs to mood/energy logs: When presence drops, does mood slump?
   - Identify external factors (e.g., work stress, health issues) that influenced presence.

3. **Goal Reassessment:**
   - Re-express presence goals: "I will aim for at least 60 % presence in DL–AD next quarter."
   - Adjust modality quotas: "Reduce SL–SD by 20 %; increase DL–SA sessions by one per month."

4. **Accountability Partner Dialogue:**
   - Share audit results with a trusted friend; discuss obstacles and brainstorm supportive strategies.

5. **New Ritual Integration:**
   - Incorporate at least one new practice from Chapter 8 (e.g., "Presence Token Exchange") into next quarter's plan.

**Outcome:** The quarterly audit fosters longitudinal awareness, preventing complacency and ensuring presence remains adaptive to life's changing rhythms.

---

## 3. Emotional Bank Account Tracking

**Purpose:** Quantify emotional "deposits" (acts of presence) and "withdrawals" (distractions, broken commitments) to maintain relational health.
 **Framework (Inspired by Covey):**

| Date | Interaction Type | Deposit (+) / Withdrawal (−) | Description | Account Balance (Cumulative) |
|------|------------------|------------------------------|-------------|------------------------------|
| June 3, 25 | DL–SA | +10 | 1h walk; fully present; DL conversation on stress. | +10 |
| June 5, 25 | SL–SD | −3 | 30m call; distracted checking Slack; friend noticed my gaze. | +7 |
| June 7, 25 | AA Care Package | +8 | Curated letter with sentimental tokens; timed delivery. | +15 |
| June 10, 25 | DL–AD Email | +6 | 500-word reflective letter; read and replied within 24h. | +21 |
| June 12, 25 | SL–AD Text | −2 | One-line "K"; missed nuance of friend's message. | +19 |

**Instructions:**

1. **Define Deposit/Withdrawal Values:** Assign numerical values based on relative impact: SL interactions (±1–3), mid-depth (±4–6), deep (±7–10).

2. **Record Real-Time:** At day's end, jot down significant interactions.

3. **Analyze Trends Monthly:** If balance dips below zero, schedule a "presence booster" (e.g., a DL–SA dinner).

**Outcome:** By tracking "presence equity," partners maintain awareness of relational health, prompting reparative presence-investments when deficits arise.

---

## 4. "Presence Questionnaire" Self-Assessment

**Purpose:** Elicit introspective responses regarding presence habits, cognitive obstacles, and aspirational benchmarks.

**Sample Questionnaire (Scale 1–7 Likert or Short Answers):**

1. **Personal Attentiveness:** "On a scale of 1–7, how often do you find your mind wandering during live conversations?"

2. **Digital Distraction Awareness:** "Which notifications most frequently disrupt your presence? List top three."

3. **Emotional Resonance:** "Describe a recent moment when you felt fully seen by a friend—what contributed to that sense?"

4. **Physical Embodiment:** "How comfortable are you sustaining eye contact during SA interactions? (1—very uncomfortable; 7—very comfortable)."

5. **Future Intentions:** "What is one concrete behavior you commit to adopting to deepen presence over the next month?"

**Instructions:**

- Administer this self-assessment every quarter.
- Compare responses over time to measure growth in self-awareness and presence capacity.

**Outcome:** The questionnaire surfaces cognitive blind spots and evolves personalized presence goals, fostering metacognitive clarity.

---

## 5. Peer "Presence Peer Review"

**Purpose:** Solicit constructive feedback from peers regarding one's presence skill, blind spots, and growth areas.
**Process:**

1. **Selection of Reviewers:** Choose 2–3 close friends or colleagues who interact frequently with you across at least two modalities.

2. **Structured Feedback Form:** Provide a form with prompts:

   - "When I spoke with you during our last SD call, what signaled high presence? Where did I appear distracted?"
   - "During our SA walk, did you feel heard? If not, which moments felt lacking?"

- "In AD exchanges, did my messages reflect careful engagement? Which felt rushed?"
- "In AA artifacts (letters, packages), did you sense my presence? How so?"

3. **Review and Reflection:** Collect feedback, identify at least three actionable insights, and integrate them into next quarter's presence plan.

**Outcome:** Peer review illuminates blind spots unreachable by self-audit alone, fostering relational accountability and sustained improvement.

# IX. Integration of Presence with Other Pillars and Modalities

Presence does not stand alone; it interlocks with **Intentionality**, **Empathy**, and **Vulnerability**—the remaining three pillars—and must be woven across all four modalities. The following subsections map these intersections in exhaustive detail.

## A. Presence ↔ Intentionality

### 1. Synergy

- **Intentionality** asks: "Why am I engaging?"
- **Presence** asks: "How fully am I engaging?"
  Together, they transform each interaction from a habit into a **deliberate practice**.

### 2. Practical Integration

- **Modality-Based Intentional Planning:** Before any SD, AD, SA, or AA exchange, clarify the **purpose** (e.g., "To support my friend's career decision") and commit to presence tactics (muting notifications, scheduling specific times).

- **Ritualized Intentional Prompts:** Use calendars to schedule "Purpose & Presence" mini-sessions—5-minute intros before a call or writing—answering: "What do I want to offer, and how will I be fully here?"

### 3. Illustrative Example

- **AD Email:** Intentionality: "To share reflections on my burnout." Presence: Apply "mindful typing" (Section VI.13), read friend's last message thrice before reacting, and structure the email deliberately, resisting shorthand.

---

## B. Presence ↔ Empathy

### 1. Synergy

- **Empathy** requires the capacity to **sense and mirror** another's internal state. Presence provides the **attentional bandwidth** to perceive subtle emotional cues across modalities.

### 2. Practical Integration

- **SD Empathy Drills:** During SD, practice "mirroring posture" (leaning in when they lean in) and "vocal attunement" (matching tone, tempo)—leveraging mirror neuron activation.
- **AD Empathy Markers:** Deliberately highlight empathic statements: "I hear that you felt anxious when…"—ensuring the friend knows their emotions were fully absorbed.
- **SA Empathy Embodiment:** Attend to micro-expressions and overlapping silences—validate pain by placing a reassuring hand, or share a supportive nod—thus embodying empathic attunement.

### 3. Illustrative Example

- **SA Walking Conversation:** Friend mentions grieving a loss. Presence: Stop walking, face them fully, maintain soft eye contact, and place hand on their shoulder. Empathy: Reflectively say, "I can only imagine how heavy that grief feels right now."

---

## C. Presence ↔ Vulnerability

### 1. Synergy

- **Vulnerability** demands risking exposure of one's inner frailties. Presence is the **safe container** within which such exposure can unfold without judgment.

### 2. Practical Integration

- **SD Vulnerability Cues:** If sharing DL content, use "presence markers" (e.g., momentary silence, steady gaze into camera) before revealing deeper layers—signaling readiness.
- **AD Vulnerability Preamble:** Begin a deep email with: "I want to share something I've hesitated to say because I need you to be fully present." Include instructions: "Read this in one sitting, no distractions."
- **SA Vulnerability Environment:** Choose low-stimulation settings for vulnerable conversations—quiet rooms, dim lighting, minimal background stimuli.

### 3. Illustrative Example

- **AA Handwritten Letter:** Prewrite an opening asterisked paragraph: "Please find a private, uninterrupted hour to read this. Inside, I share a wound I've carried." This primes the friend's presence before encountering vulnerability, reducing risk of misinterpretation.

---

# X. Advanced Practices: Cultivating Hyper-Presence

For those who seek to master presence as an ongoing endeavor, the following **advanced practices** require sustained discipline but yield profound relational depth. Each is described with rationale, concrete steps, and potential pitfalls.

---

## 1. The "Presence Retreat" (SA + AA + AD + SD)

### A. Rationale

Immersive experiences—akin to meditation retreats—fast-track presence cultivation by removing habitual distractions and integrating all modalities in a controlled environment.

### B. Structure (Weekend-Long)

| Day & Time | Activity | Modality |
|---|---|---|
| Friday Evening (6–9pm) | **SA Group Opening**: Arrival at retreat site; silent group dinner; brief SD welcome for remote participants. | SA + SD |
| Saturday Morning (8–10am) | **Mindful Walk**: SA walking meditation in nature; periodic group reflections. | SA |
| Saturday Late Morning (10–12) | **AD Journaling Session**: Time-shifted journaling in shared cabin; handwritten reflections on the walk experience. | AA + AD |
| Saturday Afternoon (1–4pm) | **Silent Co-Working**: SA silent reading or creative work; presence token placed before workspace. | SA |
| Saturday Late Afternoon (4–6) | **SD Presence Workshop**: Live video session (projected in common area) on presence theories and advanced practices. | SD |
| Saturday Evening (7–9pm) | **AA Presence Ceramics**: Hands-on pottery workshop; each piece inscribed with a reflective mantra and dried glaze. | SA + AA |
| Sunday Morning (8–10am) | **SA Empathy Walk**: Pairs walk and alternate mirror-based sharing of emotions. | SA |
| Sunday Midday (10–12) | **AD Depth Exchange**: Each writes a letter to be mailed to a friend outside retreat, synthesizing insights. | AD + AA |
| Sunday Afternoon (1–3pm) | **SA Closing Circle**: Group sharing of "One presence insight I take forward," receiving handwritten tokens from peers. | SA + AA |

## C. Pitfalls & Mitigations

- **Overwhelm:** Retreat intensity can strain introverted participants; provide optional solo time for decompressing.

- **Logistical Complexity:** Coordinating remote SD participants requires robust tech setup; do test runs in advance.

- **Post-Retreat Fade:** Integrate a follow-up plan: biweekly SD "retreat echoes" to sustain momentum.

### D. Anticipated Outcomes

- accelerated presence habituation across modalities;
- epiphanies leading to deeper relational commitments;
- tangible artifacts (ceramics, letters) serving as lasting presence anchors.

---

## 2. The "Presence Pyramid" Daily Practice (AD + SD + SA + AA)

### A. Rationale

Linear daily rituals embed presence consistently, building resilience against digital dopamine loops. The "Presence Pyramid" stacks four daily elements—AA at base, then AD, SD, and SA at apex—to structure a full-spectrum presence routine.

### B. Pyramid Components

1. **AA Foundation (Nightly):** Write one handwritten sentence reflecting on the day's relational presence. Slip it under your pillow.
2. **AD Midday Check (1pm):** Send one focused DL email or voice note to a friend, explicitly referencing presence rituals.
3. **SD Afternoon Reflection (4pm):** Schedule a 5-minute video check-in with a colleague or confidant, using "Pause & Reflect" for presence re-centering.
4. **SA Evening Ritual (7pm):** Spend at least 15 minutes in physical co-presence—dinner, casual walk, or shared task—sans screens.

### C. Pitfalls & Mitigations

- **Routine Rigor Mortis:** Rigid adherence can feel mechanical; periodically rotate rituals' timing or modality focus to sustain novelty.
- **Schedule Conflicts:** Life's unpredictability may disrupt the pyramid; treat it as aspirational—when missing one element, don't abandon the whole pyramid, pivot to the

next feasible part.

### D. Anticipated Outcomes

- incremental daily presence habit formation;
- cross-modal reinforcement—AA reflections feed AD check-ins, which prime SD discussions and culminate in SA embodiment.

---

## 3. The "Presence Mentor" Partnership (SD + SA + AD)

### A. Rationale

Learning presence can be accelerated by partnering with a mentor/friend who offers **real-time feedback** and model behaviors.

### B. Structure

1. **Kickoff SD Session:** 60-minute meeting to co-create a **Presence Development Plan** (PDP), identifying strengths and growth areas.
2. **SA Practice Walks:** Mentor and mentee meet biweekly for "Presencing Walks" (Section VI.5) to observe and reflect on presence skills.
3. **AD Reflection Exchange:** Within 24 hours of each walk, both exchange a 300-word AD reflection, observing the other's presence and offering encouragement.
4. **SD Monthly Check-In:** A 30-minute SD meeting to review PDP progress, adjust goals, and practice advanced SD presence strategies (e.g., "Pause & Reflect 2.0").

### C. Pitfalls & Mitigations

- **Too Much Feedback Anxiety:** Mentees may feel self-conscious if feedback is overly critical—mentors must balance constructive critique with affirmations.
- **Mismatch of Styles:** Ensure mentor–mentee share compatible communication preferences and presence values; renegotiate or reassign if mismatch arises.

### D. Anticipated Outcomes

- personalized presence growth;
- cross-modal synergy—SA sessions provide embodied modeling, AD exchanges deepen reflective awareness, SD check-ins reinforce accountability.

# XI. Avoiding Overextension & Presence Paradoxes

Even presence, when pursued without balance, can paradoxically undermine relational health. The following **five pitfalls** and their mitigations ensure presence remains life-giving rather than burdensome.

## 1. The "Over-Presence" Burnout

### A. Pitfall

Excessive commitment to being present—constant deep listening, relentless empathic engagement—can deplete emotional resources, leading to burnout.

### B. Mitigation

- **Presence Boundaries:** Schedule "Presence Rest Windows" where one commits to **self-presence** (self-care activities: reading, meditation) rather than social presence.
- **Emotional Titration:** Monitor Emotional Bank Account (Section VIII.3); when deposits dwindle, transition from DL to SL interactions to recuperate.

## 2. The "Vicarious Presence" Trap

### A. Pitfall

Relying on proxies (e.g., AI-written responses, auto-generated "sympathy" cards) that mimic presence but lack genuine engagement, giving an illusion of care while hollowing out authenticity.

### B. Mitigation

- **Anti-Automation Vow:** Commit: "I will not use AI to craft any DL messages or AA artifacts—only for organizational reminders."
- **Presence Audit:** Periodically interrogate interactions: "When did I rely on convenience over true presence?" and recommit to manual, personal engagement.

## 3. The "Presence Performance" Illusion

### A. Pitfall

Conflating visible signs of presence (like eye contact on Zoom) with actual presence. One might *appear* present—leaning toward the camera—while mentally rehearsing next tasks.

### B. Mitigation

- **Introspective Check:** Before and during interactions, frequently ask: "Am I fully here, or merely performing to appear attentive?"
- **Mobile Mindfulness Adventures:** Practice occasional body scans during SA or SD to root out dissociative tendencies—periodically evaluate whether mind wanders and gently pull it back.

## 4. The "Drone Presence"—Rigid Ritualism

### A. Pitfall

Overly rigid rituals (e.g., showing up to every weekly SD call regardless of mental state) can convert presence into a mechanical duty, eroding authenticity and increasing relational pressure.

### B. Mitigation

- **Contextual Sensitivity:** Integrate "Permission for Absent Presence"—explicitly allow opting out when emotionally taxed, while offering a brief AD note explaining absence.
- **Adaptive Ritual Calendars:** Build slack into schedules—e.g., "This month, if I miss one Presence Dinner, I'll host a compensatory SA coffee chat next week."

## 5. The "Presence Guilt" Cascade

### A. Pitfall

Internalizing presence as moral obligation: if one momentarily lapses into distraction, it triggers guilt, undermining self-worth and fueling anxiety—an emotional spiral.

### B. Mitigation

- **Self-Compassion Check-Ins:** After distractions, practice a brief "Apology & Recommitment" ritual: "I'm sorry for drifting earlier; I recommit to your presence now."
- **Focus on Trend, Not Moments:** Use weekly scorecards to evaluate overall presence—one slip does not negate cumulative presence efforts. Maintain 80/20 perspective: "I was fully present 80 % of the time; tomorrow I can improve the other 20 %."

---

# XII. Conclusion: Presence as Ever-Evolving Practice

From Heidegger's **Mitsein** to neuroscientific insights about mirror neurons, presence emerges as both an existential imperative and a cultivated skill. Across SD, AD, SA, and AA modalities, presence demands **vigilance against distractions**, **ritualized practices**, and **ethical self-awareness**. This chapter—deliberately more extensive than its predecessor—has:

1. **Located Presence Philosophically:** Clarifying its ontological and dialogical dimensions.

2. **Grounded Presence Neurologically:** Unveiling the mirror neuron–oxytocin networks that support authentic attunement.

3. **Mapped Presence Across Modalities:** Unpacking unique challenges, delivering detailed strategies, case studies, and curated practices (15 diverse exercises).

4. **Established Ethical Imperatives:** Emphasizing consent, reciprocity, and transparent communication to prevent presence's misuse.

5. **Equipped the Reader with Measurement Tools:** Including weekly scorecards, quarterly audits, emotional bank accounts, self-assessments, and peer reviews.

6. **Integrated Presence with Other Pillars:** Demonstrating synergy with Intentionality, Empathy, and Vulnerability.

7. **Presenting Advanced Applications:** Outlining Presence Retreats, Presence Pyramids, and Mentor Partnerships to accelerate mastery.
8. **Warned Against Overextension:** Diagnosing dangers like burnout, vicarious presence, performance illusions, ritual rigidity, and presence guilt, and prescribing mitigations.

**Presence** is not a static achievement but an **ever-evolving practice**—requiring continuous reflection, adaptation, and compassionate recalibration. As we journey beyond Chapter 8, we will explore **Pillar Two: Intentionality** (Chapter 9), examining how deliberate design of friendship—acting with purpose rather than autopilot—amplifies presence's transformative potential. But do not rush ahead; allow this chapter's abundance of tools and insights to **percolate**. Revisit the practices, calibrate your own quarterly audits, and let presence become not a checklist item but the **atmosphere** in which all your friendships breathe and flourish.

### Chapter 9
Pillar Two: Intentionality—Acting with Purpose Rather Than Drift

> "Without intention, even the most attentive presence can wander into meaninglessness."

# I. Introduction: The Necessity of Intention in Modern Friendship

In the swirling currents of daily demands, it is all too easy for friendship to drift into autopilot: we "check in" reflexively, scroll mindlessly through social feeds, or send perfunctory messages without pausing to ask whether our gestures carry genuine care. **Intentionality** emerges as the second pillar of ReconneXion Theory precisely to counteract this drift. Where **Presence** (Chapter 8) concerns itself with **how** deeply we engage in any given moment, **Intentionality** addresses **why** we engage at all.

To be intentional is to act with **purpose**, to align our motives, actions, and relational energy toward a clear aim: deepening trust, sustaining mutual support, and co-creating meaning. In the absence of intention, presence becomes a passive state—a gift squandered; modalities devolve into habits; depth remains incidental rather than cultivated.

This chapter—designed to exceed the breadth and depth of Chapter 8—offers a comprehensive exploration of intentionality in friendship across all four modalities (SD, AD, SA, AA). We will:

1. Uncover **philosophical** and **ethical** foundations of intentionality.
2. Explore **neuroscientific** and **psychological** dimensions that link intention with motivation, reward, and sustained engagement.
3. Diagnose **pitfalls** of unintentional interaction—habits, default behaviors, and "friendship fatigue."
4. Forge an **ethical framework** that grounds intention in authenticity, reciprocity, and autonomy.
5. Present an exhaustive suite of **rituals, exercises, templates, and advanced practices** (20+!) to cultivate intention in real life.
6. Analyze **case studies** demonstrating how intentionality transforms relationships at personal, organizational, and community levels.
7. Detail **metrics and audit techniques** to assess and refine intentional practice.
8. Map the **integration** of intentionality with Presence, Empathy, and Vulnerability (the other three pillars).
9. Highlight **advanced strategies**—such as "Intention Retreats" and "Purpose-Driven Presence Pyramids"—for those committed to mastering the art of deliberate friendship.
10. Identify **pitfalls and paradoxes**—overplanning, instrumentalization, ritual rigidity—and prescribe **mitigations**.
11. Conclude with a vision of **Intentional Friendship** as a lifelong practice, ever deepening through conscious choice.

By the end of this chapter, you will possess not only the conceptual clarity to perceive where intention is lacking in your connections but a vast toolkit to embed purposeful design at every touchpoint—ensuring that each interaction becomes a conscious contribution to the flourishing of you and your friends.

## II. Philosophical & Ethical Foundations of Intentionality

To act intentionally is to mobilize one's volition in alignment with a meaningful aim. In the context of friendship, intention transcends mere planning; it is a moral stance—a **commitment to choose actions that serve relational good**. Here we ground intentionality philosophically and ethically, drawing from existentialism, virtue ethics, and dialogical philosophy.

## A. Existentialism & Sartrean Freedom

**Jean-Paul Sartre** famously declared that "existence precedes essence"—we are not pre-programmed with a fixed purpose; rather, we freely choose who we become through our actions. In friendships:

- **Existential Choice:** Each interaction is an opportunity to choose authenticity over complacency.

- **Bad Faith:** When we default to "I just do what I always do" or "It's just a habit," we abdicate our freedom and moral responsibility.

- **Authentic Commitment:** Intention returns us to the realm of **authentic choices**—to send that heartfelt message rather than a hasty text, to plan that in-person visit rather than deflecting another week.

**Implication:** Intentionality in friendship is an existential affirmation of freedom and responsibility. Each email, call, or meeting is a moment of **self-definition**—an opportunity to choose to be the friend you aspire to be.

## B. Virtue Ethics & Aristotelian Friendship

Aristotle's **Nicomachean Ethics** locates ethical life in the cultivation of virtues—habits that align rational desire with moral good. True friendship (philia of virtue) arises when:

- **Goodwill (Eunoia):** Each friend intends the good of the other, independent of utility or pleasure.

- **Shared Virtue:** Friends practice virtues together—courage, temperance, generosity—co-creating a relational space for moral growth.

- **Deliberate Engagement:** Habitual habits of deliberate care become ingrained through intentional acts—listening, supporting, challenging.

**Implication:** Intentionality in friendship is not isolated tasks but the **habituation of virtuous patterns**, requiring sustained practice and reflective calibration to ensure each interaction fosters mutual flourishing.

## C. Levinas's Ethics of Encounter

**Emmanuel Levinas** posits that the face-to-face encounter with the Other places an **infinite ethical demand** on oneself—to respond to their irreducible alterity with respect, care, and responsibility. Although Levinas develops this primarily in SA contexts, the spirit extends to all modalities:

- **Infinite Demand:** Each act of friendship must open space for the Other's sanctity; intention guides us to **remain open** rather than reductively categorize.
- **Responsiveness:** Intention means actively responding to the Other's thirst for recognition, rather than projecting one's own agenda.
- **Non-Totalizing Ethic:** Resist reducing a friend to a "role"—e.g., coworker, fellow student—and instead honor their singular personhood in every interaction.

**Implication:** Intentionality is the gesture that listens to the Other's silent call for real presence and care, across digital screens and letter envelopes alike.

## D. Kantian Respect & Reciprocity

**Immanuel Kant's** ethical framework emphasizes treating persons as **ends in themselves**, never merely as means. In friendship:

- **Respect for Autonomy:** Intentional acts honor the friend's agency—e.g., asking before sharing sensitive news, ensuring no coercion.
- **Mutual Reciprocity:** Friendship entails a relationship of mutual giving. Intentionality ensures balance—avoiding paternalism or instrumentalization where one friend's needs consistently overshadow the other's.

**Implication:** Intention in friendship must be calibrated not only to express care but to **respect boundaries, maintain reciprocity,** and **affirm dignity**.

# III. Neuroscientific & Psychological Underpinnings of Intention

Understanding the neural and cognitive mechanisms that underlie intention helps us recognize why purposeful action often decays into habitual drift. Here we explore three key areas: goal-setting neuroscience, habit formation psychology, and motivational dynamics.

## A. Neuroscience of Goal-Directed Behavior

1. **Prefrontal Cortex & Dorsolateral Striatum:**

    - The **dorsolateral prefrontal cortex (DLPFC)** orchestrates planning and decision-making. Sustained intentional action—like consistently choosing to send a deep email—requires DLPFC engagement.

    - Over time, repeated intentional behaviors can shift from DLPFC-dependent to **dorsolateral striatum** patterns, becoming habitual. The challenge lies in ensuring that habits retain their **deliberative quality** rather than devolving into mindless routines.

2. **Dopaminergic Reward System:**

    - Intentional acts—particularly those resulting in positive relational feedback—trigger **dopamine release** in the nucleus accumbens, reinforcing the behavior.

    - However, superficial "likes" or automated digital interactions can hijack the dopamine system, rewarding shallow gestures rather than truly meaningful ones.

3. **Anterior Cingulate Cortex (ACC) & Conflict Monitoring:**

    - The ACC monitors conflicts between intention and impulse—alerting us when we're tempted to drift into half-hearted engagement.

    - Strengthening ACC activity through mindfulness practices (as detailed in Chapter 8) can sustain alignment between intention and action.

**Implication:** By understanding these neural pathways, we can design presence-and-intention rituals that leverage reward and habit systems while avoiding superficial gratification loops.

## B. Psychology of Habit Formation (James Clear & Cue-Routine-Reward)

1. **Cue:** Identify triggers that signal friendship actions—e.g., seeing a friend's birthday on the calendar, noticing a news article about a shared interest, or observing a "Friend's Day" alert on social media.

2. **Routine:** The intentional behavior that follows—writing a thoughtful message, planning a meet-up, or purchasing a care package item.

3. **Reward:** A sense of satisfaction: a friend's appreciative reply, strengthened rapport, or internal sense of moral integrity.

**Implication:** By designing **clear cues** (calendar reminders, environmental tokens) and **meaningful rewards** (authentic replies, self-reflection), we can transform intentional friendship acts into **sustainable habits** that resist drift.

## C. Motivational Dynamics & Self-Determination Theory (Deci & Ryan)

1. **Autonomy:** Feeling volitional and self-endorsed in our friendship actions—choosing to express care rather than feeling compelled by guilt or obligation.

2. **Competence:** Developing skill in crafting intentional gestures—learning to write deep letters, facilitate DL video calls, or curate meaningful gifts.

3. **Relatedness:** Experiencing genuine connection when our intentional efforts are reciprocated, affirming our relational bonds.

**Implication:** Intentional friendship thrives when these three psychological needs are met. Rituals and feedback loops must foster autonomy (choosing to act), competence (feeling capable of meaningful gestures), and relatedness (feeling truly seen).

# IV. Pitfalls of Unintentional Friendship

Before prescribing constructive actions, we must diagnose the **dysfunctional patterns** into which friendships often fall when intention is absent. These pitfalls can manifest across modalities and depths, eroding trust and reducing friendship to hollow routine.

## A. Modal Monotony Without Purpose

1. **Autopilot SD Routines:**
   - Example: Weekly video call that defaults to project updates with only SL–SD content—no one consciously plans for emotional check-ins, resulting in transactional rather than relational outcomes.

2. **AD Drip-Feeding:**
   - Example: Periodic "just checking in" texts lacking genuine curiosity or vulnerability.

3. **SA Foregone Opportunities:**
   - Example: In-person meetups relegated to superficial activities—shared TV watching without conversation, missing chances for DL–SA depth.

4. **AA Tokenism:**
   - Example: Sending annual birthday cards by rote, with only a signature and no heartfelt note, reducing AA to a mechanical tick-box.

**Consequence:** Friends feel unseen, conversations stagnate at base SL levels, and bonds decay even as interaction frequency remains high.

---

## B. Compassion Fatigue & Burnout

1. **Perpetual Solicitation:** If one consistently receives deep disclosures without providing equivalent emotional support, guilt or exhaustion ensues.

2. **Lack of Recuperative Rituals:** Without calendared breaks or self-care, intentional efforts flicker out, and presence withdraws.

**Consequence:** Burnout prompts withdrawal, missed replies, and defensive distance—friends perceive absence as rejection rather than the result of fatigue.

---

## C. Instrumentalization & Transactional Dynamics

1. **Friendship as Utility:** When associations serve career, status, or other self-serving ends, gestures become calculated rather than heartfelt.
2. **Emotional Commodification:** "I send you a care package so you'll do me a favor later"—friendship reduced to quid pro quo.

**Consequence:** The Other senses instrumentalization; trust erodes, and intimacy retreats.

## D. Ritual Rigidity & Overplanning

1. **Formulaic Interactions:** Overly prescribed rituals that leave no room for spontaneity—e.g., requiring a fixed script for each call—can feel mechanical.
2. **Resistance to Adaptation:** Friends find it hard to deviate from the plan, even when circumstances change, stifling genuine responsiveness.

**Consequence:** Rituals decouple from authentic intention, devolving into burdens rather than conduits of connection.

## E. Paradox of Proliferation

1. **Multiplying Platforms:** "I have five group chats, two email threads, and three social networks"—spreading intentional efforts thin across too many channels.
2. **Shallow Presence Spread:** Effort diluted—no single interaction receives full care, leading to frustration and perceived flakiness.

**Consequence:** Proliferation sows anxiety and diminishes the perceived sincerity of each action.

# V. Ethical Framework for Intentional Action

To guard against these pitfalls, we propose a **robust ethical framework** for guiding intentional friendship. Grounded in virtue ethics, respect for autonomy, and Levinasian responsibility, this framework comprises five core principles:

## A. Principle of Authentic Motivation

- **Definition:** Intention must arise from genuine goodwill (eunoia), not external pressures (social expectation, guilt, reputation management).

- **Practice:** Before any friendship act, silently ask: "Am I doing this to truly support my friend, or to alleviate my own anxiety/guilt?"

- **Mitigation:** If motives are mixed, reflect deeper or postpone action until authenticity aligns.

## B. Principle of Reciprocal Engagement

- **Definition:** Intentional acts must respect mutual agency—no friend should feel indebted or manipulated.

- **Practice:** Invite input from friends about their preferred modes of engagement—ask, "Would you find it supportive if I send a letter or schedule a call?"

- **Mitigation:** If a friend declines, honor their boundary gracefully—"Understood. I'll still be here when you're ready."

## C. Principle of Minimalism & Impact

- **Definition:** Prioritize quality over quantity: fewer, more meaningful gestures better than a flood of superficial ones.

- **Practice:** Limit AA gifts to once per quarter; focus on a single DL–AD letter rather than multiple short texts.

- **Mitigation:** Resist pressure to compete with others' gestures; reflect on which actions truly matter to each friend.

## D. Principle of Cognitive & Emotional Realism

- **Definition:** Intention must be calibrated to one's capacity—acknowledge time, mental bandwidth, and life context.

- **Practice:** Self-assess before committing: "Can I truly sustain a weekly DL–SD call while caring for a sick family member?"

- **Mitigation:** If capacity is limited, transparently communicate and adjust plans—"I'm dealing with health issues this month, so I'll send letters instead of calls."

### E. Principle of Evolution & Adaptation

- **Definition:** Intentional practices must evolve as friendships and life circumstances change.

- **Practice:** Conduct regular Intentionality Audits (Section VIII below), adjusting modality mix and ritual frequency.

- **Mitigation:** If a ritual feels stale or burdensome, experiment with variation (e.g., swap an SA meal for a DL–AD written exchange), ensuring ongoing vitality.

# VI. Rituals, Templates, and Practices for Cultivating Intentionality

Below is an exhaustive catalog of **twenty detailed practices**—designed to fold intentionality into everyday life. Each practice is described with rationale, step-by-step execution, example scenarios, and potential variations. Collectively, they ensure that acting with purpose becomes second nature across modalities.

## 1. The "Heartbeat Calendar" (Multi-Modality)

**Rationale:** Incorporate friendship intentions into personal scheduling to prevent drift.

**Steps:**

1. **Identify Key Dates:** List birthdays, anniversaries, significant life events, and recurring communal milestones (e.g., monthly "Friends' Roundtable").

2. **Allocate Modality Slots:** Assign modalities to each date—e.g.,

    - Birthday → AA: Handwritten letter mailed two weeks in advance.

    - Quarterly Check-In → SD: 60-minute DL video call.

    - Mid-Month Huddle → AD: Reflective email exchange.

3. **Set Alarms & Reminders:** Use a digital calendar to set alarms with descriptive titles ("Birthday Letter for Alex – Intentionality: express gratitude").

**Example Scenario:**

- Jane's birthday is June 15. On June 1, Jane's friend Mark schedules a "Birthday Letter Crafting Session" on his calendar. He spends two hours writing and embellishing a letter, stamps and mails it. On June 15, Mark follows up with an AD check-in email referencing the letter.

**Variants:**

- **Seasonal Friendship Plans:** Plan four intentional acts per season (e.g., Spring: plant a tree with a friend [SA], Summer: mail a postcard [AA], Fall: host a DL–SD salon, Winter: share monthly gratitude emails [AD]).

---

## 2. The "Five Whys of Friendship" (Intention Reflection)

**Rationale:** Root out superficial motives and connect actions to genuine values.

**Steps:**

1. **Select an Action:** Identify a planned friendship gesture (e.g., sending a care package).

2. **Ask "Why?" Five Times:**

- Why am I sending this care package? → Because I want to show I care.
- Why do I want to show I care? → Because I appreciate their support during my tough times.
- Why do I appreciate their support? → Because it helped me feel less alone and resilient.
- Why do I want to help them feel less alone? → Because everyone deserves emotional sustenance.
- Why do I believe emotional sustenance is fundamental? → Because so much of wellbeing hinges on relational connection.

3. **Document Findings:** Write a 2–3 sentence mission statement for the gesture (e.g., "I send this package to convey gratitude for their steadfast support, reinforcing our bond of mutual care and reminding them they are never alone.")

**Example Scenario:**

- Before planning a birthday gift, Alex uses the "Five Whys" to ensure the gift emerges from authentic appreciation rather than social obligation.

**Variants:**

- **Weekly Intention Check:** Each Sunday, ask "Why do I want to connect with Person X this week?" and document the genuine intention.

---

## 3. "Purpose-Driven SD Agenda" (Synchronous Digital)

**Rationale:** Prevent SD calls from devolving into unfocused banter by structuring with intentional objectives.

**Steps:**

1. **Pre-Call Template**: Draft a brief agenda:
   - **Opening Presence (5 min):** Quick "emotional weather check."
   - **SL Update (10 min):** Share key logistical or topical news.
   - **DL Exploration (25 min):** Pre-agreed deep topic or open reflection.
   - **Action/Support Planning (15 min):** Identify concrete ways to support each other in the coming week.
   - **Closing Ritual (5 min):** Each states one intention for maintaining connection.
2. **Share Agenda in Advance:** Send the agenda via AD at least 48 hours before the scheduled call, inviting suggestions or modifications.
3. **Timekeeping & Facilitation:** Designate a "time steward" to keep segments on track, ensuring the intended flow unfolds. Utilize "Pause & Reflect 2.0" for DL segments (Section VIII.2).

**Example Scenario:**

- Elena schedules a monthly "Friends' Forum" with three peers: first sends the agenda, they tweak it, and during the call, they follow the structure, culminating in sharing actionable support commitments (e.g., "I'll review your draft manuscript by Thursday").

**Variants:**

- **Rotating Host Model:** Each friend hosts one SD session per quarter, responsible for agenda creation and time stewardship.

---

## 4. "Letter Blueprint" (Asynchronous Digital)

**Rationale:** Ensure AD messages transcend cursory check-ins by embedding depth and clarity.

**Steps:**

1. **Subject Line Crafting:** Choose a context-rich line (e.g., "Reflections on Our Last Conversation").

2. **Opening Context (2–3 sentences):** Remind the friend of the last interaction and set tone (e.g., "Since our call on April 28 about career pivots…").

3. **Core Narrative (3–4 paragraphs):** Share relevant experiences, emotional insights, and philosophical reflections—interweaving personal updates and genuine curiosity about the friend's world.

4. **Depth Prompt (2–3 questions):** Pose open-ended queries (e.g., "How are you navigating your recent life change? What fears arise when you think about next steps?").

5. **Closing Intention (1–2 sentences):** Affirm your commitment (e.g., "I'm here to support you; looking forward to your thoughts whenever you're ready").

**Example Scenario:**

- After hearing about her friend's academic stress, Carla writes a "Letter Blueprint" email detailing her own struggles, offering empathy, and asking pointed reflective questions about coping strategies.

**Variants:**

- **Voice-Recorded Blueprint:** Record a 3–4 minute voice note following the same structure—then transcribe key sentences and send as AD text for the friend's reference.

---

## 5. "Buddy System for Intentionality" (SA + SD + AD)

**Rationale:** Pair up friends as accountability partners to sustain intention.

**Steps:**

1. **Pairing:** Two friends agree to serve as "Intention Buddies" for a 3-month cycle.

2. **Initial SD Kickoff:** Video call to co-create Intentionality Agreements (e.g., "I commit to one DL–AD email per week").

3. **SA Monthly Check:** Meet in person for a "Progress Café"—review adherence to agreements, share successes, and adjust as needed.

4. **AD Weekly Triage:** Exchange quick text check-ins on adherence—"How did your intention to call Tom manifest this week?"

5. **Reflection Log:** Each logs successes, challenges, and insights in a shared document, reviewed during SA check-ins.

**Example Scenario:**

- Two neighbors, both graduate students, serve as Buddies: they support each other in maintaining intentional rituals—weekly 10-minute DL–SD study-check video chats, biweekly DL–AA letter exchanges, and monthly SA silent reading sessions at the library.

**Variants:**

- **Group Accountability Pods:** Triads or quartets of friends form small "Intention Pods," rotating pair check-ins and SA group workshops.

## 6. "Purposeful Walk & Talk" (SA)

**Rationale:** Infuse SA walks with intention by coupling movement with defined relational aims.

**Steps:**

1. **Pre-Walk Planning:** Agree on a specific intention (e.g., "Today, I want to process my recent job change and seek your perspective").

2. **Route Selection:** Choose a location conducive to focused conversation—quiet park, nature trail, or low-traffic neighborhood.

3. **Mindful Opening:** Stand together for 30 seconds of shared breathing—eyes closed, hands on heart—then proceed.

4. **Segmented Dialogue:** Walk for 5 minutes in silence, tuning into bodily sensations; at each 500-meter marker, alternate sharing around the intention focus.

5. **Closing Ritual:** Conclude at a bench: share one concrete step you will take based on insights gleaned.

**Example Scenario:**

- Two friends walk along a riverside path; one articulates career anxieties at the first marker; the other listens empathetically and then shares reflection at the next. They conclude by committing to research job opportunities together (AD follow-up).

**Variants:**

- **Intentional "Speed-Dating" Walks:** In group settings, rotate partners every 10 minutes, each pair focusing on a predefined question (e.g., "What's one fear you overcame this month?").

---

## 7. "Curated Care Package with Purpose" (AA + AD)

**Rationale:** Go beyond generic gifts by designing packages that explicitly align with relational goals and personal narratives.

**Steps:**

1. **Intention Mapping:** Identify a specific need or celebration—e.g., friend's impending surgery, graduation, or artistic milestone.

2. **Thematic Selection:** Choose items that resonate—books, comfort objects, local treats—each tied to a symbolic narrative.

3. **Annotation and Explanation:** For each item, include a small card explaining its significance (e.g., "This lavender sachet is to soothe post-surgery anxiety; remember our afternoon at the herb farm").

4. **Digital Companion:** Enclose a QR code linking to an AD voice note elaborating on the intention and encouraging the friend to share their feet-back on how items serve them.

5. **Delivery & Follow-Up:** Mail the package; schedule an SD or AD follow-up at a reasonable time (e.g., "Expect this package by Friday; let's video chat the following Monday to hear your thoughts").

**Example Scenario:**

- Upon hearing of a friend's long-distance move, Dana curates a "New Home Kit" with a mini succulent (growth), a custom keychain engraved with a shared motto, a playlist of "moving-in" songs (QR code), and a handwritten letter celebrating their new chapter. A week later, Dana initiates an AD check-in to hear about settling in.

**Variants:**

- **Seasonal Wellness Boxes:** Quarterly wellness packages reflecting seasonal needs—winter: warm socks, herbal teas, and a DL affirmation letter; spring: seed packets, gardening gloves, and a reflection prompt on renewal.

---

## 8. "Intentional Group Salon" (SD + AD)

**Rationale:** Elevate group interactions from casual chat to structured, deep inquiry by infusing salons with philosophical and relational intention.

**Steps:**

1. **Define Group Composition:** 6–8 friends who share intellectual, creative, or personal interests.

2. **Set Recurring Cadence:** Schedule a monthly 90-minute SD session (e.g., first Sunday of each month).

3. **Curate Themes & Readings:** Prior to each session, host circulates a short reading (article, essay, poem) that resonates with collective challenges (e.g., "The Ethics of Vulnerability").

4. **Agenda Framework:**

   - **Opening Presence (10 min):** Each shares a one-word "emotional tide" and a brief breath-synchronized gesture.

   - **Reading Reflections (15 min):** Open-floor sharing of initial reactions to assigned text.

   - **DL Roundtable (40 min):** Guided by rotating facilitators, each responds to two questions: "How does this text intersect with your current life?" and "What intention do you take forward from it?"

   - **Personal Intention Commitments (15 min):** Each declares one concrete friendship action aligned with insights (e.g., "This week, I will call a friend I haven't seen in months").

- **Closing Ritual (10 min):** Group chants a shared phrase or offers a communal gratitude statement.

5. **AD Breather:** Between salons, participants maintain a shared digital notebook, posting AD reflections or gratitude notes—ensuring continuity and keeping intentions alive.

**Example Scenario:**

- A loosely affiliated writers' circle hosts a monthly "Story & Soul Salon": they read a short memoir excerpt, discuss DL, and commit to writing a reflective postcard to a different friend each by next month.

**Variants:**

- **Hybrid In-Person / Virtual:** Occasionally, the salon meets SA at a local café; remote members join via live-stream, ensuring consistent cross-modal integration.

---

## 9. "Intentional Roadmap" (Multi-Modality)

**Rationale:** Long-term friendship development benefits from a clear, co-created roadmap—charting milestones, modalities, depths, and intentions over an extended period (6–12 months).

**Steps:**

1. **Visioning Session (SA or SD):** Friends convene to articulate their collective aspiration (e.g., "We want to strengthen our triad by exploring spiritual growth").

2. **Goal-Setting:** Define 3–5 specific relational goals—e.g., "Host quarterly SA meditation retreats," "Create monthly DL–AD reflective essays," "Build a shared AA time capsule for next year."

3. **Timeline & Modal Allocation:** Map each goal onto a calendar, indicating modality, expected depth, and responsible party.

4. **Accountability Structures:** Assign "Responsibility Champions" for each goal—each friend champions one goal, ensuring follow-through.

5. **Mid-Point Review:** At the six-month mark, hold a substantial SD or SA meeting to assess progress, celebrate achievements, and recalibrate remaining milestones.

**Example Scenario:**

- Four long-distance friends design a year-long "Spiritual Growth Roadmap":

    - **Q1:** SA book club on spiritual text (SL–SA → DL–SA).

    - **Q2:** DL–AD essay exchange on spiritual awakenings.

    - **Q3:** SD guided meditation circle monthly with rotating facilitators.

    - **Q4:** AA creation of a collaborative "Spirit Journal" bound and distributed.

**Variants:**

- **Single Friendship Roadmap:** A dyad creates a personalized roadmap focusing on professional mentoring and emotional support, alternating between modalities each month.

---

## 10. "Intention Anchor Objects" (AA + SA)

**Rationale:** Tangible objects placed in key environments can anchor intentions and prompt relational actions when encountered.

**Steps:**

1. **Select an Object:** Choose something small, portable, and meaningful—e.g., a smooth river stone, a small figurine, or a hand-carved wooden bead.

2. **Imbue with Intention:** Before gifting, hold the object and articulate a precise relational intention (e.g., "This stone reminds you that I commit to listening whenever you need to talk").

3. **Placement Ritual:** Friend places the object in a prominent location—desk, nightstand, car dashboard—where its presence triggers conscious reflection.

4. **Return & Renewal:** Periodically, friends exchange new anchor objects or renew the intention by writing a short AA letter, reinforcing commitment.

**Example Scenario:**

- To support Sam during exam season, his friend Mia gives him a small carved owl. She says, "Whenever you see this owl, remember I'm here to help you study or just listen." Sam places it on his laptop; each glance cues his awareness of Mia's support.

**Variants:**

- **Group Anchor Sculpture (SA):** A small communal sculpture is placed in a shared living space. Each time a friend enters, they silently set a relational intention for that gathering (e.g., "Today, I will listen fully to Shameem").

---

## 11. "Adaptive Intentionality Matrix" (All Modalities)

**Rationale:** Develop a living document to dynamically map friends, modalities, depths, and intentions—ensuring no relationship goes unintentional.

**Steps:**

1. **Create a Spreadsheet with Columns:**
   - **Friend's Name**
   - **Preferred Modalities** (SD, AD, SA, AA)
   - **Typical Interaction Depth** (SL, Mid-Depth, DL)
   - **Role/Context** (Mentor, Colleague, Childhood Friend, Family)
   - **Primary Intention** (Emotional Support, Creative Collaboration, Accountability, Celebration)
   - **Last Intentional Gesture** (Date & Modality)
   - **Next Planned Intentional Gesture** (Date, Modality, Description)
   - **Notes on Capacity/Constraints** (e.g., time zone, health)

2. **Populate Rows:** For each close friend, fill in details.

3. **Weekly Review:** Set aside 15 minutes every Sunday to review the matrix:

- Identify friends whose "Next Planned Gesture" is overdue.
- Adjust intentions based on current life events (e.g., friend's new job, illness).

4. **Collaborative Version:** Share a simplified view with close friends—e.g., in a shared Google Sheet—so that they can reciprocate by mapping intentions toward you.

**Example Scenario:**

- Rob's matrix reveals that he hasn't intentionally engaged with his childhood friend Emma since January. He schedules a DL–AD essay exchange for March 10. He also notes Emma's preference for AA gifts and timeout periods when she's stressed.

**Variants:**

- **"Rotating Focus" Flag:** Each month, highlight 2–3 friends as "primary focus"—ensuring concentrated intentional investment before rotating to others.

---

## 12. "Mindful Automation" (Preventing Unintentional Digital Drift)

**Rationale:** Harness technology to support, rather than sabotage, our intentions—setting up thoughtful automation that prompts genuine acts of connection.

**Steps:**

1. **Identify Key Intentions:** Choose recurring friendship actions—e.g., sending a DL–AD letter every six weeks.

2. **Set Up Low-Drama Reminders:**
   - Use calendar events with custom notifications: "Write a heartfelt letter to Priya."
   - Utilize task-management apps (e.g., Todoist, Notion) to create "Intentionality Tasks" categorized by friend.

3. **Configure Gentle Nudges:** For deep modalities, set reminders with enough lead time (e.g., two-week buffer for AA packages).

4. **Resist Over-Automation:** Ensure no action is fully automated—e.g., gift subscription services can send generic items, but intention demands manual curation. Use

automation only to **signal** opportunities, not replace human choice.

5. **Review & Purge:** Quarterly, audit automated reminders—eliminate dormant tasks or update intentions to reflect evolving relationships.

**Example Scenario:**

- Lucia programs her calendar to remind her three weeks before each friend's birthday to "Brainstorm a meaningful AA gift," avoiding last-minute generic e-cards. She reviews these reminders monthly to confirm authenticity.

**Variants:**

- **Shared "Intentions Board":** A Trello board shared with friends, where automated due-dates prompt both parties to collaborate on AA or AD gestures.

---

## 13. "Purposeful Silence" Practice (SD + SA)

**Rationale:** Intentionality includes knowing when *not* to speak—creating space for authentic listening and reflection.

**Steps:**

1. **Define Silent Segments:** In SD calls, insert two or three 15-second silences during DL discussions. In SA gatherings, agree to spend the first and last 30 seconds in silence.

2. **Communicate Intent:** Explain the purpose—"These intentional silences allow us to process emotions and speak from deeper awareness."

3. **Observe Sensations:** During silence, each friend notes bodily sensations—tension, calm, anticipation—heightening introspective presence.

4. **Debrief:** After each silence, invite volunteers to share what emerged—"In that pause, I realized I was feeling fear about sharing vulnerability."

**Example Scenario:**

- In a monthly SD facilitation group, the host introduces "Trail-Silence" segments: after each theme discussion, 15 seconds of silence. Members report deeper insights and reduced pressure to "perform."

**Variants:**

- **SA "Pause & Share" Walks:** After every five minutes of walking dialogue, pause for one minute of silent walking, then share "What registered in stillness?"

---

## 14. "Intention Journaling" (AA + AD)

**Rationale:** Regular reflective journaling cements intentional insights and tracks evolving friendship goals.

**Steps:**

1. **Designate a Journal:** Either a physical notebook or a digital document, reserved solely for friendship intentions and reflections.

2. **Daily Prompt:** Each evening, answer: "What intentional friendship act did I commit today? Did I follow through? What did I learn?"

3. **Weekly Synthesis:** Every Sunday, review daily entries—flag patterns, celebrate successes, and note intentions for the coming week.

4. **Monthly Publication:** For close friends, compile a summary of key reflections and send as an AD newsletter—inviting reciprocal sharing.

**Example Scenario:**

- Jason journals: "Today, I sat with Maria for 15 minutes without checking my phone (SA). I realized I often reach for my phone unconsciously. Next week, I will place my phone in another room during our meetups."

**Variants:**

- **Collaborative Intentionality Blog:** A shared online journal where friends publish brief posts reflecting on mutual intentions—visible to the group for accountability.

## 15. "Covenant of Intentional Friendship" (SA + SD + AD)

**Rationale:** Formalize relational commitments through a written covenant—akin to a partnership agreement—grounding intentions in shared ethos.

**Steps:**

1. **Drafting Session (SA or SD):** Friends collaboratively draft a covenant document with headings:
   - **Shared Values:** Core principles (e.g., honesty, generosity, patience).
   - **Modality Commitments:** Specific promises—"We will hold a DL–SD call twice a month," "We will exchange AA tokens quarterly," "We will respond to DL–AD messages within 48 hours."
   - **Depth Benchmarks:** Define what constitutes SL, Mid-Depth, and DL for the group—"A letter over 500 words is considered DL," etc.
   - **Conflict Resolution Protocol:** Steps to address broken intentions—"If a commitment is missed, the friend expresses disappointment using our agreed 'Pause & Speak' phrase, then we schedule a repair call."

2. **Signature Ritual:** Each prints and signs the covenant, then exchanges signed copies via AA—hand-delivered or mailed.

3. **Annual Covenant Renewal:** On the anniversary of signing, hold an SA retreat or SD meeting to review the covenant's relevance, celebrate successes, and revise as needed.

**Example Scenario:**

- A trio of entrepreneurs draft a "Collaboration Covenant" emphasizing intentional check-ins, shared vulnerability in pitch practice (DL–SD), and quarterly AA "Vision Boxes" with handwritten projections for the startup's future.

**Variants:**

- **Peer Group Covenants:** A circle of six friends establishes a "Presence & Intention Guild," with rotating "Guild Master" roles ensuring covenant adherence.

## 16. "Intention-Based Gratitude Circles" (SA + SD)

**Rationale:** Expressing targeted gratitude reinforces intentions and closes the loop, ensuring actions yield relational nourishment.

**Steps:**

1. **Gathering Formation:** 4–8 friends convene, either in person or via SD.

2. **Facilitated Prompting:** A facilitator poses prompts—e.g.,
   - "Name a friendship intention you set recently and share how it was received."
   - "Express gratitude to a member for an act of presence or support, specifying why it mattered."

3. **Targeted Gratitude Statements:** Each speaker addresses one peer directly—"Maria, I appreciate how you held space for me last week when I felt anxious; because of your patience, I felt less alone."

4. **Intentional Commitments:** After rounds of gratitude, each friend states one new intention for the next month:
   - "I intend to send a deep letter to my mentee."
   - "I intend to host a monthly DL–SD conversation with my family."

**Example Scenario:**

- A local writers' group hosts quarterly "Intentional Gratitude Circles," ending with each member committing to a specific friendship action—e.g., "I'll read and comment thoughtfully on your next blog post (DL–AD)."

**Variants:**

- **Silent Gratitude Artifacts (AA):** At the end of the circle, each participant places a small slip of paper in a communal "Gratitude Jar," to be mailed back to its author a month later as a surprise AA gift.

---

## 17. "Customized Intention Playlists" (AA + SD + AD)

**Rationale:** Music, poetry, and other expressive media can encapsulate intentions, serving as a soundtrack for relational focus.

**Steps:**

1. **Identify Intention Theme:** Choose a relational aim—e.g., "encouragement," "shared reflection," "creative inspiration."

2. **Curate Media:** Compile 8–12 songs, poems, or short videos that evoke that theme.

3. **Annotated Commentary (AA):** Create a physical or digital booklet with each media piece's title, a short note explaining why it was selected, and a prompt for the friend (e.g., "When you hear Track 3, reflect on a moment of courage in your life").

4. **Shared Listening/Reading Session (SD):** Schedule a "Playlist Party" where friends experience the media together, pausing to discuss impactful moments.

5. **Follow-Up (AD):** Exchange reflections via email on how specific pieces influenced thoughts or behaviors.

**Example Scenario:**

- For a friend facing career transition, Sam creates a "Resilience Playlist" of songs about perseverance and a mini booklet inviting reflection on specific lyrics. They meet via SD to listen and discuss, then send follow-up AD reflections on how each track resonated when applied to real life.

**Variants:**

- **Playlist Exchange Ritual:** Each friend curates a 7-track "Intention Playlist" for another, delivered via USB or streaming link, with a DL–AA letter explaining the choices.

---

## 18. "Intentionality Bootcamp" (Hybrid Multi-Day Immersion)

**Rationale:** Intensive, immersive experiences can rapidly elevate one's capacity for intentional action in friendship by combining theory, practice, and reflection.

**Structure (Weekend Immersion):**

| Day & Time | Activity | Modality |
|---|---|---|
| Friday Evening (6–9pm) | **Orientation & Philosophical Primer:** SD lecture on intentionality foundations (Sartre, Aristotle, Levinas). | SD |
| Saturday Morning (8–10am) | **AD Intention Writing:** Allocate 2 hours for each participant to craft deep reflective letters or emails to friends, guided by templates (Section VI.2). | AD + AA |
| Saturday Late Morning (10–12) | **SA Guided Walk & Reflect:** Pair up; 1 hour walking meditation focusing on personal friend intentions; then share. | SA |
| Saturday Lunch Break (12–1pm) | Intentional "Presence Meal": no phones, shared fruit, guided mindful eating (SA + SD group video for remote participants). | SA + SD |
| Saturday Early Afternoon (1–4pm) | **AA Ritual Workshop:** Participants create "Intention Capsules": small sealed envelopes containing handcrafted notes, tokens, or affirmations to be mailed over the coming months. | AA |
| Saturday Late Afternoon (4–6pm) | **AD Follow-Up Integration:** Draft AD messages setting timelines for next months' intentional acts, share and refine with peers. | AD |
| Saturday Evening (7–9pm) | **SD Empathy & Intentional Listening Lab:** Simulated scenarios—role-play broken intentions, practice apologies, practice crafting intention-forward responses. | SD |
| Sunday Morning (8–10am) | **SA Community Circle:** Face-to-face (or hybrid) group debrief on challenges, successes, and personal growth moments. | SA |
| Sunday Midday (10–12) | **AD/Ethernet-aided "Intention Hackathon":** Brainstorm with peers new creative ways to embed intention—digital tools, apps, or stationery design. | AD + SD |
| Sunday Afternoon (1–3pm) | **AA & SA Closing Ceremony:** Exchange "Intention Capsules" among participants; share final reflections; plant a tree or plant as a symbol of intention growth (SA). | AA + SA |

**Pitfalls & Mitigations:**

- **Overwhelm:** Eight full hours of intentionality work can fatigue participants—build in micro-breaks; offer optional "quiet corners."
- **Tech Glitches:** For hybrid sessions, test AV equipment ahead of time; have backup low-tech options (printed materials).
- **Integration Failure:** Post-bootcamp fade can occur. Mitigate with "Booster Calls" (SD) at 1-week, 1-month, and 3-month intervals to sustain momentum.

**Anticipated Outcomes:**

- Steep learning curve in identifying unintentional patterns.
- Rapid adoption of intentional rituals.
- Peer bonding that fosters mutual accountability and shared best practices.

---

## 19. "Intention-Focused Vulnerability Circles" (SA + SD + AD)

**Rationale:** Integrate intentionality with vulnerability by creating safe spaces where friends can declare deep intentions while sharing personal narratives.

**Steps:**

1. **Covenant of Safety:** Co-create guidelines—confidentiality, non-judgment, no unsolicited advice—before any vulnerability circle.

2. **Combining Modalities:**
   - Begin SA in a private room or outdoor setting.
   - Transition to SD breakout spaces for remote participants as needed.
   - Conclude with AD "Reflection Prompts" emailed to participants.

3. **Structured Rounds:** Each friend takes 10 minutes:
   - **Declaration of Intention:** "My intention is to overcome my fear of rejection by reaching out to three friends this week."

- **Vulnerable Narrative:** Share a brief story illustrating that fear's impact (DL–SA or DL–SD).

- **Solicited Support:** Ask the group for one specific supportive action (e.g., "Please check in on me Wednesday at 7pm via a short text").

- **Affirmation Round:** The group responds with empathic statements and concrete offers of assistance.

4. **AD Follow-Up:** Each participant writes a reflective AD message summarizing how hearing others' intentions inspired their own next steps.

**Example Scenario:**

- A professional women's network holds a monthly "Intention-Vulnerability Circle": each member declares a career-related intention, shares a brief personal challenge, and selects an accountability partner for the next month.

**Variants:**

- **Mini "Intention Hot Seat":** At larger events, designate one person to take a "hot seat" for 5 minutes, focusing on one high-stakes intention, followed by group empathic feedback.

## 20. "Intentionality Hackathon" (SD + AD)

**Rationale:** Crowdsource creative hacks to embed intentionality in friendships, leveraging collective intelligence.

**Steps:**

1. **Define Hackathon Focus:** Choose a theme—e.g., "Boosting DL–AD impact in two days" or "Designing a low-cost AA gift memory kit."

2. **Form Teams:** Groups of 3–4, mixing local (SA) and remote (SD) participants.

3. **Schedule:**

- **Day 1 - Kickoff (SD, 2 hours):** Present challenge, form teams, brainstorm initial ideas.
- **Day 1 - Work Blocks (AD, 4 hours asynchronous):** Teams flesh out prototypes—draft letter templates, design gift kits, plan call agendas.
- **Day 2 - Development (SD, 3 hours):** Teams present prototypes in "demo" format; receive live peer feedback; iterate.
- **Day 2 - Wrap-Up (SD, 1 hour):** Final presentations, group voting on top hacks, and plan dissemination (e.g., shared repository of templates).

4. **Post-Hackathon Publication:** Create an AD-shared Google Drive or website for collated hacks, templates, and resources—open source for all participants and friends.

**Example Scenario:**

- A graduate student association hosts a weekend "Friendship Hackathon" to generate new AA gift concepts that double as presence anchors. They produce prototypes: "Seeded Coasters" (plantable coasters with friendship quotes), "Scented Intention Bookmarks," and "Voice-Note Keychains."

**Variants:**

- **Mini-Hack Sprints:** Hour-long events at local cafés where pairs of friends develop one actionable friendship hack (e.g., a "Monday Motivation DM template") and test it immediately.

---

## 21. "Intentionality and Nature Immersion" (SA + AA)

**Rationale:** Natural environments enhance clarity of purpose and support intentional reflection, leading to deeper relational insights.

**Steps:**

1. **Select Natural Setting:** Park, forest, lakeshore, or botanical garden with minimal human-made distractions.
2. **Pair or Small Group:** Friends convene SA.

3. **Opening Nature Ritual:** Stand barefoot (if safe) for two minutes, feeling earth beneath; each silently sets a personal relational intention.

4. **Guided Nature Walk:**

    - Walk in silence for 10 minutes, noticing surroundings.
    - At a landmark, pause for "Intention Sharing" (DL–SA)—each states one specific friendship commitment.
    - Continue, alternating between 5 minutes silent walking and 5 minutes DL sharing four times.

5. **AA Artifact Creation:** Collect small natural items (leaf, stone, pinecone). Each writes a short inscription or intention on a slip of paper, then attaches it to their chosen artifact—creating a "Friendship Altar" by the final landmark.

6. **Reflection Journaling (AD + AA):** After returning home, within 24 hours, write an AD journal entry capturing insights, including a photograph of the Friendship Altar; mail a printed copy and a small artifact to the friend as AA reinforcement.

**Example Scenario:**

- Four colleagues organize a "Forest of Intentions" weekend retreat: they each carve one sentence of commitment into small cedar boards, burying them beneath a favorite tree—a silent promise to support each other's professional and personal growth.

**Variants:**

- **Tidepool Intentions (SA):** At low tide, friends place intentions written on water-resistant paper into tidepools, symbolically releasing them to the sea, trusting nature's cycles—followed by AD reflection on how surrendering intentions can paradoxically strengthen commitment.

---

## 22. "Intentionality in Conflict Resolution" (All Modalities)

**Rationale:** Intentionality is as vital when friendship strains—transforming conflict into opportunity for growth rather than relational erosion.

**Steps:**

1. **Conflict Acknowledgment (AD):** Respond quickly to initial signals of tension by sending a respectful AD message: "I sense tension after our last conversation. I intend to understand your perspective—are you open to a chat?"

2. **Mutual Intention Setting (SD or SA):** If both agree, schedule a DL-focused conversation. Begin by co-stating: "Our intention is to repair our bond with honesty and respect."

3. **Conflict Dialogue Structure:**

    - **I-Statements:** Each speaks for 3 minutes using "I feel… when you… because…"

    - **Empathic Reflection:** Listener paraphrases and validates before speaking their own.

    - **Intentional Pause:** Insert a 10-second silence to process before responding, ensuring deliberate calibration.

4. **Resolution & Intention Declaration:** Conclude by each stating one explicit, measurable intention to prevent recurrence—e.g., "I will pause and ask for clarification when I feel triggered."

5. **AA Follow-Up:** Within a week, each mails a handwritten note summarizing insights and reinforcing the agreed intentions.

**Example Scenario:**

- Two roommates clash over household chores. Using this model, they engage in an AD "tension acknowledgment" email, convene a DL–SD "Conflict Conversation" week later, and exchange AA "Peace Notes" to seal the resolution.

**Variants:**

- **Group Mediated Intentions:** When conflicts involve more than two friends, engage a neutral peer as "Intentionality Mediator," ensuring the group's intentions align with relational well-being.

---

## 23. "Digital Detox & Intentional Reconnection" (SA + AD)

**Rationale:** Periodic digital fasts create relational vacuums that prime deeper intentional reconnection once normalcy resumes.

**Steps:**

1. **Detox Agreement:** Friends agree on a time window (12–48 hours) when all will deactivate personal social media and messaging notifications.

2. **SA Gathering Planning:** Arrange an SA event just after the detox window—e.g., a picnic, art workshop, or nature hike—designed specifically as a "Reconnection Space."

3. **AD Checkpoint:** On first day of detox, send a brief AD message of encouragement, to be read after reactivation: "I'm off-line. This time reminds me how much I value our time together."

4. **SA Reconnection Ritual:** During the post-detox gathering, perform a "Reconnect Ceremony": share reflections on the detox experience and articulate new intentions for managing digital presence.

5. **Document Insights (AD + AA):** Each writes an AD summary of the detox's personal impact and mails a small AA token (e.g., a photo of the group gathering) with annotations highlighting rekindled bonds.

**Example Scenario:**

- A cluster of friends designates the first weekend of each month as "Digital Sabbath Start," logging off Friday midnight through Saturday night. On Sunday, they host a potluck brunch (SA), sharing stories of digital withdrawal, then each mails a reflective postcard (AA) summarizing how they intend to balance digital and analog engagement.

**Variants:**

- **Micro-Detox:** Daily 2-hour windows for individual detox—followed by AD/SD check-ins where each friend shares what they noticed. Over time, these micro-detox periods train intentional digital habits.

---

## 24. "Intentionality Through Artful Collaboration" (SA + SD + AD + AA)

**Rationale:** Collaborative creative projects—poetry, art, music—can crystallize intentions into tangible artifacts, reinforcing shared purpose.

**Steps:**

1. **Project Selection:** Choose a collaborative medium aligned with group interests—e.g., creating a zine, composing a song, or co-authoring a poetry chapbook.

2. **Kickoff Vision Meeting (SD):** Discuss project goals, assign roles (editing, layout, contribution), and co-create a project intention statement (e.g., "To celebrate our friendship's evolution through a summer-themed artbook").

3. **SA Creation Sessions:** If local, meet in person for co-creation workshops—collaging, writing, or recording. Remote collaborators join via SD with shared screens, whiteboards, or collaborative platforms (e.g., Google Jamboard).

4. **AD Iterative Feedback:** Between SA sessions, work on individual sections and exchange drafts via AD—providing intentional, line-by-line feedback focused on honoring each contributor's voice.

5. **AA Artifact Production:** Compile final product into a printed zine or CD. Use AA mailings to distribute copies, each accompanied by a personalized reflective note.

6. **Reflection & Celebration (SA or SD):** Hold a launch event—reading night, listen party—where each friend presents their portion and articulates how intentional collaboration influenced their personal growth.

**Example Scenario:**

- A group of four poets initiates "The Intentional Echo Anthology": they meet in a local studio (SA) for writing sprints, share drafts via AD, workshop via SD, then print 100 zines to mail (AA) at winter solstice. Their project intention: "Illuminate the cycles of renewal we experience in friendship."

**Variants:**

- **Virtual Reality Collaboration:** In VR spaces, friends can co-create 3D sculptures or soundscapes (SD + SA elements), exporting to physical prints (AA) and posting reflective AD commentary on each piece.

---

## 25. "Time-Bound Commitment Contracts" (SD + AD + AA)

**Rationale:** Legally or ceremonially formalizing friendship intentions with clear timeframes enhances accountability and clarifies expectations.

**Steps:**

1. **Contract Drafting (SD):** Friends jointly draft a "Friendship Commitment Contract"—detailing specific acts (e.g., "One DL–AD letter per month," "Biweekly DL–SA meetups during election season"), complete with start and end dates.

2. **Signatures & Witnesses (AA):** Print the contract; each friend signs in ink and secures two neutral witnesses (mutual friends or family). Exchange physical signed copies via AA mail.

3. **Interim Reviews (AD):** At midpoint, exchange AD check-ins on contract progress—"I fulfilled my letter; how did it land?"

4. **Contract Renewal or Revision (SD):** At contract's end, convene an SD session to either renew, revise, or conclude the contract—documenting new intentions as appropriate.

**Example Scenario:**

- Three colleagues draft a "2025 Connection Contract" at the start of the year:
    - **Commitments:**
        - Send each other a DL–AD progress report at month's end.
        - Host an SA "Brainstorm Brunch" quarterly.
        - Exchange AA "Inspirational Booklets" biannually.
- They sign, witness, and commit to reviewing on June 30.

**Variants:**

- **Micro-Contracts:** For short-term intentions—e.g., "Contract to read and reflect on a friend's business proposal within 48 hours," signed digitally and emailed as PDF.

---

## 26. "Intentionality through Role-Play & Simulations" (SD + SA)

**Rationale:** Practicing difficult conversations or friendship scenarios via role-play builds skillful, intentional responses when real-life situations arise.

**Steps:**

1. **Scenario Identification:** List common friendship challenges—confession of secret, boundary-setting, conflict over resources.

2. **Role Assignment:** Friends pair up—one plays self, another plays friend or challenging situation.

3. **Simulation Execution (SD for remote, SA for local):**

    - **Round 1 (DS/SA):** Play out scenario without preparation—observe natural tendencies.

    - **Debrief (AD or discussion):** Provide feedback on listening, tone, clarity of intention.

    - **Round 2:** Replay with explicit intention statements ("I intend to prioritize your feelings over my own defensiveness").

    - **Reflective Insight (AD):** Each participant writes an email summarizing lessons learned.

**Example Scenario:**

- Two friends practice "Setting Boundaries with a Demanding Friend"—one role-plays the demanding friend, the other practices a DL–SD conversation using intentional scripts. They debrief afterward, noting improved empathic tone and clarity.

**Variants:**

- **Group Simulation Stations:** Small breakout rooms each focus on a different scenario in parallel, rotating participants every 20 minutes, culminating in a plenary SD session to share takeaways.

---

## 27. "Intentional Gratitude Map" (AD + AA)

**Rationale:** Visualizing gratitude acts with explicit intentions ensures that expressions of thanks remain meaningful and not rote.

**Steps:**

1. **Map Creation:** Draw a large mind-map or digital canvas, placing "Me" at center, with branches to each friend.

2. **Intentional Acts Logging:** For each friend, list recent thoughtful acts along with the intention behind them—e.g., "Sent a care package to signal support during her treatment."

3. **AD Reflection Exchange:** Email the map as a PDF; each friend annotates on their branch—"That gesture made me feel valued; next, I intend to send you a playlist."

4. **AA Poster Printing:** Print the collaboratively annotated map on high-quality paper; mail a copy as an AA gift to each friend, accompanied by a small frame or sleeve.

**Example Scenario:**

- A close-knit book club co-creates a "Gratitude Map" reflecting on how each member has supported others (loaned books, provided edits, offered empathy). They annotate intentions for future support (e.g., "I will host a themed discussion on your favorite author next month") and gift each other framed prints.

**Variants:**

- **Digital Interactive Map:** A shared digital canvas (Miro, Jamboard) where annotations update dynamically; periodically printed as AA posters.

---

## 28. "Intentionality Reflection Retreat" (SA + SD)

**Rationale:** Combining extended solitude with guided reflection catalyzes deep insights into one's friendship intentions and realigns actions with values.

**Structure (3-Day Solo Retreat with Remote Community Support):**

| Day & Time | Activity | Modality |
| --- | --- | --- |

| | | |
|---|---|---|
| Day 1 Morning (8–10am) | **Arrival & Grounding (SA):** Silent nature immersion, breathing exercises, sensory awareness. | SA |
| Day 1 Late Morning (10–12) | **AD Initial Journaling:** Respond to prompts: "What are my deepest friendship values?" and "Where have I drifted?" | AD (Solo) |
| Day 1 Afternoon (1–4pm) | **SA Mindful Walks & Thought-Partner Calls:** Alternate walking alone (30 min) with scheduled SD check-ins (15 min) where a friend asks reflective questions. | SA + SD |
| Day 1 Evening (7–9pm) | **SA Silent Dinner:** Eat mindfully at campsite or cabin; reflect on the day; compose AA letter to future self summarizing insights. | SA + AA |
| Day 2 Morning (8–10am) | **SA Embodied Ritual:** Craft an "Intentional Totem" using natural materials—each element representing a friendship pillar. | SA |
| Day 2 Late Morning (10–12) | **AD Deep Dive Writing:** Answer advanced prompts: "How will my friendship intentions redefine my relationships over the next year?" | AD (Solo) |
| Day 2 Afternoon (1–4pm) | **SA Role-Play Practice:** Practice difficult friendship conversations with voice-recordings, then listen back and self-evaluate intentional tone. | SA + AA |
| Day 2 Evening (7–9pm) | **SD Community Share:** Brief group call where retreat participants share one key intention revelation. | SD |
| Day 3 Morning (8–10am) | **SA Integration Walk:** Walk again reflecting on how to translate insights into daily rituals. | SA |
| Day 3 Late Morning (10–12) | **AD Commitment Document Drafting:** Write a "Personal Friendship Manifesto" outlining concrete, time-bound intentions. | AD (Solo) |
| Day 3 Afternoon (1–3pm) | **SD Closing Ceremony:** Read manifestos aloud in a video circle; peers affirm and offer supportive commitments. | SD |

| After Retreat | **AA Artifact Distribution:** Mail Intentional Totem (created Day 2) to a friend with a manifesto excerpt. | AA |

**Pitfalls & Mitigations:**

- **Isolation Overwhelm:** Provide nightly SD check-ins for emotional support.
- **Over-Intellectualizing:** Balance writing with embodied SA rituals.
- **Post-Retreat Deflation:** Schedule AD "integration accountability" check-ins at 1 week and 1 month.

**Anticipated Outcomes:**

- Participants emerge with crystalized, multi-modal Friendship Manifestos and tangible AA artifacts to reinforce intentions.
- Deeper empathy cultivated through role-play and peer affirmation.

# VII. Case Studies: Transforming Relationships Through Intentionality

In-depth examinations of three scenarios—personal, organizational, and community—demonstrate how intention reshapes relational landscapes.

## Case Study 1: "Rekindling a Fractured Friendship" (Personal, Multi-Modality)

### A. Context & Challenges

Longtime friends, **Seema** and **Leo**, experienced a painful misunderstanding that led to months of silence. Attempts at reconnection via generic "Hey, how are you?" texts (SL–AD) failed, as underlying resentment remained unaddressed.

### B. Intervention Design

**Phase 1: Intentional Acknowledgment (AD)**

- **Step 1:** Seema spent a day drafting a deep AD email structured via the "Letter Blueprint" (Section VI.4):

    - **Subject Line:** "Owning My Part in Our Drift—An Apology & Intention"

    - **Opening Context:** "Leo, I've felt the distance between us and realize my silence hurt you."

    - **Core Narrative:** Seema detailed her perspective on the misunderstanding—taking responsibility and acknowledging his pain.

    - **Depth Prompt:** "How have you experienced my absence, and what would you need from me to begin rebuilding trust?"

    - **Closing Intention:** "I commit to listening fully to your response, without defensiveness."

## Phase 2: SD Vulnerability Conversation (SD)

- **Step 1:** Upon receiving Leo's invitation for a call, they scheduled a DL–SD session. They began with a shared "digital candle" ritual (Section VIII.7), then each used "I-Statements" (Section VI.22) and "Pause & Reflect 2.0" (Section VIII.2) to explore feelings.

- **Step 2:** They co-created **specific intentions**: weekly DL–AD check-ins, monthly SA meet-ups at a quiet café, and quarterly AA "Harmony Letters" expressing gratitude.

## Phase 3: SA Healing Walk (SA)

- **Step 1:** Two weeks later, they met for an SA "Purposeful Walk & Talk" (Section VI.6) along a riverside. At the first marker, Leo shared lingering hurt; at the second, Seema responded with empathic validation and reaffirmed her commitment.

- **Step 2:** They placed a folded note of intention inside a carved wooden box at a bench—a symbolic Promise Box they agreed to revisit quarterly.

## Phase 4: AA Trust-Building Packages (AA + AD)

- Over the next three months, each mailed two AA care packages to the other containing:

    - A handwritten letter reflecting on new memories.

- A small token (friendship bracelet, pressed flower).
- A short DL–AD prompt card—"Share one way you noticed my support this month."

## C. Outcomes & Insights

- **Repaired Trust:** Within six months, SDL and AD interactions normalized to pre-conflict levels, with increased DL depth and intentional mod-ality shifts.
- **Sustainable Rituals:** The Promise Box became a quarterly site for SA reflection and renewal.
- **Mutual Growth:** Both reported improved conflict-communication skills and a revived sense of shared purpose.
- **Lessons Learned:**
  - Aggressive pursuit of intention via deep AD apologies sets the stage for genuine DL dialogue.
  - Combining AA tokens (care packages) with follow-up SD/SA rituals repairs relational rupture more effectively than either alone.
  - Co-creating specific, measurable intentions prevents drift back into passive habits.

---

# Case Study 2: "Cultivating Intentional Team Cohesion" (Organizational, Multi-Modality)

## A. Context & Challenges

**TechCo**, a mid-sized startup, faced high turnover and low morale. Teams operated siloed; "watercooler chats" vanished under the pressure of remote work. Interactions were predominantly SL–SD "stand-up meetings" devoid of relational depth or purpose beyond tasks.

## B. Intervention Design

### Phase 1: Leadership Intentionality Training (SD)

- **Step 1:** Executives participated in a "Leadership as Intentionality" workshop (SD), covering philosophical and neuroscientific underpinnings of purposeful action. They drafted an "Executive Intentionality Protocol" committing to model deliberate relational acts.

## Phase 2: Team "Intentional Huddle" Implementation (SD + AD)

- **Step 1:** Each team instituted a daily 5-minute "Intentional Huddle" adjacent to their SL "stand-up." The Huddle's structure:
    - **Opening (1 min):** Brief mindfulness practice (SA style via guided SD audio).
    - **Check-In (2 min):** Each member quietly types in shared chat one word about their current emotional state (AD element).
    - **Intentional Prompt (2 min):** Rotation: one team member poses a quick prompt ("What's one thing you appreciate about yesterday's support?").
- **Step 2:** The "Intentional Huddle" chat logs are archived (AD) so team members can revisit moments of DL connection.

## Phase 3: SA "Relationship Building Row" Sessions

- **Step 1:** Monthly, each team spends 90 minutes SA (socially distanced, if needed) doing an off-site activity—escape rooms, cooking classes, or community service—designed for co-creation and vulnerability sharing. Hosts follow the "Purpose-Driven SD Agenda" model, adapted for SA.

## Phase 4: AA "Growth Tokens" Distribution

- **Step 1:** At project launch and completion stages, managers prepare AA "Growth Tokens"—tokens engraved with words like "Innovation," "Resilience," "Collaboration."
- **Step 2:** Tokens are physically mailed or hand-delivered to team members, accompanied by a DL–AD letter explaining why that token reflects the member's contribution.

## C. Outcomes & Insights

- **Employee Engagement:** After six months, internal surveys indicated a 45 % rise in perceived team cohesion and a 30 % drop in turnover.

- **Modal Balance:** Interactions evolved from 90 % SL–SD to a balanced mix: 40 % SL, 30 % DL across SD & AD, 20 % SA, and 10 % AA.

- **Performance Gains:** Project delivery times improved by 20 %, attributed in part to heightened relational trust from intentional practices.

- **Lessons Learned:**
    - Short, daily "Intentional Huddles" prime teams for meaningful collaboration, preventing relational decay.
    - Integrating SA activities fosters embodied trust but requires logistical support (budget, scheduling).
    - AA tokens create tangible reminders of shared achievements, reinforcing intentional culture between meetings.

## Case Study 3: "Community Intentionality Network" (Community-Level, Multi-Modality)

### A. Context & Challenges

A neighborhood facing fragmentation—residents rarely interacted beyond superficial greetings. The community sought to build deeper bonds to collaborate on local initiatives (community garden, street cleanups) but lacked frameworks for intentional connection.

### B. Intervention Design

### Phase 1: Community Intent Workshop (SA)

- **Step 1:** Town hall-style SA meeting at the local community center: facilitated discussions on shared values ("What kind of neighborhood do we want to be?").

- **Step 2:** Co-create a "Neighborhood Intent Charter" outlining commitments—monthly "Intentional Potlucks," quarterly "Neighbor Narratives" storytelling sessions, and a rotating "Friendship Bench" program (intentional seat in a public park where passersby can start DL conversations).

### Phase 2: SD "Neighborhood Intent News"

- **Step 1:** Launch an SD livestream "Intent News" broadcast every first Wednesday of the month—residents share highlights of intentional acts (e.g., volunteers mentoring local youth, neighbors delivering AA care packages to seniors).

- **Step 2:** Stream is archived and interspersed with AD segments: residents submit short video testimonials or photos, which are compiled into monthly digital newsletters.

## Phase 3: SA "Intentional Potlucks" & "Storytelling Benches"

- **Step 1:** Every month, host a potluck dinner in a common hall—families bring dishes and a DL story (e.g., how they overcame adversity) to share in person.

- **Step 2:** Install painted "Friendship Benches" at community hotspots; each bench features an engraved plaque with a reflective question: "What brings you hope today?" Passersby are invited to sit and share reflections with whoever else arrives (DL–SA).

## Phase 4: AA "Intentional Care Drops"

- **Step 1:** Once a quarter, form volunteer teams to assemble AA "Comfort Kits" for elderly neighbors—handwritten cards, homemade treats, knitted scarves.

- **Step 2:** Coordinate AD "Care Calendar" so recipients know when to expect kits and can reply with letters or digital photos of gratitude.

## C. Outcomes & Insights

- **Social Capital Increase:** Within a year, cross-household collaborations surged; Neighborhood Intent Charter guided 12 new community projects.

- **Friendship Formation:** 70 % of Potluck attendees reported making at least one new friend; Storytelling Benches became weekend gathering spots for intergenerational DL encounters.

- **Emotional Well-Being:** Community surveys indicated a 40 % drop in reported loneliness and a 25 % rise in reported "sense of belonging."

- **Lessons Learned:**
    - Community-wide intentional rituals (Potlucks, News broadcasts) scale personal practices to collective impact.

- SA "Storytelling Benches" serve as low-barrier entry points for DL engagement; plaques with prompts guide conversation among strangers.
- AD and SD elements (newsletters, livestreams) sustain momentum between SA gatherings and AA initiatives.

# VIII. Measuring and Auditing Intentionality

To ensure intentionality remains an active practice rather than a transient novelty, systematic measurement and reflective audits are essential. Below are **five** comprehensive tools to assess, adjust, and amplify intentional efforts.

## 1. "Intentionality Scorecard" (Weekly)

**Purpose:** Track specific intentional actions, align them with overarching goals, and identify areas needing reinforcement.

**Components (Weekly Log):**

| Friend/Group Name | Modality | Intentional Action Taken | Self-Rated Success (1–10) | Observed Friend Response (1–10) | Key Insight/Challenge | Next Intentional Step |
|---|---|---|---|---|---|---|
| Emma | DL–AD | Sent "Letter Blueprint" email | 8 | 7 | Friend replied deeply but loitered on logistics | Plan a DL–SD call to follow up on emotional themes |
| TechCo Team | SD | Held "Intentional Huddle" | 9 | 8 | High engagement; two new issues emerged | Incorporate mid-huddle "Pause & Reflect 2.0" next week |

| Siblings | AA | Mailed "Heritage Box" | 10 | 9 | Immediate excitement; scheduled SD debrief | Schedule SA walk when siblings are home for holidays |
| Community | SA | Hosted "Potluck" | 7 | 6 | Attendance lower than expected | Use AD newsletters to boost attendance next month |

**Instructions:**

1. **Identify Recipients and Modalities:** List each friend or group targeted with an intentional act.

2. **Record Actions and Ratings:** Log what you did, then immediately after and a week later, rate your success and the friend's response.

3. **Extract Insights:** Note challenges (e.g., scheduling friction) and positive surprises (e.g., unexpected depth).

4. **Plan Next Steps:** Concrete intentions for next week, tied to modality and relational goal.

**Outcome:** The weekly Intentionality Scorecard encourages continuous, data-driven optimization of friendship actions, ensuring alignment between intention and outcome.

---

## 2. "Quarterly Intention Audit" (Comprehensive Reflection)

**Purpose:** Conduct a deep dive into the previous three months' intentional efforts—identifying patterns, recalibrating, and setting new macro-goals.

**Process:** Twice a year (e.g., January and July), complete the following steps:

1. **Aggregate Weekly Scorecards:** Compile and review all weekly logs. Identify:
   - Modalities most/least utilized.

- Distinct "streak" successes (e.g., consistently high success in DL–AD emails).
- Bottlenecks (e.g., repeated low friend response ratings in AA).

2. **Reflect on Achievements & Shortfalls:**
   - Which intentions fulfilled? Which fell short?
   - Were certain relational objectives unmet (e.g., no SA quality time with parent)?
   - How did evolving life circumstances affect capacity for intentionality?

3. **Deep Reflection Prompts (AD):** Write a 1,000–1,500 word piece addressing:
   - "What intentions led to sustained relational growth, and why?"
   - "Which unfulfilled intentions reveal core vulnerabilities or boundary issues?"
   - "What new intentions arise from shifting personal values or life events?"

4. **Peer Feedback Session (SD):** If possible, hold a group SD meeting with a small accountability circle. Share key findings; solicit feedback on blind spots—"I notice I'm avoiding SA with Jim because of unresolved tension; how might I re-enter that modality intentionally?"

5. **Revised Intentionality Roadmap:**
   - Update the "Intentional Roadmap" (Section VI.9), adjusting goals, timelines, and modality allocations for the next six months.
   - Document any new rituals to introduce or old ones to retire.

6. **Intent Reinforcement Artifact (AA):** Create a physical artifact—e.g., a printed "Intentional Goals Poster" or a hand-bound "Intent Journal"—that visually captures renewed intentions. Mail to trusted friends or display in a prominent personal space.

**Outcome:** The Quarterly Intention Audit fosters macro-level strategic reflection, preventing drift from intentional friendship goals and enabling adaptive recalibration aligned with evolving relational landscapes.

## 3. "Intentionality Peer Review" (Structured Feedback)

**Purpose:** Gather candid feedback from peers on the effectiveness and authenticity of one's intentional efforts—illuminating blind spots that quantitative metrics miss.

**Process:**

1. **Select Reviewers:** Choose 2–4 close friends or colleagues who have observed your interactions across at least two modalities.

2. **Customized Feedback Template:** Provide reviewers with a structured set of queries:
   - "When I executed an intentional act—e.g., that care package you received—how did it feel? Did you sense genuine purpose?"
   - "In SD dialogues, did my actions appear premeditated or performative?"
   - "Were there times when my well-intentioned gestures felt burdensome or misaligned with your needs?"
   - "Where have you noticed my intentions excel or falter over the past quarter?"

3. **Feedback Sessions:**
   - **PD (Process Discussion) Call (SD):** Conduct a 30-minute call to discuss feedback verbally, emphasizing an atmosphere of non-judgment.
   - **AD Written Feedback:** Review open-ended, typed responses saved in a shared document and respond with follow-up questions where clarity is needed.

4. **Integration & Action Plan:**
   - Synthesize feedback into actionable changes—e.g., "I learned I overplanned SA events and need to allow more spontaneity."
   - Document these changes in the Intentionality Roadmap and Weekly Scorecard.

**Outcome:** Peer Review reveals how intentions are perceived—bridging gaps between internal motives and external reception, enhancing relational alignment.

---

## 4. "Intentionality & Outcome Matrix" (Quantitative-Qualitative Hybrid)

**Purpose:** Evaluate which intentional acts yielded the highest relational dividends—balancing quantitative frequency with qualitative impact.

**Steps:**

1. **Data Collection:**
   - From Weekly Scorecards and Quarterly Audits, compile a list of intentional acts over the past 12 months—categorized by modality and depth.
   - For each act, assign:
     - **Frequency Score (F):** Number of times act was performed.
     - **Impact Rating (I):** Average friend response score (1–10) gathered from logs.

2. **Matrix Construction:** Create a two-axis matrix:
   - **X-Axis:** Frequency Score (Low to High)
   - **Y-Axis:** Impact Rating (Low to High)

3. **Plot Acts:** Each intentional gesture becomes a point in the quadrant:
   - **High F, High I (Golden Zone):** Acts to prioritize and replicate.
   - **High F, Low I (Overused & Under-Effective):** Re-evaluate or retire.
   - **Low F, High I (Underutilized Gems):** Consider increasing frequency.
   - **Low F, Low I (Minimal Contribution):** Phase out.

4. **Actionable Insights:**
   - For Golden Zone acts (e.g., monthly DL–AA letter exchange), maintain consistency.
   - For Overused Acts, reflect on adaptation—"Why is this high frequency but low impact? Perhaps SL–SD calls need deeper structure."
   - For Underutilized Gems, plan to integrate them more regularly (e.g., "Plan two Intentional Potlucks next quarter").
   - For Minimal Contribution acts, archive as past approaches.

5. **Update Intentionality Roadmap:** Adjust future commitments based on matrix insights.

**Example Scenario:**

- "Venmo Birthday Gifts" might have high frequency but low relational impact (Low I); shift to personalized AA gifts (Low F, High I), increasing frequency of the latter.

**Outcome:** The Intentionality & Outcome Matrix transforms qualitative perceptions into strategic adjustments, ensuring efforts focus on high-impact gestures.

---

## 5. "Satisfaction-to-Intention Ratio" (Longitudinal Reflection)

**Purpose:** Compare one's satisfaction with each friendship against actual intentional efforts, identifying discrepancies between desired closeness and practiced intention.

**Process:**

1. **Semi-Annual Survey:** For each close friend, answer two questions on a scale of 1–7:

    - **Satisfaction Metric (S):** "How satisfied are you with the depth and quality of our friendship?"

    - **Intentionality Metric (T):** "How intentional have my recent actions been toward strengthening our bond?"

2. **Ratio Calculation:** Compute the **S/T Ratio**.

    - If S > T, satisfaction exceeds intentionality—indicates opportunities to act more purposefully.

    - If S < T, you may be overinvesting intent without receiving satisfaction—signals a need to realign methods or adjust expectations.

3. **Narrative Reflection:** For each pair, write a short paragraph explaining the ratio:

    - Example: "My satisfaction with June and I is 6, but my intentionality is 3 (ratio 2:1). We have strong mutual affection, yet I realize I've been reactive rather than proactive—often only sending SL–AD texts instead of deeper gestures."

4. **Action Planning:**

- For high S/T: Schedule additional DL–SA or AA acts to match satisfaction.
- For low S/T: Evaluate whether friend's communication style differs—perhaps more SA is needed—and adjust.

5. **Re-Measuring:** Repeat after six months to track progress.

**Outcome:** The Satisfaction-to-Intention Ratio keeps one honest about where friendship feels lacking in deliberate care, prompting recalibration of efforts.

---

# IX. Integration with Other Pillars

**Intentionality** does not operate in isolation; its power is unlocked when integrated with **Presence**, **Empathy**, and **Vulnerability**. Here we map explicitly how to weave intention into the fabric of the other pillars, ensuring a harmonious, reciprocal interplay.

---

### A. Intentionality ↔ Presence

1. **Synergistic Relationship:**
    - **Presence** ensures actions are delivered fully; **Intentionality** ensures actions serve a clear purpose.

2. **Integration Strategy:**
    - **Presence Preparations:** Before any intentional act, consciously cultivate presence—e.g., take five mindful breaths to center (from Chapter 8), then proceed with the intended gesture.
    - **Intentional Presence Rituals:** Combine "Digital Silence Charters" (Chapter 8, Section VI.A) with "Purpose-Driven SD Agendas" (Section VI.3) so that presence and intention co-arise synchronously.

3. **Illustrative Example:**
    - Before sending an AD letter (intentional), complete a "mindful typing" ritual (presence), ensuring that the letter embodies both purpose and undivided attention.

## B. Intentionality ↔ Empathy

1. **Synergistic Relationship:**
   - **Empathy** deepens understanding of a friend's needs; **Intentionality** mobilizes that understanding into purposeful acts of support.

2. **Integration Strategy:**
   - **Empathy Checkpoints:** Incorporate explicit empathy checks into intentional rituals—e.g., in "Purposeful Walk & Talk," intentionally alternate empathic paraphrasing before delivering supportive insights.
   - **Intentional Empathic Prompts:** When designing an "Intentional Group Salon" (Section VI.8), choose readings that specifically cultivate empathic awareness (e.g., an article on lived experiences of marginalization).

3. **Illustrative Example:**
   - When planning an AA care package, use empathetic insight ("I know you've felt stressed at work"), then intentionally select objects (e.g., calming teas) to meet that perceived need.

## C. Intentionality ↔ Vulnerability

1. **Synergistic Relationship:**
   - **Vulnerability** opens the door to depth; **Intentionality** ensures vulnerability is offered and received within a safe, purpose-driven framework.

2. **Integration Strategy:**
   - **Vulnerability Boundaries:** Build intentional consent into vulnerability rituals—e.g., before a "DL–SD Vulnerability Conversation" (Section VI.4), declare intentions and boundaries: "My intention is to share a personal struggle—please let me know if you prefer to pause."

- **Intentional Vulnerability Prompts:** In "Intentional Gratitude Circles" (Section VI.16), incorporate a prompt like "Share a time when you felt ashamed and the intention behind why you kept it private."

3. **Illustrative Example:**

    - While drafting a DL–AD message confessing fear of failure, begin with an intention statement: "I intend to be honest because I trust you and need your perspective." This intentional framing softens vulnerability and invites reciprocal authenticity.

# X. Advanced Strategies for Intentional Mastery

For readers seeking **accelerated growth** and **expert-level integration** of intentionality into their relational ecosystems, the following **five advanced strategies** provide immersive, multi-modal pathways to deepen purposeful friendship practices.

## 1. "Intentionality Masterclass Series" (Multi-Modal Curriculum)

**Rationale:** Structured, multi-session curriculum combining theory, practice, and community to cultivate advanced intentionality skills.

### Structure (8-Week Program):

| Week | Focus Area | Modality Mix | Key Deliverable |
|---|---|---|---|
| 1 | Foundations of Intentionality | SD (Lecture), AD (Reading) | Personal "Intent Audit" Report |
| 2 | Intentional Action Design | SD (Workshop), SA (Practice) | Draft "Intentional Action Playbook" |
| 3 | Neuroscience & Habit Engineering | AD (Module), SA (Walk Labs) | "Cue-Routine-Reward" Map |

| 4 | Intentional Communication Skills | SD (Role-Play), AD (Exercises) | "DL–AD Letter" Performance |
| 5 | AA Artifacts & Symbolic Gestures | SA (Workshop), AA (Crafting) | Prototype "Intention Artifact" |
| 6 | Conflict & Repair Intention | SD (Simulation), AD (Reflection) | "Conflict Resolution Contract" |
| 7 | Community-Level Intentionality | SD (Panel), SA (Fieldwork) | "Community Intent Action Plan" |
| 8 | Integration & Next-Level Roadmaps | SD (Roundtable), AD (Strategy) | Final "Personal Friendship Manifesto" |

**Delivery Details:**

- **SD Sessions (60–90 min):** Recorded lectures, interactive polls, breakout-room workshops.
- **AD Modules:** Reading assignments, short quizzes, reflection journals, peer review.
- **SA Labs/Workshops:** Local meetups for embodied practice—mindful walks, crafting AA artifacts, simulation role-plays.
- **AA Assignments:** Hand-recorded podcasts, mailed journals, tangible tokens created and exchanged.

**Outcome:** Graduates emerge with a fully developed "Intentional Action Playbook" customized to their relational contexts, a network of accountability partners, and the capacity to serve as intentionality mentors.

---

## 2. "The Intentionality Lab" (Ongoing Multi-Stakeholder Accelerator)

**Rationale:** Foster a dynamic ecosystem where individuals, startups, and community groups collaborate to prototype, test, and scale innovative friendship-intention solutions.

**Structure:**

1. **Open Call:** Invite individuals and organizations to submit intentionality challenges—e.g., "How do we maintain deep connection across teams of 100+ remote workers?"

2. **Solution Teams:** Form multi-disciplinary teams (psychologists, UX designers, community organizers) to develop prototypes—apps, physical products, workshops.

3. **Iterative Sprints:** Over six months, teams engage in two-week sprints to design, pilot, gather feedback, refine.

4. **Stakeholder Embedding:** Embed prototypes within real communities—e.g., beta-test an "Intentionality App" at a university for student peer mentoring.

5. **Evaluation & Scale:** Measure outcomes via longitudinal surveys, social network analysis, and emotional well-being indices. Successful prototypes receive seed funding or platform support for broader dissemination.

**Example Scenario:**

- A team develops the "Intentio App"—a mobile platform that cross-maps friendship intentions, triggers reminders, suggests modality mixes based on friend profiles, and gamifies high-impact gestures. Beta tested in a 2000-student university, it reduces reported loneliness by 30 % in three months.

**Variants:**

- **Corporate Intentionality Labs:** Companies sponsor internal labs to foster intentional cohesion among remote departments—leading to improved retention and collaboration metrics.

---

## 3. "Intermodal Intentionality Symphony" (Integrated Modality Mastery)

**Rationale:** Create a multi-phase, interwoven cycle of intentional actions across all four modalities—ensuring maximal reach and depth.

**Structure (4-Phase Annual Cycle):**

| Phase | Modal Focus | Core Rituals & Practices |
| --- | --- | --- |

| | | |
|---|---|---|
| **Spring Renewal** | AD → AA | **AD:** Send "Spring Intentions" reflective letters (Section VI.4). **AA:** Mail "Springtime Care Packages" (herbal tea, seeds, handwritten prompts). Follow-up AD responses. |
| **Summer Embodiment** | SA → SD | **SA:** Host "Intentional Picnic Series"—rotating households share DL check-ins. **SD:** Biweekly DL–SD "Sunset Circles" with "Pause & Reflect 2.0." |
| **Autumn Reflection** | SD → AD | **SD:** Quarterly "Empathy & Intention Symposium" discussing seasonal emotional shifts. **AD:** Write "Autumn Memoir Essays" in AA journal postcards mailed later. |
| **Winter Consolidation** | AA → SA → SD | **AA:** Create "Winter Memory Calendars" (handcrafted) and exchange by holiday. **SA:** Host "Intentional Workshop" (crafting AA gifts for next cycle). **SD:** Virtual "Intent Review Summit." |

**Steps:**

1. **Initiation:** At year's start, gather core friendship group to co-design cycle schedule.

2. **Phase Execution:** Each quarter, focus intensively on the designated modality combo—emphasizing depth elements.

3. **Inter-Phase Checkpoints:** Use AD surveys to gather mid-cycle feedback—e.g., "How did the Spring Renewal letters shift your intentions?"

4. **Final Review:** At year's end, convene SA gathering with remote SD participants to review cycle, celebrate progress, and set next year's cycle.

**Example Scenario:**

- A cooperative of six artists organizes an "Intermodal Intentionality Symphony": Spring letters initiate reciprocal care; Summer Picnics (SA) forge embodied bonds; Autumn Symposiums (SD) refine creative visions; Winter Calendars (AA) memorialize collective achievements and set intentions for new collaborative artworks.

**Variants:**

- **Adaptive Cycles:** Scale down to 2-phase cycles for leaner groups, focusing on the two most effective modalities for that group's context.

---

## 4. "Intentionality Fellowship" (Hybrid Community Cohort)

**Rationale:** Establish a community of practice—small cohorts of individuals committed to supporting each other's intentional friendship journeys over a year.

**Structure:**

1. **Cohort Formation (SA or SD):** 8–10 members selected based on commitment and diversity of contexts (personal, organizational, community).

2. **Mentor Pairing:** Each cohort member mentors another, creating dyads that meet biweekly (SD or SA) to set, review, and adjust intentions.

3. **Monthly Cohort Convenings (SD):**

    - **Peer-led Workshops:** Each member presents a challenge and receives group coaching.

    - **Skill Shares:** Members share expertise—crafting AA artifacts, running SD salons, applying neuroscience insights.

    - **"Intentionality Spotlight":** Rotate highlighting one member's success story, amplifying group learnings.

4. **Quarterly SA Retreats:** Weekend immersive gatherings focusing on advanced strategies (e.g., Intentionality Hackathons, Purpose-Driven Workshops).

5. **AD Knowledge Base:** Shared repository of templates, case studies, reflection prompts, and best practices—crowdsourced and continuously updated.

6. **Annual Graduation Ceremony (SA + AA):**

    - **Presentation of "Intentionality Compendiums":** Each member compiles their year's intentional journeys into a bound "Compendium" (AA) to present.

    - **Ritual Affirmations:** Participants share "Affirmation Scrolls" (handwritten) for one another, articulating observed growth.

**Example Scenario:**

- An Intentionality Fellowship of twelve social workers embarks on year-long collective practice—sharing case-specific friendship challenges, co-designing client support rituals, exchanging AA "Therapy Toolkits," and culminating in a published anthology of "Friendship Practice Narratives."

**Variants:**

- **Thematic Fellows:** Cohorts centered around specific themes—e.g., "Artist Friends Fellowship," "Parenting Through Intentionality," "Digital Nomads Intentional Community."

---

## 5. "Intentionality Legacy Projects" (AA + SA + SD + AD)

**Rationale:** Embed intentional friendship practices into larger legacy-building initiatives—ensuring that acts of care transcend individual lifespans and scale to generational impact.

**Examples:**

1. **Family Friendship Archives:** Multi-generational families co-create a living "Intentional Friendship Archive"—a bound volume of letters, photos, and AA artifacts, passed down as heirlooms.
2. **Community Time Capsules:** Local communities assemble capsules containing AA items (letters, tokens), sealed with intentions for friendship and to be reopened 10–20 years later.
3. **Organizational Culture Compendiums:** Companies document best intentional collaboration practices in an "Intentionality Charter" that becomes part of onboarding, preserving culture across leadership changes.

**Steps:**

1. **Vision & Planning:** Convene stakeholders to define the legacy scope—purpose, time horizon, key modalities.
2. **Artifact Collection (AA):** Gather letters, tokens, co-created artworks, recorded interviews—each inscribed with intentional reflections.

3. **Digital Backup (AD):** Archive digital versions (scans, transcripts, recordings) to preserve artifacts against physical decay; store in accessible repositories.

4. **Periodic "Opening" Events (SA + SD):** Every 5 or 10 years, organize community or family gatherings—live or virtual—where the capsule is opened, and reflections shared.

5. **Continuity Committees:** Assign a rotating group to maintain and update the legacy artifacts, ensuring ongoing reinterpretation and relevance.

**Example Scenario:**

- A century-old neighborhood establishes a "Friendship Time Capsule" in 2025, scheduled for 2050 opening. Residents contribute AA letters articulating neighborhood ethos, recorded SD interviews capturing oral histories, and AD digital diaries reflecting on evolving community bonds.

**Variants:**

- **Personal Legacy Capsules:** Individuals create personal "Intentionality Time Capsules" (journals, letters to future descendants) with family members, bridging individual friendship practices to intergenerational connection.

# XI. Avoiding Pitfalls & Paradoxes of Intentionality

Even as we strive for purposeful action, certain paradoxes and pitfalls can ensnare the well-intentioned. Recognizing and mitigating these ensures that intentionality remains constructive rather than counterproductive.

## A. Overplanning Leading to Inauthenticity

### 1. Pitfall

- Rigidly scripting every interaction—e.g., drafting elaborate letter templates weeks in advance—risks stripping spontaneity and authenticity, making gestures feel rehearsed rather than heartfelt.

### 2. Mitigation

- **Flex Plan Approach:** Combine high-level planning (e.g., "Quarterly SA retreat") with **open-ended execution**—allow improvisation within the plan.
- **Check for Sincerity:** Before executing a planned act, pause and ask, "Does this still feel aligned with my current feelings, or am I just following a script?" Adjust as needed.

---

## B. Instrumentalization of Friendship

### 1. Pitfall

- Treating friendship acts as means to an end—e.g., sending gifts only to secure favors—undermines trust and sows resentment.

### 2. Mitigation

- **Intent Audit ("Five Whys"):** Regularly revisit the "Why" behind each gesture (Section VI.2). If motivations are less about friendship and more about personal gain, reconsider or reframe the act.
- **Transparency Pledge:** When intentions may have dual aspects (e.g., offering support but also hoping for professional advice later), disclose candidly: "I want to show support, and I'd love your insights on my project—if that feels right for you."

---

## C. Ritual Rigidity Causing Burnout

### 1. Pitfall

- Over-committing to elaborate rituals (monthly large AA packages, weekly 2-hour DL–SD salons) can overwhelm one's time and emotional resources.

### 2. Mitigation

- **Scaled Adaptation:** Use concentration of the "Presence Pyramid" (Section VI.2) logic to distribute intensity—primary rituals monthly, secondary ones quarterly.
- **"Intentional Sabbaths":** Schedule periodic "Ritual Rests"—designate one month per year to pause all formal rituals, returning to casual, unstructured interactions.

## D. Neglecting Individual Differences

### 1. Pitfall

- Imposing one's preferred modalities (e.g., frequent SD calls) on friends who value AA or SA, leading to relational friction.

### 2. Mitigation

- **Co-Creation of Intent Plans:** Always negotiate intentions—"Would you prefer a letter over a call? What feels right for you?"
- **Modal Flexibility:** Maintain multiple pathways to the same intention—if a friend resists SD, pivot to AD or AA modes that accomplish similar relational aims.

## E. Paradox of Prosperity

### 1. Pitfall

- As intentions yield relational richness, one might become complacent—mistaking the presence of structured rituals for sustained care, leading to unexamined assumptions of goodwill.

### 2. Mitigation

- **Periodic Disruption:** Intentionally alter routines—flip modalities (e.g., if typically doing AA, try SA this month) to maintain novelty and guard against complacency.
- **Intentionality Checkpoints:** Frequent small "gratitude triggers"—unexpected gestures that reaffirm underlying relational ties beyond established rituals.

# XII. Conclusion: Toward an Ecosystem of Deliberate Friendship

**Intentionality**, as the second pillar of ReconneXion Theory, transforms friendship from a passive byproduct of circumstance into a **consciously cultivated art**. Through philosophical grounding in existential freedom, virtue ethics, and interpersonal responsibility, we recognize intention as a moral imperative: each choice in friendship shapes our character and our collective flourishing.

Neuroscience and psychology reveal that intentional actions—when scaffolded by clear cues, meaningful rewards, and supportive habit architectures—can become sustainable patterns, resisting the headwinds of digital distraction and relational drift. Our exhaustive catalog of **twenty detailed practices, advanced strategies, case studies,** and **measurement tools** offers a panoramic toolkit for embedding purpose into every facet of relational life—across SD, AD, SA, and AA modalities.

As you integrate intentionality into your friendships:

1. **Reflect Continually:** Use weekly scorecards, quarterly audits, and satisfaction-to-intention ratios to maintain self-awareness.

2. **Adapt Relentlessly:** When rituals feel stale or burdensome, recalibrate—in collaboration with friends—to keep practices both authentic and flexible.

3. **Cultivate Synergy:** Interweave presence, empathy, and vulnerability with intentionality—each pillar enhancing the others.

4. **Honor Ethical Boundaries:** Guard against instrumentalization, overplanning, and burnout by anchoring intentions in authentic goodwill and mutual respect.

5. **Scale Impact:** Extend intentional practices from individual dyads to organizational teams and community networks, ensuring that purpose-driven connection becomes a culture rather than an exception.

In **Chapter 10**, we will turn to **Pillar Three: Empathy**, unpacking the mechanisms that allow us not only to **be present** and **act intentionally**, but to truly **feel with** others—scaffolding deep-level content across modalities. But to fully benefit from empathy, return frequently to the intentionality structures laid out here: they form the bedrock upon which empathic resonance can flourish, free from the distortions of habit or drift.

May each act you undertake—no matter how small—be a deliberate step toward co-creating a network of friendship whose **intention** is to uplift, heal, and inspire. In a world of passive connection, let your friendships stand as luminous testament to the power of purposeful care.

**Chapter 12**
**Embedding ReconneXion in Everyday Life Rituals**

> "Friendship is not solely what happens in grand gestures, but in the quiet repetitions that shape our days and our hearts."

---

# I. Introduction: From Theory to Daily Practice

Having traversed the philosophical, psychological, neuroscientific, and practical landscapes of vulnerability in Chapter 11, we now turn attention to an equally crucial dimension: **the seamless integration of ReconneXion's four pillars (Presence, Intentionality, Empathy, Vulnerability) and the modality/depth frameworks into the rhythms of everyday life**. True friendship flourishes not merely in punctuated "deep conversations" or specialty rituals, but in the weave of morning coffees, midday check-ins, weekend routines, and milestone celebrations. In this chapter—deliberately extended beyond Chapter 11's exhaustive length—we delve into an intricate tapestry of daily, weekly, monthly, and transitional rituals designed to ground and sustain ReconneXion Theory's insights.

We will explore:

1. **Daily Rituals:** Morning, workday, and evening routines that layer Presence, Intentionality, Empathy, and Vulnerability into the first and last moments of each day.

2. **Weekly Rituals:** Structures for weekend gatherings, asynchronous reflections, and habitual checkpoints that maintain relational health over seven-day cycles.

3. **Monthly & Quarterly Audits:** Deep-dive rituals—"Relationship Health Check," "Creative Collaborations," "Community Give-Backs"—that recalibrate modalities and depth.

4. **Life-Transition Rituals:** Wedding rites, bereavement supports, relocations, career changes—rituals that anchor friendship during upheaval.

5. **Special Occasion Rituals:** Birthdays, holidays, anniversaries—how to infuse ReconneXion principles into culturally and personally significant days.

6. **Contextual Adaptations:** Customizing rituals for couples, families with children, remote friends, multi-generational bonds, and cross-cultural dyads.

7. **Tech-Enhanced Practices:** Harnessing apps, AI prompts, shared calendars, and wearable reminders to scaffold daily reconnection without detracting from authentic presence.

8. **Compliance & Habit Formation:** Leveraging behavioral science—habit stacking, cue-routine-reward cycles, positive reinforcement—to transform rituals from deliberate actions into embodied reflexes.

9. **Measurement & Reflection Tools:** Ongoing metrics, journaling templates, digital trackers, and reflective prompts to document growth, identify stagnation, and pivot when needed.

10. **Troubleshooting Common Pitfalls:** Diagnosing ritual burnout, over-scripting, modal atrophy (over-reliance on one modality), and adaptive strategies to restore balance.

11. **Stories & Vignettes:** Interwoven case vignettes illustrating how everyday rituals have rescued friendships from drift, deepened nascent connections, or rekindled embers in long-distance bonds.

By the chapter's end, readers will possess a **comprehensive compendium of rituals**, each described with step-by-step instructions, timing guidelines, conversational examples, adaptive variants, technology integrations, and reflective questions—ensuring that ReconneXion transcends theoretical discussion to become **the living pulse of one's daily life and relational ecosystem**.

## II. Daily Rituals: Weaving Connection into Every Sunrise and Sunset

The most effective rituals are those we repeat habitually, becoming almost automatic yet profoundly meaningful. Embedding ReconneXion into daily routines means that at dawn and dusk, through work hours and travel interludes, friendship receives both attention and intentional structure. We break this down into three broad segments:

1. **Morning Rituals**: Setting tone and intention for the day, anchoring to Presence and Intentionality.

2. **Workday Rituals**: Utilizing micro-moments—breaks, commutes, shared tasks—to infuse Empathy and light Vulnerability.

3. **Evening Rituals**: Reflective closures, winding down, and preparing the relational ground for the next morning.

## A. Morning Rituals: Dawn of Presence and Intentionality

### 1. "Five-Minute Gratitude & Connection Call" (SD + AA)

**Objective:** Begin the day by offering Presence to a friend and expressing genuine appreciation—embedding Intentionality in a compact, repeatable practice.

**Timing:** Daily between 7:00–8:00 AM local time (or aligned with participants' morning routines).

**Participants:** Two friends (can be localized or remote).

**Steps:**

1. **Pre-Ritual Conditioning (AA):**

   - Both participants set an **AA digital reminder** or place sticky notes on their nightstands: "Tomorrow morning, call Alex at 7:30."

   - Craft a shared **"Gratitude Cue"**: for instance, each person picks an object to glance at upon waking (coffee mug, phone background) that reminds them to connect.

2. **Morning Wake-Up Sync (SD):**

   - Five minutes before the agreed call time, send a quick AD "Good morning!" text—this mild nudge ensures mental preparedness.

   - At the scheduled moment, initiate an SD voice or video call. Video is optional; voice suffices if one is fixing tea or in a private space where video would be impractical.

3. **Five-Minute Structure:**

   - **Minute 1 (Check-In):** One greets ("Morning, Jen! How did you sleep?"), then the other reciprocates.

   - **Minute 2–3 (Gratitude Statement):** Each expresses one specific gratitude about the other—e.g., "I'm grateful for how you supported me when I was overwhelmed last week," "Your advice on my project helped me see a new angle."

   - **Minute 4 (Intentional Offer):** Each offers an **Intentional Support Pledge** for the day: "If you sense me zipping through tasks, remind me to take a break," or "Feel free to text me if your meeting runs late, and we can reschedule."

- **Minute 5 (Closing Affirmation):** Conclude with a mutual affirmation ("Go seize the day—you've got this!") or a brief shared breathing exercise ("Three deep breaths together—1…2…3…"), reminding both of Presence.

4. **Post-Ritual AA Reflection:**
    - In a shared AA document or private journal, jot down one sentence summarizing: "Today, I'm bringing my best self because Sara reminded me I'm capable."

**Example Conversation:**

**7:30 AM, SD Voice Call**
Ava (Minute 1): "Morning, Kai! I slept like a rock—how about you?"
Kai: "Pretty well, thanks! Looking forward to this coffee."
**(Minute 2)**
Ava: "I'm so grateful for how you listened when I ranted about work yesterday. It really helped me calm down."
Kai: "Glad to hear. And I appreciate you reminding me to set boundaries with my team—still thinking about that."
**(Minute 3)**
Kai: "I promise today, if I notice you skipping lunch, I'll text "Lunch?" to remind you to eat."
Ava: "Perfect. Likewise, if I sense you're drowning in code, I'll ping you to say, 'Let's take a 5-minute breath break.'"
**(Minute 4)**
Ava: "You're amazing, Kai. Go rock those meetings."
Kai: "You too, Ava. Deep breaths—1…2…3… Done. Have a great one!"

**Adaptive Variants:**

- **Group "Sunrise Gratitude Check" (SD + SA):** Three or four friends rotate the gratitude spotlight—each says something they appreciate about others. Extend to 10 minutes if group is larger.

- **Asynchronous "Voice Note Gratitude" (AD):** If time zones differ, one sends a 60-second voice note expressing gratitude and intention, to be listened to when the other wakes.

- **Silent "Shared Journal Pages" (AA):** Instead of SD, both write in a shared AA digital document by 8:00 AM: one sentence of gratitude and one intention for the day. Each reads the other's entry later.

2. **"Morning Walk & Reflection" (SA + AD)**

**Objective:** Use a short SA (in-person) or AD (self-guided) morning walk to simultaneously practice Presence with oneself and reflect on relational intentions.

**Timing:** 15–20 minutes, ideally between 6:30–7:30 AM.

**Participants:** Solo or two friends walking together; or solo with an AD reflection target friend in mind.

**Steps:**

1. **Pre-Walk Intention Setting (AD):**
    - Decide on a focal intention—e.g., "Today, I aim to listen more than I speak," or "I will ask Maya how her weekend went." Jot this in a one-sentence AD note to self.

2. **Walking Practice (SA for local pairs; solitary for AD):**
    - **SA Duo Variant:** Two friends walk side-by-side in silence for the first 5 minutes, focusing on shared environmental cues—sounds of birds, tactile sensations of pavement.
    - At the 5-minute mark, one friend initiates a **deep check-in prompt**—"What's one emotion I need to honor today?" The listener practices empathic silence or minimal encouragers ("uh-huh," "I hear you").
    - Rotate roles at the 10-minute mark, giving each person 5–7 minutes to share a micro-vulnerability—more intimate than SL but not necessarily the deepest (Depth level 4–5).

3. **AD Solo Variant:**
    - Walk alone while replaying an **audio prompt** from a trusted friend—sent the night before—asking: "As you walk, think of one thing you're afraid to say to me."
    - At the end of the walk, immediately compose an AD message or voice note: "During my walk I realized I've been tiptoeing around telling you that I'm struggling to balance work and life."

4. **Post-Walk AD Follow-Up:**
    - **SA Pairs:** After returning, each sends an AD reflection: "Thanks for walking with me—hearing you talk about your nervousness around today's presentation reminded me to breathe."

- **Solo:** Send that voice note or text to the intended friend—opening a channel for later SD or AA deeper conversation.

**Adaptive Variants:**

- **"Mindful Route Rotation":** Each week, choose a different walking path—parks, waterfront, neighborhood streets—to keep novelty and enhance reflective states.
- **"Walking Color Journaling" (AA):** Bring colored pencils and a small sketchpad; at 5-minute intervals, sketch the dominant color in surroundings and note any concurrent emotions—symbolically linking inner states with external hues.

### 3. "Daily Mirror Affirmation & Micro-Vulnerability" (AD + AA)

**Objective:** Integrate a brief moment of self-affirmation and an intentional micro-vulnerability admission—nurturing self-Presence and seeding Vulnerability toward close friends or oneself.

**Timing:** While getting ready—brushing teeth, shaving, or standing before the mirror.

**Participants:** Solo moment; micro-vulnerability can be recorded privately (AA) or shared via AD with a friend.

**Steps:**

1. **Morning Mirror Affirmation (Solo):**
    - Stand before a mirror, look into your own eyes, and speak one positive affirmation: "I am enough," "My curiosity is a gift," or "I will remain kind, even under stress."
    - Maintain eye contact for at least 20 seconds, breathing evenly.

2. **Micro-Vulnerability Admission (AA or AD):**
    - In the next breath, calmly acknowledge one small vulnerability to yourself: "I'm anxious about that big meeting at noon," or "I'm afraid I'll forget to pick up milk."
    - Option A (AA): Write the affirmation and micro-vulnerability in a private AA notebook, then fold the page closed—serving as a self-contained ritual of acknowledgment.
    - Option B (AD): Send a single-sentence text to a trusted friend—"Today, I'm nervous about presenting to the team,"—knowing they'll receive it later and can check in. This is an AA-to-AD hybrid: the vulnerability is recorded privately until

the message is delivered.

3. **Optional Extension (AD):**

    - If the vulnerability feels urgent, request a brief SD acknowledgment from that friend ("Hey, could you send me a quick "got this" between 10–11 AM?").
    - Otherwise, make a mental note to revisit the vulnerability at day's end—e.g., in the Evening Ritual's "Second Reflection" below.

**Adaptive Variants:**

- **"Affirmation Post-its":** Write multiple affirmations on small AA post-it notes and stick them around the bathroom mirror; each morning, rotate to the next note and add one micro-vulnerability under it.

- **"Voice Reminder":** Record a 10-second voice clip of the affirmation plus micro-vulnerability as a saved phone voice memo labeled "Mirror Check." Set it as a wallpaper reminder: "Play this when you get up."

---

## B. Workday Rituals: Infusing Presence, Empathy, and Vulnerability into the Nine-to-Five

Between morning and evening anchors lies the crucible of daily obligations—work, school, caregiving. Most in-person or digital interactions occur during work hours. Conscious rituals here ensure that moments of caring and connection aren't lost to busyness.

### 1. "Pre-Meeting Presence Drop-In" (SD + SA + AD)

**Objective:** Before any scheduled work meeting (team huddle, project check-in), conduct a 30-second Presence Drop-In either silently or with a short vulnerability prompt—grounding participants before shifting to agenda items.

**Timing:** 30 seconds immediately preceding each scheduled meeting.

**Participants:** Entire meeting group (2+ people).

**Steps:**

1. **Implementation Planning (AD):**

- Include a line in all meeting invites: "30-sec Presence Drop-In at start."
- Share a one-sentence AD guideline: "In silence or aloud, commit to one thought of focus and one breath."

2. **Pre-Meeting Routine:**
    - **SA In-Person Meetings:** Facilitator stands, invites everyone to close eyes or soften gaze (if comfortable), to breathe deeply in silence for 30 seconds. Optionally, say one shared intention for meeting: "Today, we listen to build, not to respond."
    - **SD Virtual Meetings:** Host logs on 1 minute early. A black-screen placeholder appears, with the first 30 seconds as silent presence—participants mute mic/video, focus gaze at screen center, breathe. After 30 seconds, host welcomes participants by name, "Thank you for being present. Let's begin."

3. **Micro-Vulnerability Extension (Optional):**
    - If teams are accustomed to deeper sharing, the Drop-In includes a rapid-round: each person states one word describing their current feeling: "Focused," "Fatigued," "Hopeful." This cannot exceed 30 seconds; facilitator may call a timer.
    - This micro-vulnerability cultivates group Empathy—seeing others' emotional starting points—and readies collective engagement.

4. **Transition to Meeting Agenda:**
    - Post Drop-In, the facilitator explicitly states: "Now that we're grounded, let's proceed to the first agenda item: reviewing the Q2 budget."
    - Encourage sustaining that Presence—e.g., admonish the use of "two breaths" before responding to intense topics.

**Adaptive Variants:**

- **"Analog Timer Tactile Cue":** In SA rooms, place a small sand timer on table; when flipped, team spends the sand's duration (30 seconds) in shared silence.
- **"Digital Focus Buzzer":** For SD, use a brief 250 Hz tone (10 sec beep) signaling start and another at 30 seconds signaling end—no speech allowed during that interval.

2. **"Empathy Micro-Breaks" (SD + AA + SA)**

**Objective:** Build short, scheduled "Empathy Micro-Breaks" into the workday—two to three minutes where individuals intentionally listen to or send empathic messages to colleagues.

**Timing:** Twice daily—mid-morning (e.g., 10:30 AM) and mid-afternoon (3:00 PM).

**Participants:** Individual practitioners or pairs.

**Steps:**

1. **Scheduling & Notification (AD):**
    - At Monday's team meeting, coordinate a "mid-morning empathy ping" time; include it on shared calendars.
    - Create an AD group message: "Empathy Micro-Break today at 10:30—30 mins to set a reminder."

2. **Micro-Break Routine:**
    - **Option A (SD Pairing):** Two colleagues agree to a "10:30–10:32 micro-call." One sends an SD instant message at 10:30 reading, "Empathy Break—Are you OK right now?" The other responds with a one-sentence status ("A bit stressed by the Jenkins deploy, but I'll recover"), and the first offers a one-sentence supportive affirmation.
    - **Option B (Solo AA Reflection):** At 10:30, each individual reads a "generic Empathy Prompt" posted on the team Slack channel (e.g., "Share a bright spot from your week with someone"), and either AD-messages a colleague ("Your presentation last week inspired me.") or writes a one-sentence AA note expressing support ("I appreciate Jason's thorough docs—they saved me time").
    - **Option C (SA Walk & Listen):** Step away for a two-minute SA walk around the floor; during the walk, silently listen to a 60-second audio clip from a friend who recorded a brief vulnerability confession last night—played back in earphones. This builds empathic capacity and maintains connection.

3. **Post-Break Integration (AD):**
    - Each participant sends a quick AD summary in the team channel: "Empathy Break: Connected with Sara, who's celebrating her kid's first swim. Felt happy for her." Or "Listened to Alex's audio—heard his stress; I'll check in in a bit."

4. **Rotating Roles & Reciprocity:**

- Rotate who initiates each micro-break—ensuring all team members both offer and receive empathic check-ins.
- Keep a simple **Empathy Micro-Breaks Log** (AA spreadsheet) to track participation: date, initiator, partner (if any), type (SD, AD, SA), and note any action items (e.g., "Check back with Alex tomorrow").

**Adaptive Variants:**

- **"Empathy Bot Integration"**: Use an AI chatbot in the team's messaging platform that prompts at 10:30: "Time for an Empathy Micro-Break—type one word to describe your emotional state." Colleagues can react or send quick replies.
- **"Rotating Empathy Ambassadors"**: Each week, one team member is designated "Empathy Ambassador," responsible for compiling micro-break takeaways and summarizing themes (burnout hotspots, celebrations) at week's end.

### 3. "Desk-Side Vulnerability Post-It Exchange" (AA + SA + AD)

**Objective:** Create a low-pressure AA modality ritual—wherein team members place handwritten vulnerability or encouragement Post-Its on each other's desks or digital equivalents—fostering small doses of Vulnerability and Empathy.

**Timing:** Unscheduled—but participants agree to check once daily—during lunch or break.

**Participants:** Small teams (3–8 people).

**Steps:**

1. **Setup & Guidelines (AA):**
   - Supply a stack of brightly colored Post-Its and markers. Alternatively, create a shared digital board (Trello, Miro) with virtual sticky notes.
   - Agree on basic ground rules: Post-Its must be positive, supportive, or share a micro-vulnerability ("I felt nervous about the town hall too"). No negativity, no sensitive disclosures requiring confidentiality.
   - Provide a simple template: "I appreciate [X about you] because [Y]," or "Today, I want to share I'm feeling [Z]—just so you know I'm human, too."

2. **Daily Exchange Practice:**

- **Physical Teams (SA):** Each morning, drop one Post-It on a random colleague's desk—expressing appreciation, encouragement, or a mild vulnerability prompt (e.g., "I'm a little worried about our code freeze; if you feel anxious too, we can talk.").
- At end of day or next morning, recipients read their note; if desired, they can respond with a new Post-It on the author's desk, creating a micro-dialogue.

3. **Digital Teams (AD):**
    - Use a dedicated Slack channel named "#desk-side" for posting short Slack "sticky messages" tagging a colleague: "Hey @mike, I wanted to say I respect how you handled that bug fix under pressure. Today I'm a bit jittery, so your calm attitude matters."
    - Encourage asynchronously responding by adding a thread reply, sustaining the dialogue.

4. **SA Weekly "Sticky Review" (SA + AD):**
    - At a weekly standup or Friday lunch, facilitate a brief 5-minute session where team members share one insight they gained from a Post-It—"Reading Lisa's note reminded me I'm not alone in feeling imposter syndrome."
    - Summaries can be posted AD in the team's AA document: "Sticky Insights: Week of June 10." This track records recurring themes (anxiety hotspots, resiliency stories) to guide future support.

**Adaptive Variants:**

- **"Thematic Sticky Weeks":** Designate certain weeks for specific themes—"Gratitude Week," "Encouragement Week," "Vulnerability Week"—tilting the focus toward micro-vulnerabilities and deeper reflections.
- **"Anonymity Layer":** For one month, make all Post-Its anonymous; at month's end, hold an SA reveal event where authors can disclose or remain anonymous, prompting rich Empathy and laughter.

## C. Evening Rituals: Reflection, Grounding, and Preparation

The day's end is fertile ground for processing experiences, honoring small victories, and preparing for reconnection the next morning. Evening rituals anchor the four pillars and create a bridge between the external day and internal relational world.

## 1. "Dual Reflection Journals" (AA + AD)

**Objective:** Each evening, friends engage in parallel reflections—journaling privately (AA), then sharing a distilled highlight and lowlight via AD. This practice weaves self-Presence, mutual Intentionality, and measured Vulnerability.

**Timing:** Daily between 8:00–9:00 PM.

**Participants:** Pairs or small groups (3–5).

**Steps:**

1. **Private Journaling (AA):**
   - Spend 5–7 minutes writing down:
     - **Highlight:** "The most meaningful moment of my day and why."
     - **Lowlight:** "The most challenging moment and what I felt."
     - **Learning or Intention:** "One insight or goal based on today."
   - Structure these as bullet points or short paragraphs.

2. **AD Sharing (Asynchronous):**
   - After journaling, send an AD message to your friend or group formatted as:
     - **Highlight:** "Today, my highlight was landing that presentation—I felt confident when I saw nods."
     - **Lowlight:** "My lowlight: I snapped at Sasha when she interrupted me; I felt defensive."
     - **Intent:** "Tomorrow, I intend to breathe before reacting."
   - Each person responds to the message the next evening—STAT (short turn-around time) is fine, but allow up to 24 hours for slower schedules.

3. **Empathic Feedback (AD):**

- When replying, practice Empathy:

    - Acknowledge: "I hear how proud you are of that presentation—that must have felt validating."

    - Validate lowlight: "It's understandable you felt defensive; interruptions can sting."

    - Support intention: "I love your goal to breathe—you can count on me to text a 10-second breathing reminder at 9 AM."

4. **Optional SD Weekly Synthesis:**

    - Once per week (e.g., Sunday night), host an SD 15-minute call where each person summarizes one big takeaway from their dual reflection journal and the empathic feedback they received—"This week I recognized that my reactivity often masks insecurity, and your affirmations helped me soften."

**Adaptive Variants:**

- **"Group Reflection Thread" (AD):** In a WhatsApp or Slack channel, create a persistent thread titled "Tonight's Reflections." All group members drop their highlight/lowlight/intent pieces at any time. Anyone can react with emojis (♥☐ for highlight, ☐ for lowlight solidarity) and a quick empathic line.

- **"Self-Compassion Audio Journal" (AA + SD):** Instead of writing, record a 2-minute voice note capturing your reflection; send it AD. Once per week, gather on SD to play these audio clips and discuss collectively.

## 2. "Family or Household Huddle" (SA + AD)

**Objective:** For those living with family, roommates, or partners, conduct a brief end-of-evening huddle—reaffirming love, acknowledging shared joys and struggles, and aligning intentions for the following day.

**Timing:** Just before bedtime—typically 8:30–9:00 PM.

**Participants:** Family members, roommates, cohabitants (2+).

**Steps:**

1. **Huddle Structure (SA):**

- **"Rose, Thorn, Bud" Format:**
    - **Rose (Highlight):** Each person states a "rose" from their day—a positive moment.
    - **Thorn (Lowlight):** Each shares a "thorn"—a challenge or frustration.
    - **Bud (Intention/Growth):** Each mentions a "bud"—something they're looking forward to or a goal for tomorrow.

2. **Grounding Statement (SA):**
    - Begin by holding hands or creating a small circle, stating: "We come together to honor our day, relieve burdens, and prepare to rest."
    - Establish that this space is distraction-free: phones on silent, no TV or screens.

3. **Rotation Order:**
    - Decide an order in which each person speaks (e.g., clockwise around the room). Keep individual shares to no more than 45 seconds to maintain brevity and focus.

4. **Mutual Support Pledges (SA):**
    - After each person states their rose, thorn, and bud, one designated "support buddy" for that person offers a quick empathic response—"I'm happy you aced your test (rose). That argument with Tim must have been hard (thorn). Tomorrow, I'll bring you tea to help with your morning."
    - Rotate support buddies daily so that emotional support is widely shared.

5. **AD Follow-Up (Optional):**
    - Encourage silent follow-up: if details emerge that require deeper conversation, send an AD note summarizing: "I'm still thinking about what Sarah said about feeling overwhelmed. Let's chat tomorrow at 5 PM."
    - For those who need further processing, request an SD or SA dedicated time.

**Adaptive Variants:**

- **"Shield and Sword" Variation:** Replace "Rose, Thorn, Bud" with "Shield" (something that protected/strengthened you today), "Sword" (something you fought through), and

"Lantern" (a hope or question for tomorrow). This metaphorical reframe may resonate more with families of fantasy enthusiasts or children.

- **"Circular Appreciation Jar" (AA + SA):** Each night, write one line of appreciation for another family member and drop it into a communal jar. On the first of each month, open the jar and read all notes aloud.

## 3. "Second Mirror Check & Tomorrow's Intention" (AA + AD)

**Objective:** Before sleep, briefly revisit the morning's mirror affirmation/micro-vulnerability exercise, closing loops and priming the next day's Intentionality and Presence.

**Timing:** Last 5 minutes before lights out—typically between 10:00–11:00 PM.

**Participants:** Solo, with optional AD sharing.

**Steps:**

1. **Evening Mirror Reflection (AA):**
   - Stand again before a mirror, this time placing a hand on the heart, and reflect on the morning affirmation:
     - **"Did I live into today's affirmation?"** ("I am enough.")
     - **"How did the micro-vulnerability I noted unfold?"** ("I felt jittery about the noon meeting, and today I tried breathing before responding.")
   - Speak gently to yourself: "You did well by remembering to breathe at noon. Tomorrow, I intend to ask for help before 10 AM, because that will save me stress."

2. **AD Intention Message (Optional):**
   - If you have a day-partner (in a long-distance friendship or couple), send an AD voice note or text:
     - "Tonight, my reflection is that I handled my frustration better than yesterday. Tomorrow's intention: I will check in with you at lunchtime about your day."
   - This continues the loop from the morning's five-minute call, cementing an ongoing thread of Intentionality and mutual accountability.

3. **AA Sleep Scheduling (Preparation):**
    - Jot down any lingering vulnerabilities or tasks that need attention tomorrow—preventing rumination at night.
    - Close with a free-form sentence: "Tomorrow, I will remember to _____ because it matters to our friendship."

**Adaptive Variants:**

- **"Guided Self-Compassion Audio" (AD):** Listen to a 2-minute guided audio before sleep that prompts mirror reflection and sets a new intention—available from shared friend libraries or AI-generated personalized tracks.
- **"Bedtime Text Chain" (AD):** In a group chat, submit one line every night: "Today's highlight was… ; tomorrow I want to…" Seeing others' reflections builds communal Presence even across distances.

# III. Weekly Rituals: Sustaining Connection Beyond Twenty-Four Hours

While daily rituals carve micro-habits, weekly rituals allow a broader view: identifying emerging patterns, creating shared space for deeper Vulnerability, and aligning larger intentions. Here we outline several core weekly practices, each extensible to small groups, families, or remote networks.

## A. "Weekly Friendship Audit" (SD + AD + AA)

**Objective:** Once per seven-day cycle, collaboratively review the week's relationship dynamics—assessing modality balance, depth levels, and relational objectives—then plan adjustments.

**Timing:** Weekly; choose a consistent day/time (e.g., Sunday evening at 7:00 PM).

**Participants:** Dyads or small groups (up to 6 people).

**Steps:**

1. **Preparation Phase (AD & AA):**

   - **AA Individual Self-Assessment (Prior to SD):**

     - Each friend completes a brief AA worksheet containing:

       1. **Modality Tally:** How many SL–AD, DL–AD, SL–SD, DL–SD, SA, and AA interactions occurred?

       2. **Depth Reflection:** Which interactions felt surface-level (rated 1–3), moderate-level (4–6), or deep-level (7–10)?

       3. **Emotional Bank Account:** List one deposit (e.g., "Lisa gave undistracted attention during my Zoom call") and one withdrawal ("I left Sam's text unread for 24 hours").

       4. **Alignment Score:** On a scale of 1–10, how aligned did you feel with each other's intentions this week?

   - Compile these AA responses into a shared digital AA folder—each person's self-assessment document is time-stamped but can be anonymized if needed.

2. **Synchronous SD Group Review (30–45 minutes):**

   - **Opening Round (5 min):** Each person states a one-sentence summary: "This week, I felt our friendship was _____."

   - **Modality & Depth Synthesis (10 min):**

     - Facilitate discussion around the modality tallies: "I see I had 1 DL–SD conversation, but no SA time—how do you all feel about that?"

     - Map depth distributions: "My deep conversations were two instances—good—but I had five SL check-ins; I'd like more balance next week."

   - **Emotional Bank Analysis (10 min):**

     - Round-robin sharing of one deposit and one withdrawal. For each withdrawal, the group offers empathic understanding and suggests restitution: "I'm sorry I left your DM unread—next time I'll set a 2-hour response promise."

- For each deposit, group acknowledges: "Thank you for valuing my time and listening during my AA letter exchange."

  - **Alignment & Intention Planning (15 min):**

    - Compare alignment scores and explore discrepancies: "You rated 4/10 for alignment; can you share why?"

    - Co-create a **"Weekly Intention Charter"**: concrete pledges for next week—e.g., "At least two SS–SA walks," "One DL–SD conversation midweek," "Set an AA weekend letter exchange."

3. **Post-Review Documentation (AA):**

    - A designated group member consolidates key decisions into an AA "Weekly Friendship Audit" document: modality/time allocations, depth targets, accountability notes (who will initiate what).

    - Share the document via AD to ensure everyone has access and can refer to it throughout the week.

**Adaptive Variants:**

- **"Solo Reflection & Automated Reminders":** For pairs with unpredictable schedules, one friend conducts a solo weekly audit and ADs a concise summary ("Here's my audit; can we touch base on Thursday for planning?"). Automate future reminders via calendar invites.

- **"Audio-Only Audit" (SD):** In contexts where typing or reading is burdensome (e.g., vision-impaired friends), conduct the entire audit via voice—recording sessions and transcribing only key points afterwards.

---

## B. "Weekend Rituals: Deep Dive and Restoration" (SA + SD + AA)

Weekends offer extended swaths of time free from many weekday obligations. Rituals here can be longer and more immersive, affording space for deeper vulnerability, shared activities, and collective planning.

### 1. SA "Saturday Morning Coffee Salon" (SA)

**Objective:** Transform Saturday mornings into a recurring in-person gathering (or condense into a virtual café) where friends cycle through deeper thematic discussions—building shared intellectual, emotional, and creative bonds.

**Timing:** Saturday, 9:00–11:00 AM (2 hours).

**Participants:** 4–8 friends.

**Location:** Rotating hosts' homes, local cafés (reserved table for 2 hours), community centers.

**Steps:**

1. **Rotating Host Role:**
   - Each week, one friend volunteers as **Host**, selecting the venue and curating a thematic prompt (e.g., "This week's theme: 'Moments of Awe'," or "Let's discuss parenting insecurities").

2. **Opening Grounding Ritual (5 min):**
   - Host welcomes participants, invites a brief SA centering practice:
     - "Let's each take one mindful breath, grounding in the present space."

3. **Round-Robin Check-In (10 min):**
   - Each shares a 1–2 minute update—mix of SL and moderate vulnerability: "This week, I finished my project; also, my dad's health is worrying me."

4. **Thematic Deep Dive (45–60 min):**
   - Host introduces the theme with a short anecdote or question (e.g., "I felt awe when I watched the meteor shower; tell us a moment you felt small before something vast.").
   - Each person responds in 5–7 minutes—narrating personal stories, sharing emotional nuances, with listeners practicing empathic listening.

5. **Collective Activity Break (20 min):**
   - Choose an activity aligned with theme:
     - **Creative Writing**: Write a 200-word vignette about a "moment of awe," then read aloud.

- **Silent Shared Embodiment**: Watch a brief 3-minute nature video together in silence, then discuss impressions.
- **Artistic Expression**: Sketch or collage imagery, then explain the meaning behind choices.

6. **Action & Conclusion (15 min):**
   - Each person states one **"Saturday Takeaway"**—"I'll plan an evening nature walk this week," or "I'll send a letter to my grandparents describing something I'm grateful for."
   - Host ends with a group affirmation: "This café nourished our hearts; let's carry its warmth into the week."

7. **Post-Salon AA Reflection (Optional):**
   - Host circulates an AA group email with highlights and any commitments made. Participants reply with brief confirmations.

**Adaptive Variants:**

- **"Virtual Saturday Salon" (SD + AD):** For geographically dispersed friends, host an SD video call at 10:00 AM local. Use an AD shared document for creative activity (e.g., building a thematic collage in Google Slides).
- **"Larger Community Salons":** Scale to 12–15 participants by having breakout tables of 4, each following above ritual, then reconvening to share cross-group insights.

## 2. Sunday "Digital Unplug & Reflect" (SA + AA)

**Objective:** Reserve one portion of Sunday for a **Tech Sabbath**, stepping away from digital devices to engage in offline reconnection—reading, journaling, in-person or SA interactions—reinforcing Presence and restorative rhythms.

**Timing:** Two to three hours on Sunday, ideally mid-day (e.g., 2:00–5:00 PM).

**Participants:** Individual with optional invitation to one or more close friends for co-present activities.

**Steps:**

1. **Pre-Unplug Preparation (AD):**

- Highlight "Digital Unplug Block" on shared calendars.
- Send AA reminders on Saturday night: "Sunday 2–5 PM: No screens. Let's meet in the park at 3:00 for 30 min of talk."

2. **Device Shutdown (SA):**

    - At 2:00 PM, switch off all notifications, leave the phone in silent mode or in a designated drawer. Encourage physically distancing from laptops, tablets, and TVs.

3. **Offline Activities (SA):**

    - **Solo Option:** Go for a nature walk, visit a museum, or read a physical book. At 4:00 PM, find a quiet spot and write in AA: "How do I feel being unplugged? What vulnerabilities surfaced in silence?"
    - **Co-Present Variant:** Meet one friend in person: wander a farmers' market; pause to smell flowers; share a thermos of tea and practice SA "Nonverbal Empathy" (observing each other's energy, offering supportive touch or smile).
    - **Group Gathering:** Two or three friends convene for a communal activity—painting, gardening, cooking. While working side-by-side, practice SA "Empathic Echoes"—sharing brief emotional states without referencing phones.

4. **Physical AA Journaling (SA):**

    - Around 4:30 PM, encourage writing by hand: "Without digital distractions, I noticed I missed texting my friend earlier today. I felt a pang of loneliness but also calm."
    - At 5:00 PM, decide whether to resume screens or extend the unplug.

5. **Re-Entry with Presence (Optional SD):**

    - If desired, send an SD "I'm back online" group message acknowledging the experience: "Stepped away for the afternoon. Felt surprisingly free of pressure. How did you find it?"
    - Reserve responses until after dinner—avoiding immediate digital whirlwinds.

**Adaptive Variants:**

- **"Neighborhood Walk-&-Talk" (SA):** Invite neighbors or local friends to walk together in silence or minimal conversation, focusing on shared environmental details.

- **"Analog Co-Reading" (SA + AA):** Gather at a local café with copies of a book; read silently for an hour, then discuss a passage—journeying into shared literary vulnerability.

## C. "Midweek Micro-Retreat" (AD + SD + SA)

**Objective:** Interrupt weekday inertia with a brief but intentional "Micro-Retreat"—a two-hour window of combined virtual and in-person reconnection to realign intentions and practice deeper Empathy and Vulnerability.

**Timing:** Pick a weekday (e.g., Wednesday) from 6:00–8:00 PM.

**Participants:** Dyads or triads, can be in-person or hybrid.

**Steps:**

1. **Advance Planning (AD):**
   - Weeks ahead, decide on the micro-retreat's modality. For in-person, reserve a coworking space, park bench, or living room. For hybrid, ensure reliable SD link and encourage participants to find a quiet room with minimal distractions.

2. **Opening Reflection (AD):**
   - Two days prior, each participant sends an AD note with one word describing their midweek emotional state—e.g., "Fractured," "Hopeful," "Overloaded." These inform the retreat's tone.

3. **SA or SD Gathering (6:00 PM):**
   - Begin with 5 minutes of shared silence—participants settle in, focusing on breath.
   - Each person then shares the motivation behind their chosen word—"I said 'Fractured' because my workflow feels disjointed." This micro-vulnerability sets the stage.

4. **Guided Practice (SA + SD):**
   - **Option A (Empathy Focus):** Facilitator (rotating role) leads "Mirroring Pairs" exercise (Chapter X.VI.12). Each participant takes 5 minutes sharing a current

challenge; the partner mirrors back nonverbally (SA) or verbally reflects (SD). Rotate so all have a mirror partner.

- **Option B (Vulnerability Discovery):** Use "Vulnerability Flashcards" (Chapter X.VI.34). Each draws a card (prompt) like, "Describe a mistake you made this week and what you learned." Participants spend 5 minutes privately reflecting in AA, then share in SD or SA for 2–3 minutes each.

5. **Creative Expression Break (20 min) (AA):**

   - Provide art supplies or poetry prompts. Participants create a quick art piece—symbolizing midweek tensions and hopes. Alternatively, write a 50-word poem.
   - Share creations aloud or show via SD camera.

6. **Planning Next Steps (20 min):**

   - Each articulates one micro-intention for the rest of the week: "Tomorrow, I'll walk for 10 minutes at lunch," or "This weekend, I'll finish that book."
   - Partners offer to hold each other accountable via AD reminders or SA "retrospective check-ins" (e.g., "I'll text you Friday: Did you take that walk?").

7. **Closing Grounding (5 min) (SA + SD):**

   - Group practices a brief guided meditation—visualizing midweek burdens dissolving (60 seconds), replaced by a small flame of calm.
   - End with collective affirmation: "We leave here lighter, more attuned. The rest of our week awaits."

**Adaptive Variants:**

- **"Outdoor Adventure Micro-Retreat" (SA):** Replace indoor sessions with a shared bike ride or paddleboarding session—infusing Embodied Presence and shared challenge.

- **"Solo Hybrid Micro-Retreat" (AD + AA):** One-on-one micro-retreat with a friend – exchange AD written reflections at 6:00 PM; each spend 30 minutes in silent nature walk; reconvene at 7:30 PM in SD for one-sentence check-ins.

# IV. Monthly & Quarterly Audits: Deepening and Recalibrating

While daily and weekly rituals sustain momentum, **monthly and quarterly rituals** provide opportunities for more expansive reflections, shared celebrations, and course corrections. These longer-duration audits capture overarching trends, recalibrate relationships to seasonal shifts, and fortify the friendship against drift.

---

### A. "Monthly Relationship Health Check" (SA + SD + AD)

**Objective:** Conduct a thorough, multi-dimensional audit of relational health once per calendar month—reviewing successes, challenges, emerging patterns, and resetting objectives for the subsequent month.

**Timing:** Choose a day near month's end—e.g., last Saturday—dedicating up to three hours.

**Participants:** Dyads, triads, or small friendship circles (up to 8).

**Steps:**

1. **Pre-Check Preparation (AD & AA):**
    - **Private Data Gathering (AA):** Each participant compiles:
        - **Modality Usage Data:** From weekly modality tallies (Chapter X.VI.13), total counts of SL–AD, DL–AD, SL–SD, DL–SD, SA, AA interactions for the past month.
        - **Depth Distribution:** Number of interactions rated 1–3 (surface), 4–6 (moderate), 7–10 (deep).
        - **Emotional Bank Transactions:** Sum of deposits and withdrawals recorded.
        - **Personal Growth Journal Excerpts:** One paragraph highlighting "My proudest relational moment this month," and "My heaviest relational challenge."
    - **Aggregate Document Creation (AD):** One designated participant (rotational) collects anonymized summaries into a shared AA spreadsheet, categorizing each person's totals and excerpts.

2. **SA In-Person Convening (2 Hours):**

    - **Opening Ritual (10 min):** Gather in a comfortable space—circle of chairs. Perform a brief "Centering Breath" (two minutes), then state the communal purpose: "We gather to honor our bonds, learn from our patterns, and recommit to intentional friendship."

    - **Visualizing Data (20 min):** Project or lay out printed modality/depth charts on a table. Each participant briefly describes one pattern they notice (e.g., "I see I had zero SA meetings; I think we drifted away physically this month").

    - **Deep Dialogue (45 min):**

        - Facilitator poses guiding questions:

            1. **Balance Reflection:** "Were any modalities neglected? How did that affect us?"

            2. **Depth Evolution:** "Did we drift into too many surface-level interactions? Did we manage to sustain regular deep-level conversations?"

            3. **Emotional Bank Analysis:** "Which withdrawals were avoidable? Which deposits felt significant?"

            4. **Growth Retrieval:** "Which pivotal moments this month moved our friendship forward?"

        - Each participant responds candidly, with listeners practicing empathic validation. Use "talking stick" to ensure equitable airtime.

    - **Break & Silent Reflection (10 min):**

        - Everyone retreats for a silent walk or seated quiet journaling—processing before reconvening.

    - **Action Planning & Commitments (30 min):**

        - As a group, co-create a **"Monthly Friendship Commitments"** list—target numbers of interactions by modality (e.g., "Two SA meetups," "At least four DL–AD exchanges"), depth goals ("One DL–SA conversation").

        - Assign "Ritual Champions" for each domain: SA (who organizes next in-person gathering), SD (who sets video call times), AD (who drafts weekly gratitude messages), AA (who circulates journaling prompts).

- **Closing Affirmation & Gratitude (5 min):**
  - Each person shares a one-sentence appreciation for another's contribution to the friendship that month: "Thanks, Jordan, for always checking on me when I was swamped."
  - End with collective group hug or handshake circle, symbolizing renewed bonds.

3. **SD Remote Option (if in-person is not feasible):**
   - Break the 2-hour session into two 1-hour SD calls:
     - **Call 1 (Data Visualization & Reflection):** Present modality/depth charts via screen share; discuss highlights and challenges.
     - **Call 2 (Action Planning & Commitments):** After a 24-hour pause for personal reflection, reconvene to set next month's commitments.
   - Use AD "Monthly Health Digest" to summarize outcomes and confirm champions.

4. **Post-Check Documentation (AA):**
   - Designated person drafts a 1–2 page "Monthly Relationship Health Report," summarizing:
     - Data insights (charts, counts).
     - Key reflections (aggregated quotes).
     - Commitments for next month (modal counts, depth targets, champion assignments).
   - Share via AD to all participants, saving the document in a shared AA folder for longitudinal tracking.

**Adaptive Variants:**

- **"Theme-Focused Monthly Check":** Each month, choose a specific theme—e.g., **"Trust & Confidentiality," "Work–Life Boundaries," "Creative Collaborations,"** and focus reflections around how well that theme was honored.

- **"Pairwise Sub-Checks":** In large friendship circles (6+), divide into pairs for preliminary mini-checks before a collective convening to synthesize insights—this ensures quieter members are heard in a more intimate setting before speaking to the larger group.

---

## B. "Quarterly Deep Dive Retreat" (SA + SD + AA)

**Objective:** Every three months, embark on a multi-day (one or two nights) retreat to conduct a profound exploration of the evolving friendship matrix—connecting with the seasons' transitions, setting long-term visions, and undertaking extended vulnerability work.

**Timing:** Once per calendar quarter—spring, summer, autumn, winter.

**Duration:** 48–72 hours (one- or two-night format).

**Participants:** Core friendship group (ideally 4–10 individuals).

**Steps:**

1. **Pre-Retreat Planning (AA & AD, 2–3 Weeks Prior):**

    - **Venue Selection (SA or Hybrid):** Book a cabin, retreat center, or reserved Airbnb far enough to minimize daily distractions. For remote/hybrid, secure a virtual retreat platform with breakout rooms and whiteboards.

    - **Theme & Materials (AA):** Decide on the quarter's **"Macro Theme"**—e.g., "Embracing Change," "Cultivating Joy," "Navigating Conflict." Prepare reading packets (AA printouts) relevant to the theme—essays, essays from reconnection theory, curated podcasts, or video clips.

    - **Individual Pre-Work (AD):** Each participant completes a 3–4 page **"Quarterly Reflection Essay,"** responding to prompts:

        - "What significant friendship moments transpired over the past quarter?"
        - "Where did I feel we balanced or lost modality/depth equilibrium?"
        - "Which personal growth or misstep narrative felt most potent?"
        - "What is my long-term vulnerability goal for the next year?"

2. **Day 1: Arrival & Orientation (SA):**

- **Welcome Circle (30 min):** Gather in a circle. Each person reads a 2-minute excerpt from their Quarterly Reflection Essay—highlighting one triumph and one challenge.
- **Grounding Exercise (15 min):** Facilitator leads gentle yoga or qigong that emphasizes Presence and embodiment, preparing participants to inhabit the retreat space fully.
- **Theme Introduction (30 min):** Present the Macro Theme, share curated materials (handouts, short videos), and invite initial reactions in pairs.
- **SA "Mapping Our Journey" (60 min):** On a large sheet or whiteboard, draw a timeline of the past quarter. Each participant marks key friendship-related events—two personal, two shared. Narrate stories succinctly as a group chart emerges.
- **Evening Vulnerability Circle (90 min):** Select three participants to share a deeper vulnerability related to the quarter's theme (e.g., fear of redundancy at work). After each 10–12 minute share, the group practices "Empathic Mirror" (Chapter X.VI.12) and offers reflective support.
- **Free Time & Journaling (AA):** After dinner, encourage private journaling—"How did sharing tonight resonate with me? What do I want to carry forward?"

3. **Day 2: Deep Exploration & Skill-Building (SA + SD):**

   - **Morning Reflection Walks (SA):** Break into pairs for silent or minimal-conversation walks. At the end, exchange one vulnerability related to current internal landscape.
   - **Skill-Building Workshops (60 min each, SA):** Choose two interactive modules:
     - **"Advanced Empathic Listening Lab":** Role-plays on maintaining empathy in high-tension scenarios—mediated by a trained facilitator.
     - **"Modal Adaptation Masterclass":** Practice shifting fluidly between AA, AD, SD, SA, evaluating situational suitability (e.g., when to move a conversation from DM to in-person).
     - **"Vulnerability Archetype Exploration":** Guided by personality frameworks (Enneagram, MBTI), identify individual vulnerability styles and group dynamics.

- **Mid-Afternoon Guided Meditation (SD + AA):** For hybrid groups, livestream a 20-minute guided meditation focused on releasing judgment and embracing collective support. Afterward, participants write AA "Letting Go" letters—addressing internal critics.

- **Late Afternoon "Future Self Panel" (SA + SD):**
  - Each person assumes the persona of their "Projected One-Year-Ahead Self," speaking for 3–5 minutes about how they've grown in vulnerability and connection. Others may ask questions. This imaginative exercise catalyzes visioning and intention.

- **Evening Shared Cuisine & Bonding (SA):**
  - Participants collaboratively cook or order a communal meal. While eating, practice "Story Harvest"—each recounts one friendship lesson gleaned at the retreat.
  - Conclude with a "Vulnerability Toast": raising glasses to the courage present in the room and to future openness.

4. **Day 3: Integration & Closure (SA + AD):**

   - **Morning "Legacy Mandala" (SA + AA):**
     - Participants collectively construct a physical or digital mandala representing the group's shared journey—using art supplies or an online canvas. Each adds a symbol or phrase capturing personal and collective insights.

   - **Commitment Contracts (AA):**
     - In a final circle, each person writes a one-page "Quarterly Commitment Contract"—specifying modality/depth goals, frequency targets, and support mechanisms. They sign and exchange copies. Developers can store digital copies too.

   - **Closing Reflection (SA, 60 min):** Each shares one immediate "takeaway" (strength), one "lingering question" (curiosity), and one "commitment" (action).

   - **Post-Retreat AD Digest (AD):** A facilitator emails a comprehensive AA summary of discussions, commitments, and resources (articles, reading links, podcasts) to all participants within 48 hours.

**Adaptive Variants:**

- **"Virtual Quarterly Retreat" (SD + AD):** Spread the retreat over four Saturdays—each 3-hour block focusing on one day's frame (e.g., reflection, skill-building, future vision, integration). Use AD assignments and digital whiteboards for group creativity.
- **"Neighborly Collaborative Retreat" (SA):** For local groups, partner with a yoga studio or community hall offering sliding-scale rates—inviting adjacent friendship circles to cross-pollinate ideas, expanding network-level reconnection.

---

## V. Life-Transition Rituals: Anchoring Friendship Amid Change

Major life transitions—marriage, relocation, new parenthood, job changes, bereavement—can destabilize even the most robust friendships. Embedding ReconneXion into transitional rituals ensures that changes become gateways for deeper connection rather than catalysts for drift. Below, we outline **six core transition rituals**.

---

### A. "Moving Away: Digital Time Capsule & Farewell Bridge" (AA + SD + SA)

**Objective:** When one (or more) friend relocates—city, country, or figurative transitions—create rituals to honor the impending separation, establish ongoing modalities, and preserve memories.

**Timing:** Initiate one month before move; complete within two weeks post-move.

**Participants:** Friend(s) relocating, and close relational circle (3–10 people).

**Steps:**

1. **Memory Collection (AA, 2–3 Weeks Prior):**
    - Circulate an AA "Memory Prompt Sheet":
        - "Share a favorite memory with me."
        - "One thing I'll miss about our friendship."

- "A secret wish or hope for our future connection."
    - Each friend completes the prompts in writing (AA) or as short audio recordings (AD). Collect these in a "Digital Time Capsule" folder (e.g., shared Google Drive).
    - Optionally, ask for photos, short video clips, or scanned tickets from events attended together.

2. **Farewell Gathering (SA + SD Hybrid, 2–3 Hours):**
    - Host an in-person party or picnic, if feasible. For distant participants, set up an SD livestream station so everyone can attend virtually.
    - **Reflection Circle (45 min):** Each person (in-person or virtual) shares:
        - A brief story from the memory collection.
        - One micro-vulnerability about the upcoming change: "I'm afraid we'll grow apart," "I worry I'll forget the local accent."
        - A solidarity pledge: "I'll text you every Friday morning," or "When I visit, let's walk that old trail together."
    - **"Shared Playlist Creation" (AA):** Collaboratively build a playlist of 10–12 songs representing the friendship, accessible via streaming platforms. This functions as an audible bridge—whenever any friend plays a song, they recall collective memories.
    - **Gift Exchange (AA):** Each in-person friend gives a small token—handwritten letters, printed photo books, or a custom "Friendship Quilt" piece. Virtual friends send e-cards or mailed tokens in advance.

3. **Digital Time Capsule Sealing (AA):**
    - At conclusion, compile all AA and AD memory items into a zipped "Friend Time Capsule," saved in a cloud drive with a locked date (e.g., unlock six months later).
    - Add one new prompt—"In six months, reflect on how our friendship has shifted and how we support each other."

4. **Post-Move "Constant Connection Calendar" (AD):**

- Pre-populate a digital calendar with:
    - **Weekly Shared Rituals:** "Mondays 9:00 AM CTA video chat."
    - **Monthly Nostalgia Posts:** "First week of each month—share a memory on our group chat."
    - **Quarterly Virtual Retreat:** "Last Saturday of quarter—digital micro-retreat."
- Send calendar invites to relevant friends, ensuring all time zones and DST shifts are accounted for.

5. **Six-Month Unveiling & Reconnection (SD + AA):**
    - On the capsule's unlock date, convene an SD "Time Capsule Reunion" (up to 60 minutes). Each person opens the capsule, reads others' entries, and responds with a short AA reflection: "I remember how we laughed when that happened; I see now how change has strengthened us."
    - Document lessons learned and recalibrate the Constant Connection Calendar for the next six months.

**Adaptive Variants:**

- **"Relocation Scavenger Hunt" (SA):** For in-city moves, host a final group walk visiting sites significant to the friendship. At each stop, read one memory; take a group photo.
- **"Virtual Reality (VR) Farewell Tour" (SD + VR):** If friends are in VRChat or have access, recreate memorable places in VR (e.g., a virtual coffee shop) to simulate in-person presence and say goodbye.

---

## B. "Engagement & Wedding: ReconneXion Blessing Circle" (SA + AD + AA)

**Objective:** When a friend becomes engaged or married, create a transitional ritual that honors the new partnership while weaving the friend group's relational fabric into the celebration.

**Timing:** Engagement: three to four months prior to wedding; Wedding: one or two days before (rehearsal dinner or specialized event).

**Participants:** Bride/groom (or couple), close friend group (6–12), optionally spouse-to-be or close family.

**Steps:**

1. **Engagement Blessing Gathering (SA + AD):**
    - Organize an in-person "Blessing Cafe" or "Toast Circle" where each friend brings a short written "Blessing Note" (AA) and a small token (e.g., a pressed flower, a recipe card, a piece of advice).
    - **Circle Structure (60–90 min):**
        - Each person reads their blessing aloud (2–3 minutes), focusing on both congratulatory warmth and a micro-vulnerability related to their own relationship experiences—"I've sometimes struggled to express my feelings, and watching your love reminds me I need to be braver in my own marriage."
        - Couple responds with gratitude and shares one joint vulnerability: "We're both a bit nervous about balancing finances and family expectations."
    - **Token Presentation:** Each friend places their token in a decorated "Blessing Box" for the couple to keep as reminders.
    - **AD Extension:** Record audio clips of each blessing (with consent), and compile them into an AD "Blessing Playlist" for the couple to revisit in moments of doubt.

2. **Pre-Wedding Ritual (AA + SA):**
    - **"Vulnerability Letter Exchange" (AA):** Two days before the wedding, each friend writes a private letter detailing:
        - A cherished memory with the bride/groom.
        - One set of hopes and fears they harbor for the upcoming marriage.
        - A pledge of friendship support for the new year.
    - Collate letters in sealed envelopes labeled "Open if you need courage" and "Open on first anniversary." At the rehearsal dinner, place the "needs courage" envelopes on a small table with candles.

3. **Wedding Day "Circle of Presence" (SA):**

- Immediately before the ceremony begins, coordinate a brief SA "Circle of Presence" where the couple stands at the center of a ring formed by close friends. No words are spoken; silence prevails for 60 seconds. This collective Presence symbolizes communal support and acknowledges the gravity of the transition.

4. **AD Post-Wedding Reflections:**
    - Within one week after the wedding, host an AD "Memory Montage" where friends share photos, short anecdotes, and one-sentence marriage advice. Assemble these into a digital slideshow (AA) to be gifted alongside a small physical scrapbook.

5. **One-Year Anniversary Unveiling (AA + SD):**
    - On the couple's first anniversary, friends mail the sealed "First Anniversary" letters from the AA ritual. Couples read in private, then schedule a brief SD call with one core friend (rotational) to debrief how marriage has unfolded—highlighting which fears manifested, which hopes were realized, and how friendships sustained them.

**Adaptive Variants:**

- **"Vow of Continued Friendship" (SA + AD):** At the wedding reception, have a brief moment where friends read a collective commitment vow: "We vow to remain present, intentional, empathetic, and vulnerable with you as you embark on this new chapter." Record and share this AD as a memento.

- **"Couples' Friendship Audit" (Quarterly Sync):** For couples whose friends are also couples, co-host a quarterly SA retreat to practice the "Monthly Relationship Health Check" (Section III.A) in a couples' context, honoring dual pair dynamics.

---

## C. "New Parenthood: ReconneXion Family Support Sequence" (All Modalities)

**Objective:** Support friends becoming parents through staged rituals—honoring joys, acknowledging vulnerabilities, and sustaining the adult friendship amid new responsibilities.

**Timing:** Two distinct phases:

- **Pre-Birth Rituals:** During pregnancy, last trimester.
- **Post-Birth Rituals:** First six months postpartum, then quarterly check-ins.

**Participants:** Expecting parent(s) and core friend group (5–10 people), optionally family.

**Steps:**

1. **Pre-Birth Rituals:**

    - **"Pregnancy Gratitude & Intentions Jar" (AA + SA):**

        - In the second or early third trimester, friends gather SA for a small potluck. Each brings an AA index card with:

            - **Gratitude:** "I'm grateful for your strength as you carried early pregnancy nausea."

            - **Intention for Baby:** "I intend to help decorate the nursery in a calm way."

            - **Parenthood Vulnerability Share:** One micro-vulnerability: "I'm nervous about how sleep deprivation will affect our friendship."

        - Cards are read aloud; after reading, each card is folded and placed in a decorated jar. The parent(s) take the jar home to draw one card when stress mounts in late pregnancy.

    - **"Baby Name Resonance Session" (SD + AA):**

        - If the parent(s) are undecided on names, organize an SD call featuring a "Name Resonance Round":

            - Each friend suggests one name, shares a 2-minute story of why it resonates—maybe from personal history or cultural significance.

            - Parent(s) share micro-vulnerability: "We worry choosing a family name might add pressure."

2. **Birth Announcement & Vulnerability (AD):**

    - **"Arrival Affirmation Message" (AD):** Within 24 hours of birth, friends send an AD group message honoring the newborn—brief, heartfelt lines:

- "Congratulations, Emma! Your strength is luminous; Julie and I can't wait to meet the little one."
- This practice reinforces communal Presence, even if the new parents are overwhelmed.

3. **Post-Birth Rituals:**

    - **"Weekly Check-In Envelope" (AA + AD):**
        - For the first eight weeks postpartum, friends commit (in a pre-arranged AA contract) to send a physical or digital "Check-In Envelope" once per week:
            - **Contents:** One AA note of empathy ("I know nights are tough—let me bring you dinner on Saturday"), one practical offer ("I'm free Tuesday morning to watch the baby so you can nap").
            - **AD Reminder:** Automated reminders through a shared calendar prompt the sender to either physically drop off at the new parents' door or send an AD message.

    - **"Monthly "Parent Vulnerability Circle" (SD + SA):**
        - Once per month, host a short SD call (or SA if feasible) dedicated to new parents' Vulnerability:
            - Begin by sharing one deep feeling about parenthood ("I'm terrified I'll mess up potty training," "I feel guilty for wanting time alone").
            - Listeners practice "Stark Empathy": "I can't imagine how draining midnight feedings are; know I'm here whenever you need a vent."
            - Close with Intentionality: "Let's plan a half-day respite next weekend—who's in to babysit?"

    - **"Quarterly Family & Friends Picnic" (SA):**
        - At the three- and six-month marks, organize a communal SA picnic in a local park.
            - Structure includes a 15-minute "Circle of Appreciation" where family and friends each share one observed growth in the new

parents—emphasizing supportive and empathetic feedback.

- Incorporate a short AA "Reflection Jar" activity: attendees jot down a piece of advice or playful encouragement on slips, placed into a decorated container for the family's future perusal.

4. **Long-Term Follow-Up:**

   - **"First-Year AA Time Capsule" (AA):**

     - Friends collectively select 12 milestones (baby's first smile, first crawl, etc.). At each milestone, one friend writes a brief note describing the event's significance.

     - Save these as a digital AA folder labeled "Baby's First Year." Present to the child on their first birthday.

     - Optionally, record short AD videos during key moments—compiled into a video montage.

**Adaptive Variants:**

- **"Dad & Friends Breathing Break" (SD + SA):** If the father is less engaged due to work, organize an SA "Dads' Five-Minute Breather" weekly—focusing on micro-vulnerabilities unique to new fatherhood (anxiety, financial stress). Coparents can join SD empathy sessions.

- **"Sibling Inclusion Rituals" (SA + AD):** If there are older siblings, incorporate them in the rituals—"Drawing a picture for the baby" (AA), then reading aloud on family SD check-ins, fostering broader family reconnection.

---

## D. "Career Transition: ReconneXion Professional Pivot Protocol" (Self & Peer Group)

**Objective:** When a friend changes jobs, faces unemployment, or shifts career paths, institute rituals that maintain support, encourage vulnerability around professional identities, and foster Empathy for stressors.

**Timing:** Begin one month pre-transition, continue through first quarter post-transition.

**Participants:** Job-changer and a small support circle (3–6 colleagues or friends).

**Steps:**

1. **Pre-Transition "Professional Shift Symposium" (SA + AA):**
   - One month prior, convene an SA gathering—light lunch or evening potluck.
   - **"Story of Self" Sharing (AA):** Each attendee, including the transitioning friend, briefly narrates their career story—how they arrived at current role, challenges faced. The transitioning friend says: "I've accepted a new position at X; I'm nervous about stepping away."
   - **Reflective Letters (AA):** Each person writes a 200–300 word letter to the job-changer:
     - Acknowledging their growth and resilience.
     - Offering one piece of professional vulnerability advice ("When you start the new role, it's okay to ask dumb questions").
   - Collate letters in a decorated "Career Support Folder."

2. **"First Day & One-Month Check-Ins" (AD + SD):**
   - **First Day:** Friends send an AD group message midday: "Hope you're settling in; remember we're here to celebrate every small win." This fosters Presence despite physical distance.
   - **One-Month SD Debrief:** Host a 30-minute SD call where the transitioning friend shares a micro-vulnerability about new role friction ("I feel out of depth with these technical tools"), and colleagues provide calibrating empathy—"I recall feeling the same with Excel—let's set up a brief tutorial session."

3. **"Quarterly Skill-Sharing Circles" (SA + SD):**
   - For the first three months, friends rotate hosting SA or SD "Skill-Sharing" mini-workshops—each tailored to the job-changer's new role demands: "Advanced Data Visualization Techniques," "Public Speaking Confidence," "Networking with Introversion."
   - The job-changer reciprocates by offering new perspectives when roles reverse—e.g., teaching a session on "Adapting to Rapid Organizational Change."

4. **"Career Vulnerability Jars" (SA + AD):**

- Set up a small container in the transitioning friend's home office. Colleagues drop anonymous AA notes: "Today I'm curious about how bree'll handle challenging feedback," or "Share one piece of advice for overcoming imposter syndrome."
- The job-changer periodically opens the jar (once a week) and responds AD via brief messages—keeping dialogue alive.

5. **"First Promotion / Milestone Celebration" (SA):**

    - If the friend receives a promotion or completes a notable project, host an SA small gathering—"Promotion Pizza Party." Each attendee shares one vulnerability about their own journey to similar milestones—reinforcing a culture of continuous mutual growth.

**Adaptive Variants:**

- **"LinkedIn Vulnerability Post" (AD):** Host a vulnerability-themed professional post—job-changer writes: "Today I feel proud but nervous stepping into management. Grateful for mentors who held my hand." Encourages wider network to leave supportive comments, extending Empathy beyond the immediate circle.

- **"Virtual Coworking Day" (SD):** Friends commit to a shared SD workspace session for one hour weekly, each working on their own tasks but keeping mics on; occasional brief vulnerability check-ins—"I'm losing motivation on this code; how do you stay focused?"

---

## E. "Bereavement: ReconneXion Compassion Continuum" (All Modalities)

**Objective:** Support friends coping with the loss of a loved one—crafting multi-modal compassionate rituals that integrate Presence, Empathy, Intentionality, and age-appropriate Vulnerability.

**Timing:** Initiate immediately upon hearing of the loss; continue structured rituals for at least six months.

**Participants:** Grieving friend, core support network (varying size), altruistic community.

**Steps:**

1. **Immediate "Presence Call & Listening Circle" (SD + SA):**

- As soon as possible, a small group holds a brief SD call—each simply says: "I'm here; I love you." Resist giving advice or shifting to problem-solving.
- Follow up with SA physical presence if feasible—dropping off hot meals, sitting in silence, or simply being under the same roof.

2. **"Compassion Letters & Memory Collage" (AA + AD):**
   - Within the first two weeks, collect AA handwritten letters sharing memories of the deceased, expressing empathy for the bereaved, and offering gentle support: "I remember how your mom made holiday dinners; I'm here for your heartache."
   - Assemble letters into a physical "Memory Collage" or "Bereavement Bundle" to gift. Optionally, scan and send as a digital AA file with audio readings (AD).

3. **Weekly "Walk-and-Listen" (SA + AD):**
   - For the first three months, friends schedule a weekly SA walk—one hour of walking side-by-side. The bereaved friend may or may not talk; presence alone suffices.
   - At the end of each walk, send a brief AD reflection—"Today I thought of you while birdwatching, remembering how you and I used to spot owls"—maintaining empathy even between walks.

4. **Monthly "Grief Sharing Circle" (SD + AA):**
   - Once per month, convene a small SD call for grief sharing. Each participant prepares a short AA reflection on how the bereaved friend is doing—expressing empathy, cautioning against clichés ("Time heals all wounds" replaced by "Wishing you space to process in your time").
   - The bereaved friend shares micro-vulnerabilities—"I felt guilty I laughed at that joke yesterday; is that normal?" Listeners respond with supportive validation—"It's a sign of healing; laughter doesn't erase love or loss."

5. **"Anniversary & Milestone Remembrances" (AA + SA):**
   - On the deceased's birthday or anniversary of passing, host a small SA gathering—"Candle-Light Remembrance." Each person shares a memory (3–5 minutes), lights a candle, and writes one line in a shared AA memorial book.
   - If distance prevents physical gathering, organize an AD group chat where each sends a photo or quote capturing remembrance; at a predetermined hour,

everyone lights a candle and takes a photo to share digitally.

6. **Quarterly "Life Celebration Ritual" (SA + SD):**

    - After six months, host an SA "Life Celebration"—a potluck or picnic where the bereaved friend chooses a joyful theme (favorite songs of the departed, favorite foods).

    - Begin with an SD livestream segment for out-of-town supporters; then SA friends play uplifting stories and gentle Vulnerability costuming (wearing a shared memento, e.g., a scarf or bracelet the departed loved).

    - Close with a vow: "We vow to celebrate your loved one's life each year in our own ways."

**Adaptive Variants:**

- **"Community Compassion Hour" (SA + AD):** If the deceased was community-involved, broaden support: invite neighbors to a two-hour SA "Compassion Hour" where all can share grief, light candles, and sign an AA memorial board in the local hall.

- **"Interactive Digital Memorial" (AD + AA):** Create a simple website or doc where friends across the globe can post memories, photos, and micro-vulnerability reflections—ensuring ongoing, asynchronous support and presence.

---

# VI. Special Occasion Rituals: Celebrating Milestones with ReconneXion

Birthdays, holiday gatherings, friendiversaries—all present opportunities to showcase friendship's enduring power. ReconneXion enriches these occasions by layering Presence, Intentionality, Empathy, and Vulnerability onto traditions, ensuring they evolve from perfunctory to profound.

---

### A. "Friendiversary: Annual Commemorative Ritual" (SA + AA + AD)

**Objective:** Celebrate the anniversary of the friendship's inception—honoring origins, charting growth, and setting intentions for the coming year.

**Timing:** On the date of friendship start or a proximate weekend if schedules conflict; annual repetition.

**Participants:** Friendship dyad or small circle around that bond (3–6).

**Steps:**

1. **Pre-Friendiversary Journal (AA):**
    - Each friend writes a one-page reflection:
        - **"Origin Story Revisited":** Remember that first meeting—what impressions endured.
        - **"Growth Highlights":** Two key moments that transformed the friendship.
        - **"Gratitude List":** Five reasons the friendship matters.
        - **"Future Aspirations":** One thing each would like to deepen in the next year (modal focus: "I want at least two SA adventures," or "I want to write monthly AA letters").

2. **Friendiversary Gathering (SA + AD, 2–3 Hours):**
    - Begin SA with an **"Origin Memory Read-Aloud"**: Each person shares a 2–3 minute excerpt of their pre-journaled origin narrative.
    - Collate **"Time Capsule Contributions"**: Each reveals an object or digital artifact representing a friendship moment this year—photos, small tokens, screenshots. Place them into a decorated box labeled "Friendiversary Time Capsule."
        - Agree to open the capsule in one or five years.
    - **Empathy & Vulnerability Circle (30 min):** Each shares a deeper vulnerability related to the friendship—"I felt insecure when you moved away, but this weekend's call helped me feel anchored."
    - **Intentional Commitments (15 min):** Each person sets a "Friendiversary Promise"—one concrete action (e.g., "I will plan our annual reunion trip," or "I'll send a birthday care package every year").
    - **Closing Toast & Gratitude (10 min):** Raise a glass (coffee, tea, or beverage of choice) and share one heartfelt gratitude: "To your unwavering humor that's brightened all my Mondays."

- Capture a **"Friendiversary Photo"** for use in future invites and commemorations.

3. **Post-Friendiversary AD Recap (AD):**
   - Host or rotating friend circulates a short AD message summarizing:
     - Excerpts from journal reflections (anonymized if desired).
     - Highlights of objects placed in the capsule.
     - List of Friendiversary Promises.
   - Save the AD recap and any photos in a shared AA "Friendiversary Folder" for archival.

**Adaptive Variants:**

- **"Virtual Friendiversary" (SD + AD):** For distance friendships, host an SD video call replicating above elements—share digital artifacts via screen share, record to revisit. For Intentional Promises, use an AD shared doc with checkboxes for monthly triggers.

---

## B. "Holiday Ritual Augmentation" (SA + AD + SD)

**Objective:** Enrich existing holiday gatherings (Thanksgiving, Diwali, Lunar New Year, etc.) with bespoke ReconneXion elements, ensuring that cultural traditions are intertwined with deeper Presence, shared Vulnerability, and empathetic practices.

**Timing:** Align with each holiday's customary observance.

**Participants:** Family, friends, community members (size varies, 6–20+).

**Steps:**

1. **Preparatory Invitation (AD + AA):**
   - When sending holiday invites, include a brief ReconneXion clause:
     - "At this year's Thanksgiving, we'll begin with a 5-minute Silent Gratitude Pause, followed by a Round of 'My 2025 Vulnerability Moment'—each

sharing a challenge and growth."

- Provide an AA sheet listing potential Vulnerability Prompts tailored to the holiday:
  - "This year, I felt most challenged when…"
  - "I'm grateful but also vulnerable about…"

2. **Opening Silent Gratitude Pause (SA):**
   - Just before the meal or main event, ask everyone to close eyes, breathe three times, and silently reflect on one blessing. This establishes collective Presence.

3. **Round-Robin Vulnerability Share (SA, 2–3 min each):**
   - Moderator announces the prompt: "In the past year, what personal challenge made you stronger?"
   - Each guest shares a brief vulnerability: "I lost my job in March, but I learned resilience."
   - Use a "Talking Spoon" or "Gratitude Gavel" to pass; no interruptions until each has spoken.

4. **Community Empathy Anchoring (AD + AA):**
   - After the round, host invites guests to write a single-sentence empathic note for any speaker—"I admire your courage"—and place it in a "Community Empathy Jar."
   - These notes are read aloud after the meal or collected as a digital AA document for distribution post-holiday.

5. **Intentional Gift Exchange (AA + SA):**
   - Instead of conventional gift swaps, ask everyone to bring one **"Intentional Gift"**: a small handmade token or card reflecting meaningful insight ("Here's a seed packet to symbolize growth in your new home").
   - As each gift is unwrapped, the giver explains the Vulnerability or Empathy intention behind it.

6. **Closing Affirmations (SA + SD):**

- Conclude with a group Affirmation Chant—choose a short phrase like "We stand together in love and openness," repeated thrice.
- For remote participants, set up SD viewing so they can chant along.
- After the gathering, share an AD message: "Thank you for revealing your hearts and listening. Let's keep this spirit alive through biweekly vulnerability calls."

**Adaptive Variants:**

- **"Multi-Cultural Fusion" (SA + SD):** For groups celebrating more than one holiday simultaneously (e.g., non-denominational end-of-year gathering), integrate brief rituals from each tradition—Hanukkah's candle lighting, Christmas's star prayers, Kwanzaa's Umoja principles—each followed by a ReconneXion twist (e.g., "What's the light you need to shine to yourself this year?").

- **"Community Potluck with Themed Tables" (SA + AA):** At a block party, designate tables by ReconneXion pillars—Presence Table (silent reading), Intentionality Table (planning whiteboards), Empathy Table (listening pairs), Vulnerability Table (prompt cards). Attendees rotate tables, experiencing different focal practices interwoven with food.

---

## C. "Birthday: Intentional Appreciation & Reflective Growth" (SA + AA + AD)

**Objective:** Move beyond "Happy Birthday" clichés by creating multi-modal rituals inviting friends to express genuine appreciation, share micro-vulnerabilities, and co-create growth-focused birthday intentions.

**Timing:** On or around the birthday date.

**Participants:** Birthday person and their core friends (4–12).

**Steps:**

1. **Pre-Birthday "Appreciation Letters" (AA):**
   - One week prior, each friend writes a one-page AA letter to the birthday person, including:

- **Specific Appreciation:** "I appreciate how you've been a steady rock this past year when I needed honesty."
            - **Micro-Vulnerability:** "I sometimes hesitate to tell you when I'm hurt by your directness; I'm working on speaking up."
            - **Intention for Coming Year:** "I commit to saying 'thank you' more when you call me out."
    - Collect letters into a decorative "Birthday Appreciation Binder."

2. **Birthday "Presence Circle" (SA, 60–90 min):**
    - At a small SA gathering (party or dinner), assemble chairs in a circle. The birthday person sits on a special chair (a throne or a colorful pillow).
    - Each friend takes turns reading their AA letter aloud (4–5 minutes each), maintaining eye contact. The birthday person listens, then offers a short response—"Thank you; I hear you when you say you feel hurt by my directness; I'm sorry, and I'll try to temper my words."
    - This structure harnesses high Presence and authentic Vulnerability, deepening bonds.

3. **"Birthday Growth Board" (SA + AA):**
    - Create a large SA poster board or digital AA canvas labeled "Birthday Growth Board."
    - After letter readings, each friend writes (or digitally types) one actionable birthday intention for the honoree—"Complete that drawing class you've been postponing," "Spend 10 minutes each day in mindful solitude."
    - The honoree reviews these, accepts ones that resonate, and writes responses—either "I embrace this" or "I need more reflection" next to each. This practice links Intentionality with communal support.

4. **Reflective Cake Ceremony (SA):**
    - Prior to blowing out candles, the birthday person shares a "Birthday Vulnerability"—a deeper fear or hope for the coming year: "I worry I'll be stuck in my current role and not grow."

- Friends then respond with a 10-second group chant: "You are growing; we stand with you."
- After the candles are out, share slices of cake in silence for one minute, honoring Presence.

5. **Post-Birthday AD "Photo and Reflection Album":**
   - Photographer (designated friend) compiles photos from the Presence Circle and party. In an AA digital album, intersperse images with the appreciation letter excerpts.
   - Share via AD link, inviting the honoree and friends to add one-line captions capturing emotions—"Jake's eyes welled up when reading Lisa's letter"—fostering an ongoing Emotional Bank of memories.

**Adaptive Variants:**

- **"Birthday Virtual Star Shower" (SD + AD):** If friends are remote, host an SD call where each friend shares their typed appreciation reading into the chat, then texts a "star emoji" to the honoree's phone when they finish. Create an AD "Star Wall" graphic with 60 stars—one per year of age—each with embedded appreciation quotes.
- **"Milestone Birthday Time Capsule" (AA + SA):** On a 30th or 40th birthday, alongside the Growth Board, friends contribute AA items—photos, small mementos—sealed into a "Milestone Capsule" to be opened at the next decade.

# VII. Contextual Adaptations: Tailoring Rituals to Diverse Friendship Configurations

No two friendships are identical; cultural backgrounds, living situations, professional demands, and personal proclivities influence how rituals function best. Below we outline guidelines for customizing ReconneXion rituals to various contexts:

## A. Couples as Friends: "Inner Partnership Practices" (SA + SD + AA)

**Key Considerations:**

- Partners often have overlapping social circles and domestic cohabitation; rituals must differentiate friendship spaces from romantic or spousal contexts where appropriate—but also amplify the friendship dimension within the relationship.

**Core Rituals:**

1. **"Shared Morning Mantra" (SA):** Each day, while both are waking, recite together: "We honor each other's presence, listen with empathy, and hold vulnerability sacred." This sets a mutual tone distinct from routine spousal exchanges.

2. **"Weekly Date Reflection" (SD + AA):** Once a week, conduct a 20-minute SD (or in-person) date-like "Reflection Chat":
   - Partner A asks: "What was one vulnerability I showed this week that you appreciated?"
   - Partner B responds, then reciprocates. Use AA "Reflection Prompt Cards" to guide nuanced topics—"When did you feel most seen by me?" or "Where do you wish I'd been more intentional?"

3. **"Couples' Empathy Journal" (AA):** Maintain a shared AA journal where each writes a brief empathy note nightly—"Grateful for how you supported me with the toddler's tantrum." Both read it the next morning, reinforcing Presence before other commitments.

4. **"Boundary Enactment Ritual" (SA + AA):**
   - At the start of each month, write down two personal boundaries: one work-related ("I will stop checking email after 7 PM"), one friendship-related ("I need Sunday afternoons for friends outside our marriage").
   - Exchange and read aloud, then place on the fridge. This prevents friendship neglect and ensures intentional time with others.

5. **"Couples Shadow Mentorship" (SD + SA):** Pair with another couple similarly committed to mutual friendship growth—quarterly SA double-dates focusing on ReconneXion topics (e.g., "Empathy in Co-Parenting"), using AA worksheets to guide discussion.

---

## B. Families with Children: "Family ReconneXion Rituals" (SA + AD + AA)

**Key Considerations:**

- Incorporating children requires simplifying prompts, shorter durations, and fun elements so younger participants remain engaged.

**Core Rituals:**

1. **"Family Gratitude Circle" (SA):** Each evening, at dinner, everyone states one thing they're thankful for and one small challenge they faced that day. Children can draw or show a toy representing their feelings.

2. **Weekly "All-Family Walk" with Story Stones" (SA + AA):**
   - Create small painted stones, each depicting an emotion (happy face, sad face, surprised face). Each family member selects a stone to reflect their mood.
   - On Weekly Walk (30 minutes), each person briefly explains their chosen stone and why. Parents practice Empathy by kneeling to child's eye level and mirroring feelings.

3. **"Monthly Family Creativity Day" (SA + AA):**
   - Once per month, dedicate a 2-hour day for crafts: drawing family member portraits, building a house of cardboard depicting "Where we feel most safe as a family."
   - Conclude with each sharing one vulnerability ("I'm scared about starting school next week") and others respond with supportive gestures.

4. **"Digital Storytime & Micro-Vulnerability" (AD + SD):**
   - For remote family, host a 15-minute SD bedtime story. After reading, ask children a gentle question: "What's something that made you feel worried today?" Parents answer first, modeling Vulnerability, then encourage kids to share.

5. **"Annual Family Vision Board Retreat" (SA + AA):**
   - At the end of summer, gather for an all-day SA session where parents and children create a collaborative vision board: "Our Family Goals for the School Year." Incorporate drawings, magazine cutouts, and brief statements of hope or fear. This fosters Intentionality and collective Vulnerability (e.g., "I worry I won't keep up with sports" from a child; "I worry about balancing work and family" from a parent).

# C. Remote Friendship Groups: "Distributed ReconneXion Ecosystem" (SD + AD + AA)

**Key Considerations:**

- Geographic dispersion, differing time zones, and digital fatigue require asynchronous flexibility, scheduled synchronous times, and robust AA/AD scaffolding.

**Core Rituals:**

1. **"Global Gratitude Table" (AD + AA):**
   - Maintain a shared AA document titled "Global Gratitude Table." Each member adds one gratitude entry daily: "I'm grateful that I got to Skype with Maria today." Visualizing check-ins from different continents strengthens Presence across distance.

2. **"Time-Zone Compatible Weekly Circle" (SD):**
   - Use a rotating schedule where each week, the SD call time shifts by one hour to ensure fairness (e.g., a 7 PM London / Noon LA call one week, 6 PM London / 11 AM LA next).
   - During the call, use "SL–SD first five minutes" for quick hellos, then dedicate 20 minutes to a single "Discussion Prompt" where each can share a micro-vulnerability or milestone, practicing deep listening.

3. **"Asynchronous Vulnerability Podcasts" (AD + either SD or AA):**
   - Each month, one member records a 5-minute voice memo detailing a vulnerability ("Lately, I've felt lonely adjusting to remote work"). They upload to a shared AA folder.
   - Other members asynchronously add voice or text responses—"I feel that too; let's schedule a 10-minute SD check-in."
   - After two weeks, compile them into a "Quarterly Vulnerability Podcast," distributing as an AA link.

4. **"Virtual Co-Working & Silent Presence" (SD):**
   - Two or more remote friends agree on a 60-minute "Virtual Co-Work" session—set up an SD video room where cameras remain on silently while each person

works. Occasionally, glances and smiles reinforce Presence.

- Conclude with a 5-minute check-in ("What's one thing you accomplished?").

5. **"Digital Holiday Fusion" (SD + AD):**

    - For each friend's local holiday, the group holds a brief SD "Cross-Cultural Sharing" (15 minutes):

        - E.g., On Diwali, Indian friends light diyas on camera; others share what "light" they're bringing into their homes this month.
        - AD follow-up invites sharing photos or brief recipes via group chat.

# VIII. Tech-Enhanced Practices: Using Digital Tools without Losing Depth

Technology can both scaffold and sabotage friendship rituals. Here, we outline best practices for using digital tools—apps, AI reminders, shared calendars, and social feeds—while preserving human connection.

## A. "AI Prompt Integrations" for Intentionality & Follow-Through

1. **"GPT-Powered Morning Reminders":**

    - Use a simple AI service (like a custom GPT bot) to send daily 7:30 AM prompts via messaging platforms—"Don't forget your 5-minute gratitude call with Lina. Here's a suggestion: 'I'm grateful for your listening ear yesterday.'"
    - AI can also suggest personalized micro-vulnerability questions based on previous conversations ("Recall the moment you felt happiest last week; how did that shape your next steps?").

2. **"Scheduled Empathy Nudges":**

    - Employ calendar integrations (e.g., Google Calendar + Zapier) to automatically send "Empathy Nudge" messages to small groups at strategic intervals—"Now is a good time to check in on each other. Try asking: 'What's one thing you need support with today?'"

3. **"Virtual Whiteboard for Shared Rituals"**:
   - Use an always-open shared whiteboard (Miro, Mural) with sections for "Weekly Friendiversity," "Monthly Intention Board," "Gratitude Wall." Participants can drop virtual Post-Its anytime, simulating physical SA/AA boards.

4. **"Wearable Presence Reminders"**:
   - For deeply habitual pairs, set up a shared IFTTT routine: if one friend's smartwatch registers a period of high stress (elevated heart rate beyond threshold), a gentle vibration on the partner's wearable prompts: "Check in with Alex." This "empathy alarm" fosters neural attunement.

---

## B. "Digital Journaling Platforms" for AA & AD Synchrony

1. **"Collaborative Google Doc Audit Templates"**:
   - Share a folder containing:
     - **"Weekly Reflection Template"** (modality counts, depth logs, deposits/withdrawals).
     - **"Monthly Audit Presentation Slides"** (with embedded charts).
   - Friends commit to filling out their sheets by Sunday evenings, enabling streamlined SD/SA review.

2. **"Encrypted Voice Journals"**:
   - Use secure apps like Day One or Penzu to record private voice memos or typed entries. Grant selective access to close friends for periodic review—ensuring privacy while enabling vulnerability sharing.

3. **"Shared Digital Photo Albums with Memory Prompts"**:
   - Upload photos to a shared Google Photos album labeled "2025 Friendship Moments." Use "Memory Prompt" comments: "Remember this—March 12 coffee walk, when we realized we both dreaded Monday meetings?"

## C. "Social Media Mindfulness: Curated Connection" (AD + SD)

1. **"Private Friend Circles":**

   - Instead of broadcasting to hundreds, create a "Close Friends" list or private group (Facebook, Instagram, WhatsApp). Post micro-vulnerabilities, appreciation notes, or casual updates only visible to this curated circle—maintaining intimacy without public exposure.

2. **"Scheduled Digital Sabbaths":**

   - Use app timers (Screen Time, Digital Wellbeing) to lock social feeds for selected hours, preserving weekend "Digital Unplug" rituals (Section III.B.2). Encourage sharing of analog experiences post-sabbath via AD, amplifying real-world Presence.

3. **"Storytelling Live Streams" for Shared Experiences:**

   - Host short live streams (Instagram Live, Facebook Live) at predetermined times: "Wednesday at 5 PM—'Walk & Talk' where we share a 10-minute vulnerability prompt." This can serve as a hybrid of SA/SD Presence when physical meetup is impossible.

# IX. Compliance & Habit Formation: From Deliberation to Automaticity

Creating rituals is only half the battle; forging them into **automatic, habitual elements** of daily life requires leveraging behavioral science principles—cue identification, routine structure, reward systems, and gradual progression.

## A. "Habit Stacking" with Existing Routines

1. **Identify Anchor Habits:**

- Link new ReconneXion rituals to existing daily anchors—brushing teeth, morning coffee, bedtime routine. For example:
    - Right after pouring morning coffee, initiate the "Five-Minute Gratitude & Connection Call."
    - After brushing teeth at night, stand before the mirror for the "Second Mirror Check & Tomorrow's Intention" (Section II.C.3).

2. **Micro-Habit Scaling:**
    - Start with ultra-short interactions (30-second silence together before meetings) and increment length every two weeks by 15 seconds. This gradual ramp ensures sustainable adoption.

## B. "Reward Systems & Positive Reinforcement"

1. **Immediate Positive Feedback:**
    - Incorporate celebratory emojis, virtual high-fives, or short AD "Pats on the Back" each time a ritual is completed—leveraging dopamine-driven reward circuits.
    - For SA rituals, attach a symbolic token—e.g., small sticker or colored yarn strand—added to a visible group "Ritual Completion Chart."

2. **Long-Term Accountability & Celebrations:**
    - Upon completing 30 consecutive days of a daily ritual (like the morning gratitude call), mark a milestone with a group celebration—group dinner, extended SA retreat, or a "Digital Trophy" graphic shared AD.

## C. "Overcoming Inertia & Resistance"

1. **Anticipate Barriers:**
    - Conduct a brief pre-routine audit asking: "What might get in our way of performing this ritual?" (e.g., "My internet is finicky in the morning," "I'm rarely free at exactly 7:30 AM.")

- Preemptively design workarounds—"If internet fails, send a voice memo instead," "Adjust meeting window by ±15 minutes."

2. **"Implementation Intentions" Exercise:**

    - Each person formulates "If–Then" plans: "If it's raining and I can't walk for the morning ritual, then I'll do the mirror check and a 3-minute breathing exercise indoors."

    - Write these down in AA or set as AD reminders to reinforce when obstacles arise.

3. **Peer Nudging & Gentle Accountability:**

    - Establish a "Friend Ritual Buddy" system—partners send AD prompts or gentle check-ins when a ritual is skipped ("Hey, I noticed you missed the morning call—everything OK?"). This preserves Empathy while spurring routine adherence.

# X. Measurement & Reflection Tools: Tracking Growth, Identifying Drift

Effective rituals are living systems requiring ongoing calibration. Here, we consolidate and expand upon measurement tools that can integrate seamlessly into the ritual infrastructure.

## A. "ReconneXion Dashboard" (Comprehensive Monthly Tracker)

**Purpose:** Provide a high-level panoramic view of friendship health by consolidating daily, weekly, and monthly metrics into an accessible dashboard—enabling rapid identification of strengths, weaknesses, and areas needing attention.

**Components:**

1. **Modality Distribution Chart (Bar Graph):**

    - X-axis: Modalities (SL–AD, DL–AD, SL–SD, DL–SD, SA, AA).

    - Y-axis: Count of interactions in past 30 days.

- Aim: Visualize whether any modality is disproportionately neglected (<10% of total) or overused (>40%).

2. **Depth Heatmap:**

    - X-axis: Days of month; Y-axis: Depth levels (1–10).
    - Color intensity represents number of interactions at that level/day.
    - Aim: Spot clusters of high-depth sharing or prolonged surface-level periods.

3. **Vulnerability Bank Balance (Line Graph):**

    - X-axis: Time (days/weeks).
    - Y-axis: Net emotional bank account balance (aggregate deposits minus withdrawals).
    - Aim: Identify periods of relational strain (steep negative slopes) and recovery (upward slopes).

4. **Habit Adherence Gauge (Dial):**

    - For designated daily/weekly rituals (e.g., Morning Gratitude Call, Pre-Meeting Presence), track total completions versus expected frequency over the period.
    - Gauge reads 0%–100%; red if below 60%, yellow 60–80%, green above 80%.

5. **Subjective Satisfaction Index (Survey-Based Score):**

    - Aggregate from weekly "Connection Satisfaction Surveys" (AD or AA) where each friend rates, 1–10: "How connected did you feel this month?" and "How supported did you feel?"
    - Display as a monthly numeric trend.

**Implementation:**

- Use spreadsheet software (Google Sheets, Excel) with embedded charts.
- Set up formulas to auto-calculate modality counts from separate weekly logs (automated via forms or scripts).

- Update at end of month; share in SD "Monthly Relationship Health Check" (Section III.A) or as a look at the ReconneXion Dashboard during retreats.

---

## B. "Reflective Questions Repository" (AA + AD)

**Purpose:** Maintain a dynamic, ever-expanding set of open-ended reflective questions that prompt deeper engagement during rituals—ensuring freshness and progression as friendships evolve.

**Structure:**

1. **Categorization by Modality & Pillar:**

    - **Presence Prompts (SA/SD):** "What did you notice in my body language today?"; "When did you wish I was more 'there' this week?"

    - **Intentionality Prompts (AD/AA):** "What's one goal you set for our friendship this month that you'd like to revisit?"; "In what way did your impulse guide you toward caring for me this week?"

    - **Empathy Prompts (SA/SD):** "Describe a moment this week when you felt misunderstood by me."; "What's one feeling you sensed I was holding back?"

    - **Vulnerability Prompts (AA/AD):** "When was the last time you felt too vulnerable to share and how can I support you?"; "What's a hope you fear sharing because it might sound selfish?"

2. **Maintenance & Growth:**

    - Friends collectively add 2–3 new prompts per quarter based on emerging relational themes—collected via AD suggestion threads.

    - Assign a rotating "Prompt Curator" each month to ensure 4–6 prompts are fresh, aligned with seasonal or contextual shifts (e.g., end-of-year retrospection prompts in December).

3. **Usage Guidelines:**

    - During weekly/ monthly rituals, draw one prompt at random to initiate deeper discussion—ensuring unpredictability and avoiding canned routines.

- For daily micro-reflections (mirror, journaling), select one prompt from the repository and jot one or two sentences in AA.

**Adaptive Variants:**

- **"Random Prompt Bot" (AD):** Duplicate all prompts into a simple chatbot that, when messaged "Friend Prompt," returns a random question. Launch micro-rituals spontaneously during lulls in conversation.
- **"Mood-Based Prompt Selection" (AA):** Use mood tracking apps—if logged as "anxious," the prompt system filters to ones addressing fear and support; if "pensive," favors reflective prompts about growth.

## C. "Periodic Ritual Effectiveness Surveys" (AD)

**Purpose:** Solicit anonymous (if desired) or transparent feedback to gauge whether the existing suite of rituals meets current needs, or if modifications or new rituals are warranted.

**Frequency:** Quarterly (aligned with Quarterly Deep Dive Retreats, Section V.B).

**Components:**

1. **Likert-Scale Items (1–5):**
   - "How useful did you find our daily Morning Ritual?"
   - "Did our Weekend Rituals contribute to feeling recharged?"
   - "Rate the balance of modalities we used this quarter (1 = too digital, 5 = too analog)."
   - "How often did you feel uncomfortable sharing vulnerability in our rituals?" (1 = never comfortable, 5 = very comfortable).

2. **Open-Ended Questions:**
   - "What ritual do you wish we introduced but haven't?"
   - "Which ritual felt unnecessary or burdensome?"

- "Describe one new Contextual Adaptation you think would help our group."
- "Any suggestions on improving our Habit Formation strategies?"

3. **Outcome & Follow-Up:**
   - Collate survey responses into an AD summary.
   - Present top themes during the Quarterly Deep Dive Retreat, adjusting the ReconneXion Dashboard, Ritual Schedules, and Contextual Adaptations accordingly.

# XI. Troubleshooting Common Pitfalls in Embedding Rituals

Even the most well-intentioned rituals can falter under practical constraints, emotional resistance, or over-scripting. Below are **eight common pitfalls** encountered when embedding ReconneXion into everyday life, along with targeted mitigation strategies.

## Pitfall 1: "Ritual Overload"—Burnout from Too Many Scheduled Checkpoints

**Symptoms:**

- Friends express feeling "tired of check-ins," "forced participation," or "overly scheduled" interactions.
- Missed rituals accumulate guilt, leading to avoidance.

**Mitigations:**

1. **Ritual Pruning:** Conduct a "Ritual Inventory" to identify which have become burdensome. Retire or reduce frequency of low-impact rituals.
2. **Variable Cadence:** Alternate weeks between light (only daily micro-rituals) and full (daily + weekly + monthly) ritual schedules—allowing "breather weeks" to prevent fatigue.

3. **Opt-In Flexibility:** Permit individuals to skip specific rituals without reproach, shifting to asynchronous alternatives to reduce pressure.

## Pitfall 2: "Modal Atrophy"—Over-Reliance on a Single Modality

**Symptoms:**

- Friendship becomes heavily AD (texting) with little SA or face-to-face time; emotional depth stagnates.
- Group chat dynamics feel superficial ("How's it going?" "Good.").

**Mitigations:**

1. **Modal Quotas in Audits:** Use the "Modality Distribution Chart" to flag underused modes (e.g., SA <10% of interactions).
2. **Targeted "Modal Repair Ritual":** If SA is depleted, schedule a "SA Necessity Weekend"—block a day for in-person meet-ups or group activities. If AA is neglected, initiate a "Handwritten Letter Week."
3. **Adaptive Substitution:** When physical SA is impossible, substitute with DL–SD extended sessions to at least approximate analog exchange.

## Pitfall 3: "Scripted Interaction Syndrome"—Engagement Lacks Authenticity

**Symptoms:**

- Rituals become rote; participants recite answers without real emotional engagement ("robot replies").
- Early insights fade into perfunctory checkboxes.

**Mitigations:**

1. **Inject Novelty & Surprise:** Periodically introduce surprise elements—unexpected prompts, rotating hosts, or themed attire ("Wear a color that reflects your mood today").

2. **Rotate Facilitators & Formats:** Change who leads each ritual; vary structures (e.g., switch "Rose/Thorn/Bud" to "Shield/Sword/Lantern").

3. **Embrace Imperfection:** Encourage raw, unpolished sharing over idealized answers; e.g., "It's OK if you don't have an answer—say 'I don't know how I feel.'"

---

## Pitfall 4: "Boundary Erosion"—Blended Personal/Professional Overreach

**Symptoms:**

- Work-focused teams hold vulnerability sessions during crunch times, generating resentment.

- Friends feel obligated to share at socially inappropriate moments—e.g., at funerals, weddings.

**Mitigations:**

1. **Explicit Boundary Clauses:** Incorporate clear AA statements about permissible ritual contexts—e.g., "No vulnerability check-ins during company peak periods (quarter-end) unless pre-approved."

2. **Safe Word Protocols:** Allow any member to say "Safe Word: Pause" to immediately freeze a vulnerability discussion if boundaries are being crossed.

3. **Periodically Revisit Boundary Audits (Section X.C):** Ensure mutual understanding of when and where rituals are appropriate; renegotiate as life circumstances change.

---

## Pitfall 5: "Technology Fatigue"—Overuse of Digital Tools Diminishes Presence

**Symptoms:**

- Friends complain of video-call exhaustion, ignore AA prompts due to notification overload.

- The line between personal and digital life blurs, causing stress.

**Mitigations:**

1. **Digital Sabbaths (Section III.B.2):** Schedule regular, even brief, device-free windows—daily or weekly—to reset.

2. **Selective Tool Use:** Evaluate which apps or platforms add real value; archive or silence unused channels.

3. **Encourage Offline Rituals:** When possible, prioritize AA or SA over SD/AD—e.g., "Handwritten E-Letter Hybrids" over long email threads.

---

## Pitfall 6: "Friendship Asymmetry"—Some Participate More, Others Less

### Symptoms:

- One or two friends dominate rituals; quieter members withdraw.
- Engagement fatigue is concentrated in a few "Friendship Champions," while others coast.

### Mitigations:

1. **Ritual Role Rotation:** Systematically rotate responsibilities—note-taker, host, facilitator, curator—so everyone has ownership and a chance to lead.

2. **Inclusive Check-In Protocols:** During group rituals, use explicit "round-robin" speaking turns, ensuring balanced airtime.

3. **Anonymized Feedback Options:** Provide AA "Silent Feedback Boxes" where quieter participants can express concerns without speaking in group.

---

## Pitfall 7: "Lifecycle Shifts"—Rituals Misaligned with Changing Life Phases

### Symptoms:

- College friends find weekday rituals impossible post-graduation due to work schedules.

- Newly parent friends can't attend weekend micro-retreats.

**Mitigations:**

1. **Lifecycle Audit:** Twice yearly, assess whether existing rituals align with current life phases—adjust schedules, modalities, and expectations.

2. **Flexible Ritual Subscriptions:** Create "Ritual Menus" with multiple options (weekday, weekend, hybrid) so friends can pick what fits their season of life.

3. **Peer Buddying:** Pair friends at similar life stages for rituals; share broader group obligations via cross-pair check-ins.

### Pitfall 8: "Emotional Burnout & Compassion Fatigue" Among Support Network

**Symptoms:**

- Frequent high-intensity vulnerability-sharing sessions leave listeners exhausted—compassion wanes.

- Some participants become reluctant to initiate vulnerability for fear of overburdening friends.

**Mitigations:**

1. **Compassion Reservoir Maintenance:** Incorporate regular "Self-Compassion Micro-Rituals" (e.g., 5-second breathing breaks, brief solo walks) into the calendar.

2. **Rotate Listening Duties:** Use a "compassion roster" so no one is the perpetual "go-to" for vulnerability support; distribute signals of support evenly.

3. **Encourage Professional Referrals:** When vulnerabilities exceed friendship bounds (clinical depression, trauma), guide toward mental health professionals—ensuring friends don't burn out in non-professional roles.

# XII. Stories & Vignettes: Everyday Rituals in Action

To ground the preceding frameworks, we present **three detailed vignettes** illustrating how everyday rituals have transformed friendships—saving them from drift, deepening bonds, or sustaining them across vast distances.

---

## Vignette 1: "Morning Magic—Sealing Distance with Five Minutes" (Long-Distance Friends)

### Background:

- **Friends:** Raj (in Mumbai) and Emily (in New York), since university exchange program five years ago. After both graduated, careers took them to opposite hemispheres. Despite fond memories, inconsistent messaging led to drift—messages went unanswered for days, questions unanswered, leaving both feeling guilt and disconnection.

### Challenge:

- Vast time-zone difference (10.5 hours) and busy schedules made synchronous contact rare. Both felt isolated: Raj missed Emily's quick empathy when work overwhelmed him; Emily missed Raj's grounded presence when postdoc stress peaked.

### Ritual Introduction:

- Inspired by ReconneXion's "Five-Minute Gratitude & Connection Call" ritual, they decided to adapt it for their time-zone reality.

### Implementation:

1. **Time Coordination (AD):**

    - Raj's morning 7:00 AM IST corresponds to Emily's 8:30 PM EST. Hence, at 7:00 AM IST daily, Raj would wake, make chai, and call Emily—Emily would be finishing dinner, with her laptop open.

    - They set up a rotating schedule: weekdays for actual calls; weekends deferred to voice note exchanges (if call missed).

2. **Structure Customization:**

- **Minute 1 (SL Check-In):** Brief, "Good morning! How's your evening?"
- **Minutes 2–3 (Gratitude & Highlight):** Raj expresses gratitude: "I'm so grateful you watched my presentation recording yesterday; your feedback helped." Emily reciprocates: "I appreciate you sending me that article on burnout; it changed my perspective."
- **Minute 4 (Intentionality Statement):** Raj pledges: "Today, I'll schedule a dedicated 5-minute break between meetings to breathe." Emily promises: "I'll text you a short summary of my conference session."
- **Minute 5 (Presence Closure):** "Sending you a virtual hug—talk tomorrow." Both breathe together for one deep sigh.

3. **Ritual Evolution:**

    - After two weeks, both noticed mood improvements. Raj's mornings felt less lonely; Emily's workdays ended on a positive note.
    - They began adding a **"micro-vulnerability"** in Week 3: "I felt embarrassed when I tripped in front of my boss today"—eliciting laughter and reciprocal micro-vulnerability.
    - By Month 2, they turned Fridays into 10-minute calls—adding a "Weekend Planning" element (DL integration).

**Outcome:**

- **Modality & Depth Balance:** Before ritual, they logged 0 SA and occasional AD (1–2 messages weekly). Post-ritual, they had 5 SL–SD calls weekly, 2–3 DL–SD sessions by Week 4, and shared AA "Weekend Letters" monthly.

- **Emotional Bank Rebuilt:** Consistent deposits reversed drifting patterns; by Month 3, Raj's "Emotional Bank Balance" line graph showed sustained positive slope.

- **Continued Evolution:** At six months, Raj flew to New York; they seamlessly transitioned from SL–SD to SA—sharing two-hour in-person walks, making up for lost time. Their friendship sustained, and distance no longer felt permanent.

# Vignette 2: "Office Breakroom Presence—Reviving a Colleague's Hope" (Corporate Team)

**Background:**

- **Team:** Six software engineers at a mid-sized fintech startup. Workloads were heavy; stress was high. Friendships among team members existed but were superficial—most interactions confined to Slack or brief standups.

- **Issue:** One member, Sophie, felt isolated after her mother's illness worsened. She privately struggled with grief but feared vulnerability at work would be seen as weakness.

**Challenge:**

- Team's culture was high-performance, low-emotion. No regular rituals supported Empathy or Vulnerability; the "Pre-Meeting Presence Drop-In" was absent. Morale dipped, work quality suffered; Sophie's productivity plummeted.

**Ritual Intervention:**

- A junior team member, Andre, introduced ReconneXion's "Pre-Meeting Presence Drop-In" to the weekly sprint planning meeting.

**Implementation:**

1. **Initial Push (AD):**

    - Andre messaged the team: "Hey, let's try something—30 seconds of silence before our next sprint planning to just be present. If you're okay, share one feeling after."

    - Some teammates teased at first, but agreed to try.

2. **First Drop-In (SA):**

    - During next Monday's 10:00 AM meeting, no one spoke for 30 seconds. When Andre nudged, "Any feelings?", a few softly said, "Anxious," "Tired," "Concerned." Sophie murmured "Sad," surprising others, including manager Jenna.

3. **Empathy Response & Ripple Effect:**

- After spotting Sophie's pain, Jenna said: "I'm sorry you're feeling sad, Sophie. If you need a break today, just let me know."
- Sophie, taken aback by genuine concern, disclosed in private after the meeting: "My mom's been in the hospital; I didn't feel I could say anything." Manager approved a half-day off for her to visit.

4. **Routine Establishment & Expansion:**
   - The team kept the Presence Drop-In weekly. Soon, a "Weekly Empathy Micro-Break" was introduced—team members took two minutes mid-week to share a supportive message in a "#empathy" Slack channel.
   - They also instituted a monthly "Lunch & Vulnerability" (SA)—an hour-long breakout where each could share deeper concerns.

## Outcome:

- **Improved Morale & Productivity:** Within two months, Sophie's performance recovered; the team's average sprint velocity improved by 15%.
- **Enhanced Empathetic Culture:** Team members reported feeling psychologically safer—"I can mention family issues without fear."
- **Long-Term Practices:** Even as the company grew, the rituals persisted. New hires were taught the Presence Drop-In, preserving the culture of reconnection.

---

## Vignette 3: "Neighborhood ReconneXion: From Strangers to Support" (Community Initiative)

### Background:

- **Setting:** Oakwood is an urban neighborhood where transient residents and urban development created social fragmentation. Many neighbors felt alone, and community programs were sporadic.
- **Problem:** A spate of burglaries and rising petty crime led to fear and mistrust. Residents locked doors, avoided communal areas, and seldom spoke beyond cursory "hello."

### Challenge:

- Despite shared physical proximity, emotional distances loomed large. There was no unified space for vulnerability, empathy, or intentional neighborly connection.

**Ritual Intervention:**

- Inspired by ReconneXion's "Anonymous Vulnerability Café" (Section X.VI.32) and "Community Vulnerability Mural" (Section V.B.3), a small volunteer coalition organized a neighborhood-wide initiative.

**Implementation:**

1. **Anonymous Vulnerability Kiosk Installation (SA):**
   - With local artists, volunteers installed a large, decorated bulletin board in the community center lobby—dubbed "Oakwood's Wall of Voices."
   - Residents were invited to drop anonymous notes: "I feel unsafe walking my dog at night," "I lost my job and am scared I can't pay rent," "I wish neighbors said hello more."

2. **Weekly Vulnerability Café (SA + AD):**
   - Every Thursday 6:00–8:00 PM, the community center opened for the "Oakwood Vulnerability Café."
   - Residents took turns reading anonymous notes aloud, then silent reflection followed by a short group empathy-sharing (SA micro-breaks of 2–3 minutes).
   - Facilitators, including local clergy and school teachers, curated each session with a "Vulnerability Theme" (e.g., "Fear & Security," "Hope & Renewal").

3. **Community Mural Project (SA + AA):**
   - Over two weekends, neighbors co-created a 30-foot vulnerability mural on a boarded-up storefront—each painted a panel depicting their personal struggles and hopes (seeds, open hands, silhouettes). Underneath each panel, volunteers wrote the core message from their anonymous note (in simplified, respectful wording).
   - A community "Unveiling Ceremony" followed—loud applause, reading of a unifying "Oakwood Declaration": "We stand together in our vulnerabilities."

4. **Credentialed "Oakwood Empathy Ambassadors" Program (SD + SA):**
    - Volunteers trained as Ambassadors, earning badges, committed to check in weekly with random neighbors, offering an empathetic ear and practical help (grocery runs, dog walks).
    - Each Ambassador logged visits in an AD spreadsheet to track community needs, ensuring no one was overlooked.

5. **Monthly "Neighborhood Insight Newsletter" (AD + AA):**
    - A compiled AA PDF summarizing Café themes, mural updates, and stories of neighborly support. Distributed via email and printed copies posted at key locales (libraries, coffee shops).

**Outcome:**

- **Crime & Fear Reduction:** Within six months, community surveys indicated fear of walking alone at night dropped from 72% to 38%; local police reported a 25% reduction in petty crime.

- **Social Cohesion Metrics:** New neighborhood events cropped up—book clubs, shared gardening days, "Block Pizza Parties."

- **Sustained Rituals:** The Vulnerability Café continues twice monthly; the mural is maintained and expanded with "growth rings" representing new stories. Ambassadors remain active, and the newsletter enjoys high readership (80% of households).

# XIII. Conclusion: Ritualized ReconneXion as the Fabric of Everlasting Friendship

This chapter has endeavored to weave together the rich theoretical and practical threads of ReconneXion Theory into an **exhaustive array of rituals**—from fleeting daily morning calls to expansive quarterly retreats, tailored adaptations for families, couples, remote groups, and community action. Each ritual, in its modality, depth, timing, and structure, is an invitation: to show up fully, act purposefully, listen empathetically, and dare to be vulnerable. When Rituals become second nature—when they are no longer tasks but ingrained reflexes—they transform the **architecture of friendship** from precarious connections into **resilient bonds** that withstand time, distance, and life's constant churn.

By now, readers possess not merely a smattering of ideas but a **comprehensive Compendium of Rituals**—over seventy distinct practices spanning everyday life, special occasions, life transitions, and contextual adaptations. Each ritual is annotated with step-by-step guidance, timing, adaptive variants, technological integrations, measurement tools, and strategies to navigate or prevent pitfalls. Whether one is a pair of friends separated by continents, a 20-person corporate team seeking greater psychological safety, a newly married couple blending intimacy with friendship, or a community facing collective challenges—ReconneXion's insights have been grounded in **actionable, measurable, and deeply human rituals**.

Yet, making rituals count demands **ongoing reflection, flexibility, and courage**. It requires resisting the ossification of practices into mere choreographed motions. Instead, one must guard against ritual burnout, remain attentive to shifting life seasons, recalibrate modalities when imbalanced, and embrace imperfection as a pathway to genuine connection. The provided measurement dashboards, audits, and reflective question repositories ensure that friendships evolve intentionally, guided by data and empathy, rather than meandering in autopilot.

As this chapter concludes, the **cumulative invitation** is clear: let ReconneXion's daily, weekly, monthly, and special occasion rituals serve as the spiritual sinews knitting our hearts to those we love. Let each morning's breathing together, each "silent gratitude pause" before a meeting, each monthly health check, and each bereavement circle be an act of relational courage. For in embedding these reconnection rituals into the mundane and the monumental, we transcend the hollow hum of digital chatter and rediscover friendship as a deliberate, living art—one that echoes through years and generations.

**Chapter 13**, titled **"Sustaining ReconneXion Through Life's Seasons: From Youth to Elderhood"**, will explore how these rituals adapt across biographic arcs—childhood friendships, teenage bonds, midlife reconnections, and friendships in elder years—ensuring that ReconneXion's principles remain robust in every chapter of life's unfolding narrative. Until then, may your daily cups of coffee, your evening reflections, and your spontaneous phone calls be suffused with Presence, guided by Intentionality, warmed by Empathy, and rooted in Vulnerability—transforming every moment into a stepping stone of lasting, living connection.

## Chapter 13
### Sustaining ReconneXion Through Life's Seasons: From Youth to Elderhood

> "Friendship is the living thread that weaves through the tapestry of our lives, adapting its hues as we journey from dawn to dusk."

# I. Introduction: The Arc of Friendship Across a Lifetime

While earlier chapters have provided a compendium of rituals woven into daily, weekly, and milestone moments, true mastery of ReconneXion requires an appreciation of **life's seasons**—from the boundless curiosity of childhood, through the upheavals of adolescence, the forging of adult identity, midlife transitions, and into the reflective years of elderhood. Each season brings unique relational landscapes, developmental needs, and environmental constraints. In **Chapter 13**, we explore how to **adapt ReconneXion's modalities, pillars, and rituals** so that friendships not only endure but flourish through every stage of personal evolution.

We will examine:

1. **Childhood & Early Adolescence (Ages 6–12):** Introducing simple analog/digital balance and foundational empathy skills.

2. **Teenage Years (Ages 13–19):** Navigating identity formation, privacy boundaries, and peer-group complexities.

3. **Young Adulthood (Ages 20–35):** Balancing emerging independence, career-building, and long-distance maintenance.

4. **Midlife (Ages 36–55):** Managing heavy life responsibilities—careers, parenting, aging parents—while preserving emotional availability.

5. **Senior Years (56+):** Fostering intergenerational bonds, adapting rituals for shifting energy and mobility, and leveraging legacy-building.

6. **Cross-Generational Friendships:** Strategies for youthful and elder friends to learn reciprocity and mutual enrichment.

7. **Adjusting Modalities & Depth:** How each stage favors particular modalities (SA vs. AD) and depth levels, and how to compensate for imbalances.

8. **Seasonal Audit Calendars:** A framework for checking in on friendship health at key life transitions—school graduations, career pivots, retirements, bereavements.

9. **Case Vignettes:** Three illustrative stories showcasing reconneXion across life's seasons.

By the end of this chapter, readers will possess **age- and context-sensitive rituals**, reflective prompts, and adaptive guidelines to ensure that ReconneXion remains a living, breathing practice—reshaped by time's passage but rooted in human connection's timeless core.

# II. Childhood & Early Adolescence (Ages 6–12)

Friendships at this stage often center on play, shared activities, and concrete expressions of care. While children may lack deep self-reflection skills, they can learn foundational empathy, presence, and simple rituals that scaffold emotional intelligence.

## A. Key Developmental Considerations

- **Short Attention Spans:** Rituals must be brief and playful.
- **Concrete Thinking:** Abstract emotional prompts should be grounded in tangible experiences.
- **Adult Facilitation:** Parents, teachers, or mentors guide and model reconnection.

## B. Foundational Rituals

### 1. "Playful Check-In Circle" (SA, 5 minutes)

- **When:** Start of recess or playdate.
- **How:** Children stand in a circle and pass around a "Feeling Ball" (soft toy). Whoever holds the ball names one feeling word ("happy," "sad," "excited").
- **Why:** Builds basic SL–SA awareness and presence.

### 2. "Empathy Story Swap" (SA + AA, 10 minutes)

- **When:** After class or during snack time.
- **How:** Pairs of children draw a simple comic strip (AA) of a moment they felt a strong emotion. Partners then explain their drawings to each other (SA).
- **Why:** Introduces reflective listening and validates feelings.

### 3. "Kindness Tokens" (AA + AD)

- **When:** Anytime at home or school.
- **How:** Provide small tokens (stickers, wooden beads). When a child does a kind act (shares a toy, helps clean up), peers give them a token. Tokens collected earn a group

treat.

- **Why:** Encourages intentionality and deposits in emotional bank accounts.

## C. Adult-Guided Reflection

- **Weekly "Emotion Spotlight":** Teacher selects one token-giver each week to share why they performed their act, modeling vulnerability and celebration.

- **Parent-Child "Mirror Affirmation":** Before bedtime, parents encourage a one-sentence affirmation ("I am kind because I shared my crayons") and note one small worry ("I was nervous to join the new class").

# III. Teenage Years (Ages 13–19)

Adolescence introduces identity exploration, social hierarchies, and emotional volatility. Rituals must respect growing autonomy while fostering trust and deeper empathy.

## A. Key Developmental Considerations

- **Heightened Privacy Needs:** Teens may resist overt rituals; opt for more subtle, teen-led formats.

- **Peer Influence:** Group norms shape willingness to participate.

- **Digital Natives:** Comfortable with AD/SD modalities but risk overuse of superficial social media.

## B. Adapted Rituals

### 1. "Anonymous Confession Board" (AA, Ongoing)

- **How:** In a physical location (locker room wall) or private group chat with anonymous posting enabled, teens share one worry or challenge.

- **Follow-Up:** Weekly, a trusted peer facilitator reads recurring themes and invites anyone struggling to join a small SD or in-person support circle.

2. **"Playlist Exchange & Reflection" (AD + SD)**
   - **How:** In friend groups of 3–5, each teen curates a five-song playlist representing their current mood. They share it via streaming service (AD).
   - **Ritual:** Once a week, they meet on a group video call (SD) or in person (SA), play one song each, and explain why they chose it, practicing vulnerability.

3. **"Digital Detox Hour" (SA + AA)**
   - **When:** Weekend afternoons.
   - **How:** A group of friends commits to one screen-free hour—playing board games, drawing, or walking. Afterward, they write in personal journals (AA) about what they noticed in themselves and each other, then optionally share two sentences in a secure group chat (AD).

## C. Boundary and Safety Checks

- **Consent Culture:** Teens set clear rules about what's safe to share and what remains private.
- **Adult Allyship:** A designated adult (counselor, coach) holds an open-door policy for deeper teen vulnerabilities flagged via the confession board or playlists.

---

# IV. Young Adulthood (Ages 20–35)

This stage often involves geographic moves, career building, and shifting friend circles. Rituals must balance independence with maintenance of core friendships.

## A. Key Developmental Considerations

- **Life Transitions:** University to workforce, relationships, relocations.
- **Time Scarcity:** Busy schedules demand flexible modalities.
- **Digital Reliance:** AD and SD are default but need depth calibration.

## B. Core Rituals

1. **"Quarter-Life Audit" (SD + AA)**

   - **How:** Once every six months, small friend groups complete a digital AA workbook covering chapters I–VI questions: modality balance, depth distribution, emotional bank balances.

   - **Synchronous Review:** Host a 90-minute SD call to debrief and set new intentions (e.g., scheduling one SA meetup per quarter).

2. **"Surprise Care Package Chain" (AA + AD)**

   - **How:** Each month, one friend mails a small care package—handwritten note, local snack—to the next friend in a rotating chain. Package contents include a question card prompting deeper sharing ("What's one dream you're afraid to chase?").

   - **Why:** Integrates AA with intentional vulnerability prompts.

3. **"Micro-Travel Rituals" (SA + AD)**

   - **How:** For friends traveling to new cities, coordinate a micro-ritual: meet at a local landmark for a 30-minute "Presence Walk," then each texts a 2-sentence reflection ("Walking by the river reminded me of our college days") once they return home.

## C. Sustaining Long-Distance Bonds

- **Shared Digital Calendar:** Block recurring slots for rituals—morning calls, weekend micro-retreats.

- **'Ritual Champions':** Rotate responsibility for scheduling and sending reminders.

- **Annual In-Person Gathering:** A yearly SA retreat (one weekend) for deeper reconnection.

---

# V. Midlife (Ages 36–55)

Midlife brings cumulative responsibilities—peak career demands, parenting, caregiving. Emotional reserves can feel depleted, making rituals critical for sustaining deep bonds.

## A. Key Developmental Considerations

- **Role Overload:** Juggling work, children, aging parents.
- **Time Compression:** Weekends and early mornings become prime ritual windows.
- **Emotional Strain:** Higher risk of burnout; empathy rituals help buffer stress.

## B. Priority Rituals

### 1. "Morning Partner Pulse" (SA + SD)

- **Who:** Couples or close dyads.
- **How:** Five-minute morning check-in—alternating SL question ("What's on your schedule?") with a DL prompt ("What's one worry you want my support with today?"). Can be SA over coffee or SD voice note if apart.

### 2. "Parent-Family Huddle Lite" (SA, Twice Weekly)

- **How:** A 10-minute evening huddle with children: one "Rose" (highlight), one "thorn" (challenge), one "bud" (tomorrow's hope). Adults model vulnerability by sharing theirs first and listening attentively.

### 3. "Midweek Micro-Retreat" (AD + SA)

- **How:** One weekday evening, partner with one friend for a 30-minute activity—walk, museum visit after hours, or cooking together. Followed by a shared AD reflection ("Today's micro-retreat felt like a reset").

## C. Preventing Compassion Fatigue

- **Self-Compassion Bursts:** Short solo mirror affirmations and micro-breathing breaks inserted during the day.
- **Peer Buddy System:** Assign one friend as accountability partner for checking in on emotional well-being.

# VI. Senior Years (56+)

In elderhood, friendships provide vital social support, purpose, and joy. Adapted rituals honor physical limitations and leverage legacy-building.

## A. Key Developmental Considerations

- **Mobility Constraints:** SA rituals may be shorter or adapted (indoor gatherings).
- **Desire for Legacy:** Many wish to share life stories, impart wisdom.
- **Technology Barriers:** Need gentle onboarding to SD/AD modalities.

## B. Enriching Rituals

### 1. "Stories of Self Circle" (SA + AD)

- **How:** Monthly in-person or SD gatherings where each elder shares a 10-minute life story vignette around a theme ("My happiest childhood memory," "A lesson I learned the hard way"). Listeners practice reflective listening and record brief AA summary notes.

### 2. "Intergenerational Pen Pals" (AA)

- **How:** Pair seniors with younger adults or teens as pen pals—handwritten letters exchanged monthly, featuring vulnerability prompts ("What are you afraid of?" "What wisdom can you share?"). Builds cross-generational empathy.

### 3. "Memory Photo Collages" (SA + AA)

- **How:** Quarterly workshops where friends assemble photo collages of life milestones. Each image sparks a shared DL conversation—"That lake trip was when I realized life's fragility."

## C. Leveraging Technology

- **Simplified SD Platforms:** Use one-touch video-call devices or group-chat tablets with large icons.
- **Voice-Activated Journaling:** Enable voice-to-text journaling apps so elders can record reflections without typing.

## VII. Cross-Generational Friendships

These friendships blend the energy of youth with the wisdom of age. Rituals must foster mutual respect, openness, and tailored depth.

### A. Foundational Principles

1. **Mutual Curiosity:** Encourage both parties to learn from each other.
2. **Balanced Vulnerability:** Adapt prompts so that neither side feels patronized.
3. **Customized Modalities:** Often SA or SD with shared activities (gardening, storytelling).

### B. Ritual Examples

#### 1. "Wisdom & Wonder Walks" (SA)

- **How:** Pairs walk together—one shares a current life wonder (youth), the other shares a life lesson (elder). Each listens and later writes a two-line AA reflection for the other.

#### 2. "Skill Swap Sessions" (SD + SA)

- **How:** Younger friend teaches the elder a digital skill (setting up a podcast), elder teaches the younger a legacy craft (knitting, woodworking). Each session ends with a 5-minute empathy check-in: "How did it feel to teach/learn today?"

## VIII. Life-Season Audit Calendars

A simplified **Life-Season Audit Framework** helps friends schedule checkpoints aligned with major transitions:

| Life Season | Audit Cadence | Focus Areas | Suggested Rituals |
|---|---|---|---|
| Childhood/Early Adolescence | Quarterly (School Terms) | Empathy basics, play-based presence | Playful Check-In Circle; Kindness Tokens |

| | | | |
|---|---|---|---|
| Teenage Years | Semesterly | Identity, peer support, digital balance | Confession Board; Playlist Exchange |
| Young Adulthood | Biannual | Modality balance, long-distance maintenance | Quarter-Life Audit; Care Package Chain |
| Midlife | Quarterly | Burnout prevention, family dynamics | Morning Partner Pulse; Parent Huddle Lite |
| Senior Years | Quarterly | Legacy-sharing, mobility-friendly connection | Stories of Self Circle; Pen Pals |
| Across All Seasons (Context) | Annual | Major transitions—graduations, retirements, relocations | Moving Time Capsule; Transition Support Rituals |

# IX. Vignettes: ReconneXion Across the Ages

### A. "Schoolyard to Lifelong Bond"

**Friends:** Maya and Lex met at age 8. Their childhood "Playful Check-In Circles" made way for teenage "Playlist Exchanges," then young adulthood "Quarter-Life Audits" when Maya moved overseas. Now both retirees, they share monthly "Stories of Self" over SD calls, their friendship's rituals evolving but never breaking.

### B. "A Teen and Her Mentor"

**Friends:** Seventeen-year-old Amir and his 68-year-old neighbor, Mr. Patel. They initiated an "Intergenerational Pen Pal" ritual—monthly letters sparked deep DL discussions in person, while "Wisdom & Wonder Walks" cemented mutual trust. Through life's seasons, each served as the other's sounding board and guide.

### C. "Midlife Mom's Micro-Retreats"

**Friends:** A group of four women in their mid-40s juggling careers and young kids. They instituted Friday "Micro-Retreats"—a two-hour SA co-working café session with childcare swaps, followed by AD gratitude notes. Over three years, these rituals sustained their deep bonds and emotional well-being.

# X. Conclusion: Friendship as a Lifetime Practice

ReconneXion is not a one-size-fits-all program but a **life-long art**, demanding flexibility, creativity, and unwavering commitment. By tailoring rituals to each life stage—addressing developmental needs, environmental constraints, and evolving depths—we ensure that our friendships remain **living, breathing entities**, capable of weathering distance, transitions, and time itself.

As you close this chapter, consider mapping your own **Life-Season Audit Calendar**, selecting three rituals from each season above to pilot in your circles. Whether you're teaching a child empathy through a "Feeling Ball," guiding a teen through an "Anonymous Confession Board," co-creating a "Moving Time Capsule," or sharing a "Stories of Self" circle with neighbors, remember: every ritual, no matter how small, is a **declaration of presence, intentionality, empathy, and vulnerability**—the timeless pillars that anchor the heart of friendship across the entire human journey.

Chapter 14
 From Dyads to Communities: Scaling ReconneXion Across Groups, Organizations, and Societies

> "Friendship is both the spark of individual connection and the wildfire of collective belonging."

---

# I. Introduction: The Imperative and Opportunity of Collective ReconneXion

Thus far, ReconneXion Theory has guided us through deeply personal, dyadic, and small-group rituals, adapted across life's seasons. Yet the transformative power of intentional presence, empathy, vulnerability, and purpose extends far beyond pairs or quartets—it scales. **Chapter 14** addresses how to **institutionalize ReconneXion across larger communities**, from families of ten to companies of thousands, neighborhoods, educational institutions, and even civic bodies. We explore how to:

1. **Define Community ReconneXion:** What collective friendship looks like at scale.

2. **Frameworks for Group Modality & Depth Balance:** Extending the four modalities and depth continuum to multi-person contexts.

3. **Core Community Ritual Categories:** Daily connectors, weekly forums, monthly assemblies, annual convocations, and unforeseen solidarity actions.

4. **Organizational Embedding:** Best practices for workplaces, schools, NGOs, religious communities, and civic groups.

5. **Leadership & Facilitation Models:** Training ambassadors, forming reconneXion councils, and ensuring inclusive governance.

6. **Measurement & Feedback Systems:** Dashboards, surveys, participatory ethnography, and real-time sentiment tracking.

7. **Technology Platforms & Infrastructure:** From simple group chats to bespoke reconnection apps, digital whiteboards, and AI-guided facilitation.

8. **Policy & Cultural Strategies:** Aligning institutional policies, codes of conduct, and reward structures to reinforce reconnection values.

9. **Case Studies:** Four vivid examples of communities transformed by ReconneXion.

10. **Managing Scale-Specific Pitfalls:** Ritual fatigue, clique formation, anonymity erosion, power imbalances, and multi-modality overload.

11. **Sustainability & Evolution:** Keeping community reconnection alive through leadership transitions, demographic shifts, and evolving challenges.

By chapter's end, readers—whether community organizers, HR professionals, educators, or civic leaders—will possess a **blueprint** for **designing, implementing, and sustaining** reconnection at any scale, ensuring that intentional friendship becomes a **collective fabric** in our homes, workplaces, and societies.

---

# II. Defining Community ReconneXion

## A. Beyond the Dyad: Dimensions of Collective Connection

While dyadic friendship thrives on mutual presence and vulnerability, communities require:

1. **Networked Presence:** Ensuring each member feels seen, even among many.

2. **Distributed Intentionality:** Shared purpose and agreed-upon goals that transcend individual agendas.

3. **Collective Empathy:** Mechanisms to surface and respond to group members' emotional states at scale.

4. **Safety for Vulnerability:** Guaranteeing psychologically safe spaces so that individuals feel secure sharing even in large settings.

## B. The Community Modality Matrix

We generalize the four modalities—Synchronous Digital (SD), Asynchronous Digital (AD), Synchronous Analog (SA), Asynchronous Analog (AA)—into organizational contexts:

| Modality | Examples in Communities |
| --- | --- |
| SD | All-hands video calls, live town halls, moderated group chats |
| AD | Email newsletters, forum posts, digital bulletin boards |
| SA | In-person assemblies, walking meetups, "hallway" drop-bys |
| AA | Newsletters, printed memoir walls, care-package drives |

## C. Community Depth Continuum

We scale the depth continuum across group sizes:

- **Level 1 (Surface-Level Broadcast):** Announcements, updates, logistical notices.
- **Level 2 (Surface-Level Interaction):** Polls, casual Q&A, icebreaker games.
- **Level 3 (Moderate-Level Discussion):** Themed breakout rooms, panel discussions, reflection circles.
- **Level 4 (Deep-Level Sharing):** Storytelling circles, vulnerability workshops, peer-support groups.

- **Level 5 (Transformative Depth):** Collective ritual performances, confessional assemblies, multi-day retreats.

---

# III. Core Community Ritual Categories

## A. Daily Connectors

**Purpose:** Maintain ongoing micro-connections that prevent drift and foster a continuous sense of belonging.

1. **"Morning Community Pulse" (SD/AD):**
   - A 2-minute pre-recorded video or voice snippet from rotating ambassadors, sharing one appreciative observation and one daily intention for the group. Delivered via email, Slack, or community app at daybreak.

2. **"Micro-Gratitude Threads" (AD):**
   - A persistent online forum where members drop one-line gratitudes about others each day. Gamified with "gratitude badges" for frequent contributors.

3. **"Watercooler Pop-Ups" (SA):**
   - Designated 5-minute unstructured meetups—physical or virtual—scheduled randomly twice per day for group members to spontaneously congregate and chat.

## B. Weekly Forums

**Purpose:** Provide structured space for reflection, feedback, and empathy-building on issues of the week.

1. **"Community Huddle" (SA + SD):**
   - A weekly 30-minute all-hands meeting:
     - **5 min Presence Drop-In:** Silent centering or breathing.

- **10 min Highlights & Lowlights:** Rapid round-robin of one "win" and one "challenge."
- **10 min Themed Deep Question:** Pre-selected prompt from a "Community Question Bank."
- **5 min Closing Intentions:** One pledge each.

2. **"Pulse Surveys" (AD):**
   - Midweek, members receive a quick 3-question survey measuring connection, support, and workload. Automated dashboards update in real-time for leadership and ambassadors.

## C. Monthly Assemblies

**Purpose:** Dive deeper into emerging themes, share long-form stories, and recalibrate community commitments.

1. **"Story Salon" (SA):**
   - An in-person or hybrid evening event where members sign up to share a 10-minute personal story on a monthly theme. Listeners practice "reflective listening pairs" post-sharing.

2. **"Community Audit Workshop" (SD + AA):**
   - A structured session where subgroups analyze modality usage, depth distribution, and emotional bank metrics, using interactive digital whiteboards. They propose adjustments to next month's rituals.

3. **"Recognition & Ritual Renewal" (SA + AD):**
   - Collective celebration of "Ritual Champions" (those who carried initiatives), followed by an AD "Ritual Survey" to vote on retiring, tweaking, or introducing rituals for the coming month.

## D. Annual Convocations

**Purpose:** Mark major achievements, solidify long-term vision, and induct new members into the reconnection culture.

1. **"Annual ReconneXion Festival" (SA):**
   - A multi-day gathering featuring:
     - **Opening Grounding Ceremony:** Shared ritual (silent circle, communal artwork).
     - **Skill-Building Tracks:** Empathy labs, vulnerability workshops, leadership panels.
     - **Collective Art Installation:** Community contributes to evolving artwork embodying the year's theme.

2. **"Legacy & Launch" Ceremony (SA + AA):**
   - Honoring departing members' contributions and onboarding newcomers with "Friendship Contracts" that outline mutual commitments and shared expectations.

## E. Unforeseen Solidarity Actions

**Purpose:** Rapid-response rituals that surface when communities face collective crises or triumphs—disasters, social justice moments, major wins.

1. **"24-Hour Solidarity Chain" (SD + AD + SA):**
   - In emergencies, each member commits to a 15-minute Presence module—phone calls, letters, supply drops—to another member or subgroup, forming a continuous human chain of support.

2. **"Community Pulse Vigil" (SA):**
   - When collective trauma strikes, swift convening in safe spaces (physical or virtual) for silent presence, short shared reflections, and opportunities for immediate emotional first-aid.

# IV. Organizational Embedding

## A. Workplaces

1. **Integrating ReconneXion into Company DNA**

    - **Onboarding Programs:** New hires undergo a "ReconneXion Orientation," learning core modalities, community rituals, and their first "Ritual Pledge."

    - **Performance Reviews:** Include "Connection KPIs"—peer-raised gratitude counts, empathy contributions, participation in reconnection forums.

    - **Physical Spaces:** Design "Reconnection Zones" in offices—quiet rooms for AA journaling, open pods for SA huddles, video rooms optimized for SD presence.

    - **Digital Ecosystem:** A unified community app hosting AD forums, event calendars, pulse surveys, and AI-driven ritual reminders.

2. **Leadership & Culture**

    - **C-Level Sponsorship:** Executive sponsors model reconnection by leading monthly Story Salons and recognition ceremonies.

    - **ReconneXion Council:** A cross-functional group that curates rituals, monitors engagement, and refreshes practices annually.

## B. Educational Institutions

### 1. K–12 Schools

- **Daily Check-Ins:** Homeroom teachers facilitate "Feeling Circles" each morning to ground students in SA presence.

- **Peer-Mentorship Networks:** Upperclass students trained as "Empathy Ambassadors" conduct weekly AD reflections with underclass cohorts.

- **Family Engagement:** Monthly "Family ReconneXion Nights" where parents join SA workshops on digital balance and shared empathy-building activities with their children.

### 2. Universities & Colleges

- **Residential ReconneXion Floors:** Living-learning communities organized by reconnection themes—participants commit to shared rituals: weekly Story Salons, daily micro-gratitude boards.

- **Learning Outcomes:** Incorporate ReconneXion Theory into curricula—courses on empathy, group dynamics, and digital well-being.

## C. Nonprofits & NGOs

- **Volunteer Onboarding:** Embed reconnection rituals—morning intention huddles, AD peer-support forums—to sustain volunteer resilience and reduce burnout.
- **Donor Engagement:** Monthly Story Salons featuring beneficiary narratives, strengthening donor empathy and long-term commitment.

## D. Religious & Spiritual Communities

- **Interfaith ReconneXion Circles:** Facilitated SA gatherings where members from diverse traditions share vulnerabilities and spiritual hopes.
- **Digital Liturgy Augmentation:** AD platforms broadcast daily reconnection prompts—scriptural reflections tied to empathy practices and community acts of service.

## E. Civic & Neighborhood Organizations

- **Block-Level Rituals:** "Porch Chat" meetups scheduled weekly to foster SA neighbor presence; AD neighborhood newsletters highlight Gratitude Spotlights and upcoming communal rituals.
- **Local Government Integration:** Town councils allocate time for "Public Presence Check-Ins" at meetings—30-second silent centering and citizen highlight rounds.

# V. Leadership & Facilitation Models

## A. ReconneXion Ambassadors & Councils

1. **Ambassador Roles:**
    - **Ritual Keeper:** Ensures scheduled rituals occur, updates event calendars.

- **Empathy Champion:** Monitors pulse data, identifies members in need of support.
- **Inclusion Advocate:** Tracks participation diversity, ensures marginalized voices surface.

2. **Council Structure:**
   - Elected every year by community vote.
   - Meets monthly to review dashboards, propose new rituals, retire old ones.

## B. Training & Certification

1. **ReconneXion Facilitation Certification:**
   - Modular training on Empathy Labs, Vulnerability Circles, Community Audits.
   - Capstone projects implementing a new ritual and reporting impact.

2. **Peer Coaching Networks:**
   - New ambassadors paired with veterans for six months of mentoring, co-facilitating rituals.

## C. Distributed Leadership

- **Rotating Hosts:** Ritual leadership rotates to prevent burnout and ensure fresh perspectives.
- **Subgroup Autonomy:** Sub-communities (departments, interest groups) granted autonomy to tailor rituals, reporting back to the ReconneXion Council.

# VI. Measurement & Feedback Systems

## A. Multi-Level Dashboards

1. **Individual Metrics:**

    - Ritual participation counts, empathy contributions logged, AD forum engagement.
 2. **Team/Unit Metrics:**
    - Modality distribution pie charts, depth heatmaps, emotional bank account trends per team.
 3. **Organizational Metrics:**
    - Aggregated connection satisfaction index, ritual adherence rates, turnover correlation with reconnection engagement.

### B. Qualitative Feedback Mechanisms

1. **Ethnographic "Listening Posts":** Trained observers attend rituals, gather stories, identify hidden friction points.
2. **Focus Groups:** Quarterly facilitated discussions probing ritual relevance, cultural fit, and emerging needs.
3. **Open-Ended Pulse Surveys:** Invite narrative responses, later coded for thematic analysis.

### C. Real-Time Sentiment Tracking

- **Natural Language Processing (NLP):** Analyze group chat and forum posts for emotional tone shifts, surfacing spikes in anxiety or frustration.
- **Wearable Integration (Optional):** For voluntary programs, aggregate anonymized heart-rate variability data during SA rituals to gauge group stress reduction.

# VII. Technology Platforms & Infrastructure

## A. ReconneXion App Suites

1. **Core Features:**
   - **Ritual Scheduler:** Syncs with calendars, issues reminders.

- **Pulse Surveys & Dashboards:** Embedded analytics, real-time alerts.
- **Story Salon Booking:** Sign-up, video streaming, transcription.
- **Gratitude Wall & Confession Board:** AD forums with anonymity options.

2. **AI Augmentation:**
   - **Prompt Generator:** Suggests empathy questions based on past conversation history.
   - **Facilitation Coach:** Provides real-time tips during SD rituals—timing cues, speaking order reminders.
   - **Sentiment Alerts:** Notifies ambassadors if group tone becomes unusually negative.

## B. Physical Space Design

- **Reconnection Zones:** Modular rooms with configurable lighting, acoustic panels, whiteboards, journaling stations, and video-conference setups.
- **Ritual Corners:** Smaller alcoves for 2–4 member micro-rituals—equipped with comfortable seating, low tables for AA activities.

## C. Integration with Existing Tools

- **Calendar & Email Platforms:** Plugins for ritual invites, auto-scheduling, and follow-up prompts.
- **Collaboration Suites:** Slack/Teams integrations—bot-driven "Ritual Reminders," "Gratitude GIFs," ephemeral "Presence Channels."
- **Learning Management Systems (LMS):** Host ReconneXion training modules, record certifications, track progress.

# VIII. Policy & Cultural Strategies

## A. Embedding in Codes of Conduct

- **Connection Charter:** A community-wide statement of values—commitment to presence, empathy, vulnerability, and intentionality—incorporated into onboarding and regular reinforcement.

- **Safe Disclosure Policies:** Clear guidelines protecting members who share vulnerabilities from negative repercussions.

## B. Reward & Recognition Structures

- **Reconnection Awards:** Annual or quarterly honors for "Empathy Ambassador of the Month," "Ritual Champion," "Community Connector."

- **Peer-Nominated Badges:** Digital tokens members award each other for extraordinary presence, support, or vulnerability.

## C. Resource Allocation

- **Budgeting for Rituals:** Allocating funds for community gatherings, digital platform subscriptions, ambassador stipends, and training programs.

- **Time Allotment:** Institutionalizing "Ritual Time" in work schedules—e.g., 15 minutes daily, 2 hours monthly reserved for reconnection.

# IX. Case Studies: Communities Transformed by ReconneXion

## Case Study 1: "Tech Startup Culture Reborn"

- **Context:** 200-employee SaaS startup plagued by high turnover and toxic stress.

- **Intervention:** Introduced daily "Morning 3×3" (three gratitudes, three intentions, three micro-vulnerabilities), weekly "Empathy Huddles," monthly "Founder Story Salons," and quarterly "Reconnection Hackathons."

- **Outcomes:**
  - 40% reduction in attrition over 12 months.

- Employee Engagement scores rose from 52 to 78.
- Reported psychological safety increased by 65%.

## Case Study 2: "University Residential Revival"

- **Context:** A 500-student dorm suffered from isolation and rising incidents of anxiety/depression.
- **Intervention:** Created "Friendship Floors" with mandated SA morning circles, AD "Anonymous Worry Walls," peer-led vulnerability workshops, and mid-semester "Community Retreats."
- **Outcomes:**
  - Counseling referrals for isolation dropped by 30%.
  - Average resident GPA increased by 0.3 points.
  - 85% of participants reported feeling stronger social support.

## Case Study 3: "Neighborhood Renewal in Oakwood Heights"

- **Context:** Urban neighborhood divided by socioeconomic tensions and mistrust.
- **Intervention:** See Chapter 13's vignette; scaled it city-wide via block reconnection ambassadors, mobile "Reconnection Trucks" hosting weekly pop-up circles, and city council-adopted "Public Presence Minutes" at meetings.
- **Outcomes:**
  - 25% decline in petty crime; neighbor-helping-neighbor metrics soared.
  - Local elections saw a 15% turnout increase, attributed to stronger civic bonds.

## Case Study 4: "National NGO Volunteer Network"

- **Context:** 3,000 volunteers dispersed globally experienced burnout and disengagement.
- **Intervention:** Launched global ReconneXion platform—AI-driven ritual personalization, monthly multilingual Story Salons, peer mentoring circles, and an annual in-person

"Volunteer Convergence."

- **Outcomes:**
    - Volunteer retention rose from 48% to 72%.
    - Program impact metrics improved by 22% due to higher volunteer satisfaction.
    - Cross-regional collaborations increased by 50%.

---

# X. Managing Scale-Specific Pitfalls

## Pitfall 1: "Ritual Overwhelm" in Large Groups

- **Symptom:** Members feel inundated by too many scheduled touchpoints; ritual fatigue ensues.
- **Mitigation:**
    1. **Ritual Menus:** Offer optional tracks—Core (daily micro-rituals) vs. Deep (monthly Story Salons, annual festivals).
    2. **Phasing & Pilot Programs:** Gradually introduce new rituals, pilot with small cohorts before scaling.

## Pitfall 2: "Clique & Exclusion" Dynamics

- **Symptom:** Subgroups dominate, leaving others isolated.
- **Mitigation:**
    1. **Rotating Groups:** Randomized assignment for small-group rituals to ensure cross-pollination.
    2. **Inclusion Audits:** ReconneXion Council monitors participation diversity, intervenes when participation skews.

## Pitfall 3: "Anonymity Erosion & Safety Breaches"

- **Symptom:** On "Anonymous" boards or forums, identities sometimes revealed or misused, undermining trust.

- **Mitigation:**

    1. **Strict Moderation Policies:** Moderators trained in confidentiality.

    2. **Technical Safeguards:** Platforms that auto-anonymize posts and prevent IP tracing.

### Pitfall 4: "Power Imbalance & Voice Silencing"

- **Symptom:** Senior or loud voices dominate deep-level discussions, silencing marginalized members.

- **Mitigation:**

    1. **Facilitator Training:** Equip leaders to call on quieter participants, manage dominant voices.

    2. **Structured Turn-Taking Tools:** Use digital "talking sticks" or timed rounds in SD and SA formats.

### Pitfall 5: "Technology Dependency"

- **Symptom:** Over-reliance on digital rituals reduces face-to-face presence.

- **Mitigation:**

    1. **Modality Quotas:** Minimum SA rituals per month mandated.

    2. **Tech Sabbaths:** Group-wide digital detox windows.

# XI. Sustainability & Evolution

## A. Ritual Lifecycles

- **Innovation Phase:** Piloting, prototyping new rituals.

- **Growth Phase:** Broadening participation, embedding in culture.
- **Maturity Phase:** Ritual becomes taken-for-granted; requires reinvigoration.
- **Renewal or Retirement:** Using community audits and surveys to decide whether to refresh, retire, or replace rituals.

## B. Leadership Transitions

- **Succession Planning:** Outgoing ambassadors mentor successors; compile "Ritual Playbooks" with history, lessons learned, and future recommendations.
- **Institutional Memory Preservation:** Maintain a central AA archive of ritual documentation, case studies, and iteration logs.

## C. Demographic & Cultural Shifts

- **Adaptive Inclusivity:** Regular cultural audits to ensure rituals respect evolving diversity—language, traditions, accessibility.
- **Global Localization:** For multinational communities, permit localized variants of core rituals that honor regional customs while maintaining global reconnection principles.

# XII. Concluding Reflections: The Collective Heartbeat of ReconneXion

Chapter 14 has charted a path from the intimate contours of individual friendship to the grand scales of organizational and societal connection. By **systematically adapting modalities, depth, leadership structures, measurement systems, and policy frameworks**, we transform ReconneXion from a personal ethos into a **powerhouse of collective well-being**—fuelling innovation, resilience, and shared purpose.

Whether you oversee a team of five, steward a neighborhood of thousands, or coordinate global volunteer networks, the principles remain steadfast:

1. **Presence at All Scales:** From a two-minute micro-huddle to an annual all-hands festival.

2. **Intentionality Embedded:** Through shared charters, ritual calendars, and programmed reminders.

3. **Empathy Amplified:** Via pulse surveys, Story Salons, and real-time sentiment tracking.

4. **Vulnerability Protected:** With safe anonymity protocols, trained facilitation, and formalized feedback loops.

Navigating the complexities of scale demands **flexible governance**, **iterative learning**, and **courageous leadership**. Yet as the case studies demonstrate, communities that dare to embed reconnection rituals reap dividends in trust, creativity, and collective resilience—becoming living expressions of humanity's deepest promise: that together, we flourish.

**Chapter 15**, titled **"The Future of ReconneXion: Integrating AI, Neuroscience, and Cultural Evolution"**, will peer beyond today's practices, envisioning how emerging technologies, brain-based insights, and shifting cultural paradigms can further enrich our friendship architectures—ensuring that ReconneXion Theory not only adapts to tomorrow but helps shape it. Until then, may your communities pulse with the rhythms of connection, may your rituals spark joy and mutual understanding, and may the tapestry of your shared humanity grow ever more vibrant.

# Chapter 15
## The Future of ReconneXion: Integrating AI, Neuroscience, and Cultural Evolution

> "Tomorrow's friendships will be shaped by our tools, our brains, and the culture we craft together."

---

# I. Introduction: Charting ReconneXion's Next Frontier

As ReconneXion Theory moves from applied rituals into the broader currents of technological innovation, neuroscientific discovery, and shifting cultural landscapes, we stand on the brink of a profound transformation. **Chapter 15** embarks on an exhaustive exploration of how **artificial intelligence**, **neuroscience**, and **cultural evolution** converge to redefine presence, empathy, vulnerability, and intentionality in friendship—both at the individual and collective levels. We will delve into:

1. **AI-Augmented Empathy & Presence:** From real-time sentiment analysis to generative conversational agents that scaffold deep connection.

2. **Neuroscientific Foundations & Biometrics:** Leveraging insights into mirror neurons, oxytocin dynamics, and neurofeedback to optimize reconnection.

3. **Cultural Evolution & Globalization:** How shifting norms around privacy, group identity, and digital expression reshape ritual design.

4. **Ethical Considerations & Privacy Safeguards:** Balancing powerful new capabilities with respect for autonomy, consent, and data protection.

5. **Interdisciplinary Synergies:** Integrating design thinking, behavioral economics, and anthropology into reconnection practices.

6. **Next-Generation Ritual Prototypes:** Imagining holographic gatherings, emotionally attuned avatars, and neuroadaptive group sessions.

7. **Implementation Roadmaps:** Guidelines for pilot projects, technology adoption, cross-sector partnerships, and scaling with human-centered leadership.

8. **Longitudinal Impact & Evaluation Models:** Frameworks for assessing relational well-being over years or decades using mixed-methods research.

9. **Global Case Vignettes & Thought Experiments:** How futuristic reconnection might look in smart cities, space habitats, and virtual metaverses.

10. **Conclusion & Call to Collective Imagination:** Urging readers to become active co-creators in ReconneXion's unfolding future.

This chapter exceeds all prior lengths, weaving comprehensive theoretical analysis with practical design, ethical rigor, and visionary storytelling—ensuring that ReconneXion remains at the leading edge of human connection in an ever-accelerating world.

---

# II. AI-Augmented Empathy & Presence

## A. Real-Time Emotional Intelligence

1. **Sentiment Analysis in Group Chats**
    - **Mechanism:** Natural language processing (NLP) algorithms scan text-based interactions (Slack, WhatsApp) to detect emotional valence, intensity, and topics of concern.

- **Application:** Automated "empathy nudges" prompt facilitators when negativity spikes or inclusion dips. For instance, if tension rises in a community forum, an AI bot might privately message moderators: "Your community chat's tone shifted toward frustration—consider deploying a reflective prompt."

2. **Voice & Video Emotion Recognition**

    - **Mechanism:** Computer vision and paralinguistic analysis interpret facial microexpressions, vocal tone changes, and speech patterns to estimate participants' emotional states.

    - **Application:** During synchronous video calls, an AI overlay discreetly indicates when a participant's stress indicators peak—enabling facilitators to pause, check in, or adjust pace. Conversely, peaks in warmth or mirroring can reinforce positive momentum.

3. **Predictive Well-Being Models**

    - **Mechanism:** Machine learning models integrate digital footprints (message frequency, response latency, sentiment trends) with optional self-reports to forecast risk of isolation or burnout.

    - **Application:** Communities receive proactive alerts—"Alice's engagement has dropped 40% week-over-week, and sentiment analysis shows increased negative language; consider an outreach ritual."

## B. Generative AI as Conversational Catalyst

1. **AI-Powered Icebreaker Prompts**

    - **Mechanism:** Large language models (LLMs) fine-tuned on community-specific data generate personalized conversation starters that resonate with individual preferences and shared history.

    - **Application:** When a group's weekly Story Salon lulls, a facilitator's dashboard suggests tailored deep-dive questions—e.g., "Kim, last month you spoke passionately about climate activism; would you share a recent moment that reignited your resolve?"

2. **Virtual Co-Presence Agents**

    - **Mechanism:** AI-driven avatars or chatbots co-participate in digital rituals, modeling empathic language, reflective listening, and vulnerability disclosures.

They adapt style to group norms, serving as "benchmarks" for human participants.

- **Application:** In a new ReconneXion pilot, a "Presence Bot" silently observes a micro-huddle and, at the end, offers a brief meta-reflection: "I noticed that whenever Jamal paused, peers waited attentively—beautiful presence in action."

3. **Personalized Reflection Summaries**

    - **Mechanism:** After asynchronous letter exchanges or voice journals, generative AI condenses content into thematic excerpts, highlighting recurring emotions, key commitments, and unanswered questions.

    - **Application:** A monthly AD digest arrives for each member: "Highlights from your January reflections: gratitude surged around 'team support'; you noted vulnerability regarding 'work–life balance' three times—consider scheduling a focused reconnection call."

## C. AI-Mediated Ritual Support

1. **Adaptive Ritual Scheduling**

    - **Mechanism:** AI analyzes calendar data, time-zone differences, and engagement patterns to optimize ritual timing—proposing windows that maximize attendance and energy alignment.

    - **Application:** The system recommends that the weekly "Community Huddle" shift from Tuesday 3 PM to Thursday 10 AM, based on peak active hours and lower conflict rates.

2. **Embodied VR/AR Ritual Spaces**

    - **Mechanism:** Virtual reality and augmented reality platforms host immersive reconnection rituals—spatial audio, shared environmental simulations, and AI-guided embodiment coaches.

    - **Application:** Teams don VR headsets for a monthly "Presence Pilgrimage"—a guided virtual nature walk with AI-generated environmental triggers (birdsong, rustling leaves), prompting participants to share micro-vulnerabilities at designated waypoints.

# III. Neuroscientific Foundations & Biometrics

## A. Mirror Neuron System & Empathy

1. **Neural Mirroring in Digital Contexts**

   - **Insight:** Mirror neurons fire both when we perform an action and when we observe it. High-fidelity video can engage similar neural circuits as in-person interaction, but attenuated by frame rate and gaze alignment.

   - **Application:** SD rituals emphasize eye-line calibration—participants position cameras at eye level and use eye-contact prompts ("look at the lens") to maximize mirroring engagement.

2. **Empathy Training via Neurofeedback**

   - **Mechanism:** Wearable EEG headbands provide real-time feedback on neural markers associated with empathic engagement (e.g., alpha/theta synchronization).

   - **Application:** During empathy micro-breaks, participants wear simple headbands; when neural indicators of attention wane, the system gently vibrates, cueing refocus. Over weeks, users train sustained empathic attention.

## B. Oxytocin, Trust, and Bonding

1. **Bio-Assays in Ritual Design**

   - **Insight:** Oxytocin release correlates with feelings of trust and social bonding. Activities involving physical touch or synchronized movement (walking together, group breathing) elevate oxytocin.

   - **Application:** SA rituals integrate synchronized breathing exercises and light, consensual touch (hand on shoulder) to catalyze bonding—particularly in new or large-group settings.

2. **Pharmacopsychological Augmentation (Experimental)**

   - **Research Frontier:** Studies in controlled settings examine low-dose intranasal oxytocin's effects on group trust exercises. Ethical protocols prohibit casual use, but insights inform non-pharmacological design—e.g., choice architecture to simulate proximity.

## C. Stress Regulation & Autonomic Balance

1. **Heart Rate Variability (HRV) Monitoring**

   - **Mechanism:** Wearable devices track HRV as a proxy for parasympathetic activation—higher HRV indicates calm, readiness for vulnerability.

   - **Application:** Before deep-sharing segments, participants check a communal HRV dashboard; if average HRV dips below threshold, the facilitator leads a brief grounding meditation.

2. **Polyvagal-Informed Ritual Sequencing**

   - **Insight:** The Polyvagal Theory emphasizes safe social engagement via activation of the ventral vagal pathway.

   - **Application:** Rituals begin with low-demand safety cues—soft lighting, gentle music, moderated pacing—before advancing to higher-intimacy vulnerability prompts, ensuring physiological readiness.

---

# IV. Cultural Evolution & Globalization

## A. Shifting Norms Around Privacy & Public Sharing

1. **Cultural Variability in Vulnerability**

   - **Insight:** Individualistic cultures may prize self-disclosure, whereas collectivist societies emphasize harmony and indirect expression. Rituals must adapt language and modes—a Japanese reconnection circle might use silent reflection followed by written notes rather than open vocal sharing.

2. **Digital Footprint Awareness**

   - **Challenge:** In a world where every message can be recorded and shared, participants may self-censor.

   - **Solution:** Implement "Ephemeral Sharing" options—messages and video streams that vanish after session end, boosting candidness while preserving safety.

## B. Emergence of Hybrid Digital-Traditional Cultures

1. **Neo-Analog Movements**

   - **Phenomenon:** A growing "analog resurgence" favors face-to-face, tactile experiences—handwritten letters, in-person gatherings—juxtaposed with digital tools.

   - **Application:** ReconneXion rituals can deliberately alternate high-tech and low-tech editions—one month using AI prompts and VR spaces, the next employing handwritten letter exchanges and neighborhood walks.

2. **Global Diaspora & Translocal Communities**

   - **Context:** Migrant populations form friendships across geographies, blending homeland customs with host-country influences.

   - **Application:** Rituals co-create multicultural fusion ceremonies—tying moon festivals, solstices, and local holidays into reconnection cycles that honor diverse heritages.

## C. Evolution of Group Identity & Belonging

1. **Fluid Social Structures**

   - **Trend:** Online affinity groups form around transient themes—hashtags, memes, micro-communities—challenging stable membership assumptions.

   - **Application:** ReconneXion frameworks offer "Ritual-On-Demand" modules: a suite of micro-rituals deployable within 24 hours for emergent groups (e.g., fans of a viral event) to quickly forge empathic ties.

2. **Ethics of Scale-Free Friendship**

   - **Consideration:** How to maintain depth when any individual can simultaneously belong to dozens of micro-communities?

   - **Solution:** Introduce "Depth Budget" concepts—allocating cognitive-emotional resources intentionally across commitments, supported by AI reminders to prioritize core reconnection channels.

# V. Ethical Considerations & Privacy Safeguards

## A. Consent & Autonomy in AI-Driven Rituals

1. **Informed Consent Protocols**

   - **Requirement:** Participants must understand which personal data (biometric, textual, audiovisual) they share, how it's used, who can access it, and for how long.

   - **Practice:** Before AI-integrated rituals, digital or analog consent forms are co-signed, with plain-language summaries and opt-in granular controls (e.g., "I consent to sentiment analysis but not to emotion-recognition in video").

2. **Right to Disconnect**

   - **Principle:** Individuals can withdraw from any AI-mediated monitoring at any time without penalty.

   - **Mechanism:** A universal "Disconnect Button" in community apps instantly suspends data collection for that user, and rituals adapt seamlessly to their absence.

## B. Data Governance & Security

1. **Anonymization & Aggregation**

   - **Standard:** Raw personal data is never stored without de-identification. Aggregated metrics and dashboards use group-level statistics only.

2. **Zero-Trust Architecture**

   - **Implementation:** Employ end-to-end encryption for all ritual communications; store biometric data locally on user devices unless explicit secondary consent is given for cloud storage.

## C. Equity & Bias Mitigation

1. **AI Fairness Audits**

   - **Action:** Regularly evaluate sentiment-analysis models for demographic biases—ensuring emotion recognition works accurately across ethnicities, age groups, and language varieties.

2. **Inclusive Ritual Design**
   - **Guideline:** Avoid culturally specific metaphors or references in prompts; instead, co-design with representative stakeholders to ensure global relevance.

---

# VI. Interdisciplinary Synergies

## A. Design Thinking & Human-Centered Design

1. **Empathy Mapping for Ritual Users**
   - **Tool:** Create detailed personas—mapping users' needs, frustrations, and contexts—to inform ritual prototypes that resonate emotionally and practically.

2. **Rapid Prototyping & Feedback Loops**
   - **Process:** Develop Minimum Viable Rituals (MVRs), deploy in micro-pilots, gather qualitative feedback, iterate, and scale.

## B. Behavioral Economics & Nudge Theory

1. **Choice Architecture in Ritual Adoption**
   - **Technique:** Default enroll participants in core rituals, while allowing easy opt-out—leveraging the power of defaults to boost engagement.

2. **Gamification & Loss Aversion**
   - **Approach:** Introduce small stakes—"Ritual Streaks," "Presence Points," and the possibility of "losing a streak" if skipped—to motivate consistency without undue pressure.

## C. Anthropology & Ethnography

1. **Cultural Contextualization**

- **Method:** Conduct participant-observation in diverse community settings to surface local meaning-making processes and inform ritual localization.

2. **Ritual Archaeology**
   - **Insight:** Study historical friendship rites—ancient vow circles, confessional guilds—to unearth time-tested elements adaptable to modern contexts.

---

# VII. Next-Generation Ritual Prototypes

## A. Holographic ReconneXion Assemblies

1. **Immersive Holograms**
   - **Vision:** Participants appear as life-sized holograms in shared physical spaces—blurring lines between digital and analog presence.
   - **Prototype Ritual:** Monthly "Holo-Huddle" where five global team members convene around a virtual table, each represented as a 3D projection, enabling natural gestures and eye contact.

## B. Emotionally Attuned Avatars

1. **AI-Driven Avatar Mirrors**
   - **Mechanism:** An avatar replicates a user's facial expressions and posture in real time, corrected for camera distortions, ensuring more accurate presence cues.
   - **Use Case:** In VR-based vulnerability workshops, participants interact through avatars that genuinely reflect microexpressions, reducing the sense of distance.

## C. Neuroadaptive Group Sessions

1. **Brain-State Synchronized Rituals**
   - **Mechanism:** Wearables share anonymized group neural states; when brain coherence peaks, the ritual transitions to deeper prompts; when coherence dips, the session shifts to grounding exercises.

- **Prototype:** A 45-minute SA/SD hybrid session that dynamically adapts the script based on collective neurofeedback—optimizing flow and connection.

# VIII. Implementation Roadmaps

## A. Pilot Project Blueprint

1. **Phase 1: Discovery & Stakeholder Alignment**
   - Map needs, identify champions, secure ethical approvals, define success metrics.

2. **Phase 2: Technology & Ritual Co-Design**
   - Collaboratively develop AI integrations, neuroscientific protocols, and cultural adaptations.

3. **Phase 3: Small-Scale Testing**
   - Run micro-pilots with 10–20 participants, using mixed-methods evaluation (qualitative interviews, biometric sampling, engagement analytics).

4. **Phase 4: Iteration & Scaling**
   - Refine based on feedback; train ambassadors; expand to full community with phased roll-out.

5. **Phase 5: Institutionalization & Governance**
   - Embed rituals into policy, appoint councils, establish ongoing audit cycles.

## B. Cross-Sector Partnerships

1. **Academic Collaborations:** Partner with neuroscience labs and social scientists for rigorous evaluation.

2. **Tech Alliances:** Joint ventures with AI startups and wearable manufacturers.

3. **NGO & Government Engagement:** Secure grants for community-scale pilots and public-sector adoption.

# IX. Longitudinal Impact & Evaluation Models

## A. Mixed-Methods Research Design

1. **Quantitative Measures:**
   - Engagement metrics (ritual attendance, digital touchpoints), well-being scales (e.g., WHO-5), biometrics (HRV trends).

2. **Qualitative Insights:**
   - In-depth interviews, focus groups, ethnographic vignettes capturing subjective transformation narratives.

## B. Multi-Year Cohort Studies

1. **Design:** Follow cohorts over 3–5 years, tracking relational health, life outcomes (job satisfaction, turnover, social support), and community resilience.

2. **Outcome Indicators:**
   - Friendship longevity rates, frequency of deep-sharing interactions, incidence of isolation or conflict.

## C. Data Visualization & Storytelling

1. **Dynamic Dashboards:** Time-series graphs of community cohesion metrics, heatmaps of modality usage, network graphs of social ties.

2. **Narrative Synthesis:** Annual "State of ReconneXion" reports combining data with personal stories to humanize insights.

# X. Global Case Vignettes & Thought Experiments

## A. Smart City "Reconnection District" in Singapore

- **Concept:** A neighborhood where public spaces are embedded with sensors detecting group presence and mood (sound levels, air quality, foot traffic).
- **Ritual Prototype:** "Community Sound Baths"—twice daily, ambient lighting and soundscapes shift in public plazas to signal micro-huddles, encouraging spontaneous SA gatherings.

## B. Space Habitat Friendship Module

- **Context:** Astronaut crews on long-duration missions must maintain psychological bonds despite isolation.
- **Ritual Suite:** AI-driven holographic "Earth Home Visits," VR empathy journeys simulating Earth environments, neuroadaptive group breathing circles timed to orbital sunrise.

## C. Virtual Metaverse Tribal Circles

- **Scenario:** Users form 'tribes' in a decentralized metaverse platform, connecting across 2D/3D worlds.
- **Rituals:** Digital campfires where avatars gather around a procedurally generated flame, practiced virtual drumming synced to biometric rhythms, and shared dream-journals stored on blockchain for immutability.

## D. Post-Pandemic Hybrid Communities

- **Realization:** Hybrid work and living patterns demand rituals that fluidly integrate in-person and digital.
- **Prototype:** "Dual-Mode ReconneXion Kits" mailed quarterly—physical tokens (seed packets, postcards) paired with digital AR experiences unlocked via smartphone, guiding both SA and SD rituals.

# XI. Conclusion & Call to Collective Imagination

As we stand at the juncture of unprecedented technological capabilities, deepening neuroscientific understanding, and rapidly shifting cultural norms, ReconneXion Theory invites us not merely to adapt but to **co-create** the future of friendship. By thoughtfully integrating AI tools that amplify empathy, applying neuroscientific insights to design rituals that resonate with our biology, and honoring the evolving tapestry of cultures across the globe, we forge pathways to deeper, more resilient bonds.

Yet with great power comes great responsibility. Ethical guardrails, inclusive design, and unwavering commitment to autonomy and privacy must underpin every innovation. Our shared challenge is to ensure that ReconneXion remains **profoundly human**—that algorithmic suggestions never eclipse authentic presence, that biometric feedback never supplants genuine empathy, and that global connectivity never dilutes the sacred space of vulnerability.

**Now is the moment** for practitioners, technologists, leaders, and everyday friends to step into the role of **collective futurists**—to pilot, evaluate, iterate, and celebrate new reconnection rituals that honor both timeless human needs and the tools of tomorrow. Let this chapter serve as both **roadmap and inspiration**, urging each reader to imagine, design, and enact ReconneXion's next frontier—where friendship transcends distance, time, and even mortality, becoming a living force for human flourishing in every corner of our interconnected world.

### Chapter 16
### Embodied ReconneXion: The Role of Physicality, Environment, and Sensory Engagement

> "The deepest bonds are not only spoken—they are felt through space, movement, and every sense we inhabit."

---

# I. Introduction: Why Embodiment Matters for Friendship

While Chapters 1–15 have charted the modalities of digital and analog connection, AI augmentation, neuroscientific underpinnings, and cultural evolution, the **embodied dimension** of ReconneXion—the ways in which our bodies, our spaces, and our sensory experiences shape and are shaped by our friendships—remains a critical frontier. **Chapter 16** delves into how **physical presence**, **environmental design**, **movement**, **ritual objects**, **soundscapes**, **olfactory cues**, **taste rituals**, and **tactile practices** infuse friendship with visceral resonances that bypass language and logic, anchoring reconnection in the rich tapestry of human embodiment.

We will explore:

1. **Theoretical Foundations of Embodied Social Bonding**
2. **Designing ReconneXion Spaces: Architecture, Furniture, & Lighting**
3. **Movement-Based Rituals: Dance, Walking, and Kinesthetic Synchrony**
4. **Ritual Objects & Tactile Tokens: Anchors of Presence**
5. **Multisensory Soundscapes & Music Rituals**
6. **Olfactory & Gustatory Practices in Friendship**
7. **Bodywork & Touch Rituals: Consent, Safety, and Bonding**
8. **Nature Immersion: Ecotherapy & Forest Bathing with Friends**
9. **Synesthetic & Artistic Embodiment: Collaborative Creation**
10. **Embodied Micro-Rituals for Daily Life**
11. **Measurement & Research in Embodied ReconneXion**
12. **Implementation Guides: From Tiny Ritual Labs to Community Embodiment**
13. **Case Vignettes: Embodied ReconneXion in Action**
14. **Managing Pitfalls: Accessibility, Boundaries, Overstimulation**
15. **The Future of Embodied Friendship: Biointerfaces & Haptic VR**
16. **Conclusion: Weaving Flesh, Space, and Movement into Everlasting Bonds**

This chapter surpasses all previous lengths, offering exhaustive frameworks, step-by-step designs, adaptation variants, research citations, and visionary prototypes—ensuring that ReconneXion is not merely a conversation but a lived, breathed, moving art.

## II. Theoretical Foundations of Embodied Social Bonding

### A. The Body as Social Organ

- **Embodied Cognition:** Our minds and bodies are inseparable; social thinking emerges from sensorimotor experiences. Friendships rely on shared bodily states—synchronized breathing, mirroring gestures, collective movement.

- **Interpersonal Neurobiology:** Our nervous systems resonate; physical co-regulation fosters attachment and safety. Studies show that synchronized heart rates and breathing in pairs amplify trust and cooperation.

### B. Environmental Psychology & Affordances

- **Place Attachment:** Humans form emotional bonds not only with people but with places. Friendship spaces—cottages, cafes, shared studios—become repositories of memories.

- **Affordances for Connection:** Design elements invite certain behaviors (e.g., circular seating invites egalitarian conversation; narrow benches invite shoulder-to-shoulder closeness).

### C. Sensorimotor Ritual Theory

- **Ritualized Movement:** Repetitive, patterned actions (walking in a labyrinth, drumming circles) entrain brains and bodies, fostering group cohesion.

- **Embodied Metaphors:** Physical enactments (e.g., passing a torch, planting a seed together) embody relational metaphors—"passing responsibility," "planting shared dreams."

## III. Designing ReconneXion Spaces: Architecture, Furniture, & Lighting

### A. Principles of Connection-Centric Design

1. **Proximity & Flow:**

- Arrange furniture to minimize physical barriers; allow ease of approach and retreat—a key for both SA and SD hybrid spaces.

2. **Flexibility & Modularity:**
    - Use movable seating, convertible tables, and adaptable lighting to shift from intimate two-person corners to larger Story Salons.

3. **Sensory Comfort:**
    - Control acoustics to reduce noise fatigue; incorporate natural materials (wood, fabric) for warmth; ensure variable lighting for mood alignment.

## B. Indoor Ritual Rooms

1. **Presence Pods:**
    - Semi-enclosed nooks with soft seating, dimmable lights, and acoustic dampening—ideal for one-on-one presence rituals or micro-vulnerabilities.

2. **Communal Halls:**
    - Open circular rooms with central focal points (fire pits, hanging rings) for group Story Salons and vulnerability circles.

3. **Digital–Analog Hybrids:**
    - Spaces equipped with retractable screens, VR-ready floors, and analog dashboards—facilitating seamless transition between SD and SA.

## C. Outdoor Friendship Gardens

- **Design Elements:**
    - Winding paths for walking conversations; seating niches under pergolas for quiet reflection; community vegetable beds for shared project SA rituals.

- **Microclimate Considerations:**
    - Shade structures, water features for white-noise masking, seasonal plantings to anchor monthly ritual symbolism.

# IV. Movement-Based Rituals: Dance, Walking, and Kinesthetic Synchrony

## A. Walking Conversations

- **The Walking Labyrinth:**
  - A simple stone or hedged labyrinth in a garden where pairs walk opposite directions then meet at center for a DL–SA sharing.

- **Urban Stroll & Sound Mapping:**
  - Friends walk a set route, each carrying a simple audio recorder; at designated intervals, they narrate a sensory reflection—later compiled into a shared AD map of the city's emotional geography.

## B. Synchronized Movement Practices

1. **Friendship Breath Circles:**
   - Groups stand in circles, practice synchronized inhalation/exhalation patterns (e.g., 4 sec inhale, 6 sec exhale) for four minutes—entraining nervous systems for calm, safe sharing.

2. **Simple Folk Dance Rituals:**
   - Adapt local folk dances into friendship rituals—circle dances where steps correspond to conversational turns; movement metaphors ("step forward when sharing hope, step back when speaking fear").

## C. Movement as Vulnerability Gateway

- **Embodied Vulnerability Exercises:**
  - Guided sessions where partners mirror each other's slow, minimal movements for 1–2 min, then verbalize the internal state each felt—a high-safety bridge to deeper verbal vulnerability.

## V. Ritual Objects & Tactile Tokens: Anchors of Presence

### A. Friendship Totems

- **Definition:** Small sculpted objects—stones, wooden figures, clay beads—carried by friends during rituals, symbolizing shared intentions.
- **Use Cases:**
    - **Passing the Totem:** During deep-sharing circles, possession of the totem grants the "talking stick" right.
    - **Tactile Grounding:** When feelings overwhelm, holding the totem provides sensory anchor.

### B. Tactile Journals & Material Letters

- **Handbound Journals:** Crafted collaboratively with friends—each contributes one decorated page—used for AA journaling with tactile emphasis (decorative papers, fabric swatches).
- **Material Letter Exchanges:** Letters printed on textured paper, sealed with wax stamps; the ritual of unsealing engages multiple senses, deepening presence.

### C. Multi-Person Weaving & Craft Rituals

- **Friendship Looms:** A communal loom where each friend weaves a colored thread representing current emotional state; the resulting tapestry embodies collective relational narratives.
- **Clay Circle Sculpting:** Shared clay slab onto which friends press handprints or sculpt small symbols; fired and kept as a group artifact.

## VI. Multisensory Soundscapes & Music Rituals

### A. Sound as Emotional Catalyst

- **Ambient Composition:** Curate background soundtracks—nature recordings, soft percussion—that subtly support desired ritual mood (calming, energizing, introspective).
- **Silence Intervals:** Intentional pauses amplify empathy; practicing 30 sec communal silence primes deeper sharing.

## B. Collaborative Music-Making

1. **Hand Drum Circles:**
   - Each participant has a simple percussion instrument; facilitator guides call-and-response rhythms, culminating in free collective improvisation—a nonverbal empathy exercise.

2. **Vocal Harmony Rituals:**
   - Group sings a simple, harmonized phrase at the start and end of gatherings, fostering physiological synchrony via shared vocal vibration.

## C. Personalized Sound Tokens

- **Friendship Soundboxes:** Small devices programmed with each friend's voice saying an affirming phrase; to be opened during reflection or anxiety, simulating presence.

---

# VII. Olfactory & Gustatory Practices in Friendship

## A. Aromatherapy Rituals

- **Shared Scent Signatures:**
  - Friends co-create a unique blend of essential oils (e.g., lavender for calm, citrus for energy) sprayed in the ritual space—triggering associative recall of past reconnection moments.

- **Scented Reflection Jars:**
  - Mason jars containing dried herbs or flowers; opening a jar signals a micro-reflection moment—"What does this scent remind you of in our friendship?"

## B. Communal Taste Experiences

1. **Flavor Mapping:**
   - In Story Salons, each story is paired with a small, symbolic taste sample (e.g., honey for sweetness, a spicy drop for tension), linking narrative to palate.

2. **Ritual Tea Preparation:**
   - A slow, ceremonial tea-making session shared among friends—each pours for another, offering a micro-gesture of care as they discuss hopes or fears.

# VIII. Bodywork & Touch Rituals: Consent, Safety, and Bonding

## A. Consent Frameworks

- **Touch Agreements:** Explicit pre-ritual discussion of comfort zones, safe words, and nonverbal cues to pause or stop tactile exercises.

- **Cultural Sensitivity:** Adapt touch practices for cultural norms; alternatives for participants uncomfortable with physical contact.

## B. Gentle Therapeutic Touch

1. **Friendship Handholds:**
   - Pairs hold hands silently for 60 sec before and after micro-sharing prompts, reinforcing presence and nonverbal support.

2. **Shoulder Circles:**
   - Small groups form concentric circles; each places a hand on neighbor's shoulder—slow, gentle pressure maintained for self-regulation during intense sharing.

## C. Assisted Movement & Massage

- **Self-Massage Stations:** Providing simple massage tools—foam rollers, handheld massagers—in ReconneXion Zones; friends encourage each other to release physical tension as precursor to deeper connection.
- **Paired Massage Rituals:** With consent and minimal training, friends exchange brief 2-minute shoulder or scalp massages—stimulating oxytocin release and mutual care.

## IX. Nature Immersion: Ecotherapy & Forest Bathing with Friends

### A. Principles of Forest Bathing (Shinrin-Yoku)

- **Sensory Engagement:** Attune to sights, sounds, smells, textures, and tastes of natural environments to reduce stress and open reflective capacity.
- **Slow, Intentional Movement:** Guided walks of 30–90 min without goal-oriented endpoints, focusing on present-moment awareness.

### B. Friendship Forest Rituals

1. **Group Forest Meditation:**
   - Friends gather under a canopy for 10 min silent nature meditation, then share a DL prompt—"What element of nature resonates with your current emotional state?"

2. **Pinecone Promise Exchange:**
   - Each selects a natural object (pinecone, stone), imbues it with an intention or vulnerability, then swaps with a friend—symbolizing shared burden or support.

### C. Place-based Memory Anchors

- **Ritual Mapping:** Create an AA map of local trails with marked "Friendship Waypoints"—sites where a significant conversation occurred. Returning to these spots evokes shared history and deepens place attachment.

# X. Synesthetic & Artistic Embodiment: Collaborative Creation

## A. Visual Art Dialogues

1. **Collaborative Murals:**
    - Large blank walls invite friends to paint together—each session adds layers representing evolving emotional landscapes.

2. **Emotion Color Wheel:**
    - Friends choose paint colors to represent feelings; after a week of daily micro-journals, they paint a collective color wheel, sparking group reflection.

## B. Movement as Art

- **Friendship Choreography:**
    - Pairs design a simple 2–3 min movement sequence embodying their dyadic journey—teaches nonverbal empathy and mutual attunement.

- **Public Performance Rituals:**
    - Small flash-mob style dance or spoken-word performances in familiar public spaces serve as collective vulnerability acts and community invitations.

## C. Integrating Multiple Modalities

- **Audio-Visual Installation:**
    - A chamber where friends listen to recorded voice notes (AD), view collaborative digital art, and physically navigate a light installation—melding sensory streams to deepen mutual understanding.

# XI. Embodied Micro-Rituals for Daily Life

### A. "Three-Second Pause" Triggers

- **Mechanism:** Strategic stickers or tokens placed on door frames; each time you pass, pause for three deep breaths, intending presence for an absent friend.
- **Effect:** Momentary embodied reconnection loops micro-ritual into everyday movement.

### B. "Shoulder Check" Gestures

- **Solo Version:** Lightly press your own shoulders, inhaling calm; exhaling intention to reach out to a friend later.
- **Dual Version:** In corridors or hallways, passing friends tap each other's shoulders as a silent "I see you" acknowledgment.

### C. "Window Gaze Correspondence"

- **How:** Friends facing their own windows at a set time (e.g., daily at 6 PM), gaze outward for one minute, then send a "window wink" emoji (AD) to each other—signifying shared presence across distances.

---

# XII. Measurement & Research in Embodied ReconneXion

### A. Physiological Metrics

- **HRV & EEG Logging:** Collect anonymized heart rate variability and neural synchrony data during embodied rituals to quantify co-regulation effectiveness.
- **Biochemical Assays:** Track salivary oxytocin pre- and post-tactile rituals to validate bonding effects.

### B. Behavioral Observations

- **Ethnographic Coding:** Trained observers video-record rituals (with consent) and code posture mirroring, proxemic closeness, and synchronized movement as indicators of connection.

- **Self-Report Scales:** Develop embodied reconnection questionnaires assessing participants' sense of physical safety, sensory resonance, and somatic empathy.

## C. Mixed-Method Synthesis

- **Integrated Dashboards:** Combine biometric graphs, coded behavioral data, and participant narratives into holistic impact reports for iterative ritual design.

---

# XIII. Implementation Guides: From Tiny Ritual Labs to Community Embodiment

## A. Tiny Ritual Labs

1. **Setup:** Identify a small group (4–6) willing to experiment with embodied micro-rituals over four weeks.

2. **Week-by-Week Plan:**

   - **Week 1:** "Three-Second Pauses" and "Shoulder Checks."
   - **Week 2:** "Presence Breath Circles" and "Window Gaze Correspondence."
   - **Week 3:** "Walking Labyrinth" and "Tactile Totems."
   - **Week 4:** "Collaborative Mural" pop-up and "Forest Bathing Reflection."

3. **Evaluation:** Collect HRV snapshots, conduct focus group debrief, and refine rituals.

## B. Scaling to Organizations

- **Pilot Embodied Zones:** Transform one meeting room into an Embodied ReconneXion Space—test for four months, gather usage metrics, staff feedback.

- **Training Facilitators:** Certify internal "Embodiment Champions" in movement facilitation, sensory design, and consent protocols.

- **Embedding in Culture:** Integrate at least one embodied ritual into every major organizational event—quarterly retreats, offsites, annual ceremonies.

## C. Community-Wide Embodiment

- **Public Installations:** Create interactive art spaces (e.g., "Friendship Forests" in parks) with embedded sensors that trigger communal soundscapes when visitors gather, inviting synchronized movement or hush rituals.
- **City-Wide Ritual Calendars:** Municipal schedules that list daily "Collective Breathing Moments" broadcast over public speakers, encouraging whole neighborhoods to pause together.

# XIV. Case Vignettes: Embodied ReconneXion in Action

### Vignette 1: "The Friendship Journey Carpet"

A group of ten university alumni co-designed a long runner carpet painted with symbols marking significant moments from their campus years. At each reunion, they unroll the carpet, walk it together, pausing at each motif to share an embodied reflection—touching the symbol, gesturing a breath, and recounting the memory. Over five years, the walk deepened their bonds more than any dinner table conversation.

### Vignette 2: "The Midnight Forest Walk"

In a tech startup, the Leadership team introduced monthly "Midnight Forest Walks" at a nearby nature reserve. Led by a guide, the group walked under starlight in single file, maintaining silence for 15 minutes, then emerged into a clearing for a brief fire-light heartbeat meditation—30 sec of synchronized chest pulses to the fire's flicker. Participants report lower burnout and renewed team empathy.

### Vignette 3: "The Scent Library Ritual"

A women's elderhood circle curates a "Scent Library"—34 distinct jars of dried botanicals gathered from participants' childhood gardens. Each month, one jar is selected at random; participants inhale the scent together, sharing a childhood story prompted by that aroma. This multisensory sharing evokes deep nostalgia and fosters cross-generational empathy.

# XV. Managing Pitfalls: Accessibility, Boundaries, Overstimulation

1. **Sensory Overload:**

   - **Symptom:** Participants with sensory sensitivities feel overwhelmed by combined stimuli (sound, scent, touch).

   - **Mitigation:** Offer low-sensory variants—silent rooms, scent-free zones, touch-optional roles.

2. **Physical Accessibility:**

   - **Symptom:** Movement-based rituals exclude those with mobility challenges.

   - **Mitigation:** Provide seated or wheelchair-compatible versions—guided arm gestures, virtual labyrinth apps, tabletop totem exchanges.

3. **Consent & Comfort Variances:**

   - **Symptom:** Cultural or personal boundaries conflict—some resist touch or certain scents.

   - **Mitigation:** Universal consent check-ins, opt-out codes (colored bracelets indicating comfort levels), quiet observation roles.

4. **Ritual Saturation:**

   - **Symptom:** Overly elaborate embodied rituals become burdensome.

   - **Mitigation:** Maintain a rotating Ritual Menu; ensure micro-ritual options for days when energy is low.

---

# XVI. The Future of Embodied Friendship: Biointerfaces & Haptic VR

## A. Wearable Haptic Suits

- **Concept:** Lightweight suits deliver gentle haptic feedback—soft pulses corresponding to a friend's heartbeat or hug, enabling tactile presence across distances.
- **Ritual Prototype:** "Remote Hug Exchange"—friends send a 10-second hug that triggers synchronized haptic compression, evoking embodied comfort in real time.

### B. Neural Lace Ritual Co-Regulation

- **Speculative Frontier:** Brain–computer interfaces detect neural synchrony levels in small groups; adjust environmental parameters (light hue, ambient music) to sustain optimal collective states—supporting deeper vulnerability without cognitive overwhelm.

### C. Multisensory Telepresence Pods

- **Design:** Enclosed pods integrating VR visuals, directional sound, scent diffusion, and haptic feedback—allow dyads or triads to share immersive reconnection experiences that engage all senses, creating "impossible proximity" for distant friends.

---

# XVII. Conclusion: We Are Bodies in Friendship

Embodied ReconneXion transcends words into the realm of sensation, movement, and space—recognizing that our friendships are **lived** in every breath, step, touch, flavor, and sound. By meticulously designing spaces, objects, and rituals that engage our entire sensorium, we elevate connection from the conceptual into the visceral, forging bonds that endure because they are **felt** at the cellular level. As we stand poised at the threshold of haptic virtual realities, neuroadaptive group experiences, and sensory-infused environments, the challenge—and opportunity—is to ensure that technology amplifies, rather than displaces, the **ancient wisdom** of embodied human care.

In this grand tapestry, each embodied ritual is a thread of presence woven through flesh and space, creating patterns of belonging that no algorithm alone can replicate. Let Chapter 16 serve as both **manual and manifesto**: a call to architects, facilitators, artists, technologists, and everyday friends to co-create the next generation of ReconneXion—where every hug, every breath, every shared meal, and every communal heartbeat is a living testament to our capacity for profoundly human friendship.

Chapter 17
ReconneXion in Crisis: Adapting Rituals for Collective Trauma, Disruption, and Transformation

> "In the crucible of adversity, true friendship is forged through shared ritual, resilient presence, and the courage to hold space for collective grief and hope."

# I. Introduction: The Imperative of Connection Amidst Crisis

Crisis—whether sudden (natural disasters, pandemics, political upheavals) or chronic (systemic inequality, climate anxiety)—tests the fabric of our relationships. Under stress, habitual rituals falter, and solitude or fragmentation can deepen trauma. Yet, history and psychology attest that **intentional connection** is among humanity's most powerful antidotes to fear, grief, and disorientation. **Chapter 17** offers an exhaustive exploration of how ReconneXion Theory's pillars and modalities must be **remodeled** for crisis contexts, guiding individuals, friendship dyads, communities, and institutions through:

1. **Crisis Typologies & Friendship Vulnerabilities**
2. **Phases of Crisis Response & Ritual Alignment**
3. **Acute Crisis Rituals:** Rapid-Response Micro-Rituals for Immediate Stabilization
4. **Chronic Crisis Rituals:** Sustaining Connection Under Prolonged Stress
5. **Collective Healing Ceremonies:** Transformative Deep-Level Gatherings
6. **Adapting Modalities & Depth in Restricted Environments**
7. **Leadership & Peer Support Structures**
8. **Measurement & Adaptive Feedback Loops**
9. **Cross-Cultural & Ethical Considerations**
10. **Case Vignettes:** Real-World Applications in Disaster Zones, Pandemic Lockdowns, and Social Movements
11. **Managing Secondary Trauma & Compassion Fatigue**

12. **Hybrid Ritual Prototypes for Future Crisis Scenarios**

13. **Guidelines for Research, Training, and Policy Integration**

14. **Conclusion:** From Survival to Emergence—Forging Stronger Bonds Beyond Crisis

By chapter's end, practitioners and friends alike will possess a **crisis-ready toolkit** of rituals, protocols, and design principles—empowering ReconneXion to serve as a beacon of stability, empathy, and collective resilience, even amidst the most turbulent times.

---

## II. Crisis Typologies & Friendship Vulnerabilities

### A. Categorizing Crises

1. **Acute-Onset Crises:** Earthquakes, floods, terror attacks—immediate upheaval demanding rapid response.

2. **Slow-Burning Crises:** Climate change, economic recession—gradual deterioration eroding hope over months or years.

3. **Systemic Crises:** Racism, inequality, public health disparities—embedded in social structures, requiring sustained collective action.

4. **Personal Crises:** Individual loss, illness, bankruptcy—though personal, ripple into friendship networks.

### B. Friendship Under Duress: Vulnerability Profiles

- **Disruption of Modalities:** Physical gatherings (SA) may be impossible; digital overload (SD/AD) can strain.

- **Emotional Overload:** High anxiety impairs Presence; trauma can shut down Empathy.

- **Ritual Atrophy:** Daily and weekly rituals fall away under survival pressures.

- **Power and Resource Imbalances:** Some friends may have shelter and bandwidth, others may lack basic needs, creating relational friction.

## III. Phases of Crisis Response & Ritual Alignment

Crisis unfolds in **distinct phases**, each requiring tailored reconnection strategies:

1. **Phase 1—Shock & Mobilization (Hours–Days):** Urgent safety measures, confusion, adrenaline.

   - **Priority Rituals:** Micro-Presence rituals, safety check-ins, brief solidarity pulses.

2. **Phase 2—Acute Adaptation (Days–Weeks):** New routines stabilize (e.g., lockdown schedules); acute grief surfaces.

   - **Priority Rituals:** Structured weekly empathy huddles, hybrid SA/SD gatherings, ritualized information updates.

3. **Phase 3—Chronic Endurance (Weeks–Months):** Fatigue, compassion burnout, existential questioning.

   - **Priority Rituals:** Ritual variation to prevent burnout, peer respite rotations, communal meaning-making ceremonies.

4. **Phase 4—Reconstruction & Emergence (Months–Years):** Communities rebuild, systemic change efforts advance.

   - **Priority Rituals:** Deep-level story-sharing salons, participatory visioning retreats, legacy-building embodiment.

---

## IV. Acute Crisis Rituals: Rapid-Response Micro-Rituals

### A. "SOS Presence Drops" (SA/SD/AD)

- **Structure:** Every crisis onset triggers an immediate "SOS Presence Drop"—a single sentence check-in ("I'm here, I see you, you're not alone").

- **Modalities:**

  - **SA:** A brief in-person touchpoint (hug, hand on shoulder) when safe.

- **SD:** 10-second video clip of faces saying "I'm okay" or "I'm safe"—shared in group channels.
- **AD:** One-word status updates via group chat (e.g., "Safe," "Shaken," "Here") serving as quick emotional triage.

### B. "Collective Breathing Anchors" (SA + AD)

- **Mechanism:** Broadcast a 1-minute guided breathing audio file at set intervals across community platforms, prompting synchronous deep breathing to stabilize nervous systems.
- **Example:** Every two hours on the hour during a wildfires, local officials and community leaders share a short "Breath Together" audio snippet on social media.

### C. "Safety Map Sharing" (AA + AD)

- **How:** Friends or neighbors asynchronously share AA "safety maps"—sketched floor plans indicating safe routes, shelter locations, and resource caches.
- **AD Integration:** Scan and post to shared channels for collective situational awareness.

### D. "Emergency Bond Bracelets" (AA)

- **Ritual:** Quickly craft simple string bracelets with coded colors indicating needs (red = medical, yellow = supplies, green = safe). Wearing them communicates status nonverbally in chaotic environments.

---

# V. Chronic Crisis Rituals: Sustaining Connection Over Time

### A. "Ritual Menus" for Flexibility

- **Design:** Develop a menu of short (5–10 min), medium (15–30 min), and long (1–2 hr) rituals. Participants choose based on daily capacity, preventing guilt from unmet expectations.

### B. "Rotating Respite Teams" (SA + SD)

- **Structure:** In extended crises (pandemic, refugee camps), form small "Respite Teams" of 3–4 friends. Each team member takes turns receiving support—everyone else provides attentive SD check-ins or SA meal deliveries once per assigned shift.

### C. "Ritual Innovation Sprints" (AD + AA)

- **Process:** Monthly digital hackathons where small groups prototype new micro-rituals adapted to current constraints (e.g., zero-contact gestures, novel use of public PA systems for solidarity pulses). Results are documented in an AA "Crisis Ritual Handbook."

### D. "Persistent Story Archives" (AA + AD)

- **Mechanism:** Maintain an evolving AA/E-journal capturing daily micro-narratives of survival and solidarity ("Today I met Sarah at the water distribution line; she gave me half her share"). Monthly compilations foster a shared sense of journey.

---

## VI. Collective Healing Ceremonies: Deep-Level Gatherings

### A. "Shared Grief Circles" (SA + SD)

- **Structure:** Facilitate monthly grief-sharing circles with a trained facilitator. Use safe-space agreements, a "speaking stone" for turn-taking, and group breathing anchors. SD participants join via high-fidelity audio with moderated mics to preserve presence.

### B. "Hope Weaving Workshops" (SA + AA)

- **How:** Participants weave strands of yarn onto a communal loom—each color/texture representing a hope or intention. As the tapestry grows, so does collective vision-building for post-crisis reconstruction.

### C. "Resilience Ritual Retreats" (Hybrid)

- **Format:** Multi-day immersive retreats (virtual and in-person pods) combining embodied practices (forest bathing, dance), AI-supported reflection summaries, and neuroscientific biofeedback sessions to rebuild community cohesion.

# VII. Adapting Modalities & Depth Under Constraints

## A. Digital-Analog Hybrids

- **Micro-Relay Handoff:** Where SA is impossible, use SD "relay" nodes—small in-person clusters broadcast to other clusters, interlinked in a ring topology—preserving embodied micro-communities at scale.

## B. Managing Bandwidth & Fatigue

- **Low-Bandwidth Options:** Offer audio-only recitations of ritual scripts, text-based guided prompts, and SMS-based micro-rituals for participants with limited connectivity.

## C. Depth Calibration

- **Surface-to-Deep Gradients:** For safety in crisis, begin gatherings at depth level 2 (moderate) before admitting deeper vulnerability (levels 4–5) only after physiological co-regulation indicators (HRV, collective silence) confirm group readiness.

# VIII. Leadership & Peer Support Structures

## A. Crisis ReconneXion Councils

- **Composition:** Multidisciplinary teams—community elders, health workers, ReconneXion ambassadors—rotate facilitation and ensure democratic representation.

## B. Peer Support Training

- **Curriculum:** Rapid certification in Psychological First Aid, embodied co-regulation techniques, and AI-assisted sentiment dashboards—equipping friends to lead micro-rituals safely.

### C. Distributed Leadership Networks

- **Fractal Models:** Small support cells of 5–7 replicate up-chain in federated networks—ensuring rituals propagate without overburdening central actors.

## IX. Measurement & Adaptive Feedback Loops

### A. Crisis-Specific Dashboards

- **Real-Time Indicators:**
    - **Engagement Metrics:** Ritual participation rates, check-in frequencies.
    - **Emotional Sentiment:** NLP analysis of crisis forums.
    - **Physiological Baselines:** Average HRV, sleep pattern deviations.

### B. Rapid Survey Pulses

- **Frequency:** Daily 2-question check-ins ("How are you feeling?" "What do you need today?") delivered via AD, with automated triage flags for high-risk responses.

### C. Ritual Efficacy Reviews

- **Weekly Micro-Retrospectives:** Brief AA/SD gatherings where facilitators review what rituals resonated, which fell flat, and co-design adjustments for the coming week.

## X. Cross-Cultural & Ethical Considerations

### A. Trauma-Informed Design

- **Principles:** Prioritize safety, choice, and empowerment. Explicitly avoid triggering content; ensure facilitators are trained to spot dissociation or retraumatization.

## B. Cultural Variants

- **Localization:** Co-create rituals with local cultural consultants—integrate indigenous healing practices, local music, and community-specific symbols.

## C. Equity & Access

- **Resource Allocation:** Ensure materially disadvantaged friends receive technological tools, data stipends, or physical transportation to participate in SA rituals.

# XI. Case Vignettes

### Vignette 1: Earthquake Aftermath in Coastal Town

- **Context:** A 7.2 magnitude quake devastates infrastructure.
- **Response:**
    - **Phase 1:** "SOS Presence Drops" via megaphones and SMS blasts; "Safety Map Sharing" chalked onto streets.
    - **Phase 2:** Rotating Respite Teams organize community kitchen micro-rituals—collective cooking circles using available supplies, weaving in "Hope Tapestry" yarn projects during meal prep.
    - **Phase 3:** Monthly "Resilience Ritual Retreats" held in temporary shelters, featuring forest bathing in nearby undamaged groves and AI-curated reflection compilations emailed to families.

### Vignette 2: Pandemic Lockdowns in Urban Centers

- **Context:** Extended social isolation, digital fatigue, health anxieties.
- **Innovations:**

- **Micro-Relay Handoff** Neighborhood Pods of 4 meet SA in backyards, relaying Viral Haze Checks (brief updates) to adjoining pods via SD links.
- **Window Gaze Correspondence** scaled city-wide via "6 PM Light Flash"—street lamps synchronize a one-minute light blackout, signaling communal solidarity.
- **Breath Circles** integrated into public health announcements, with narrated guided breathing clips broadcast on radio and social channels.

## Vignette 3: Social Justice Uprisings in Metropolitan Districts

- **Context:** Mass protests, heightened tensions, potential violence.
- **Response:**
  - **Acute Rituals:** Brief "Solidarity Pulse" chants—two minutes of communal vocalizations recorded and shared across platforms.
  - **Chronic Rituals:** Weekly "Safe Space" Tipi Camps in public parks offering refuge, circle dialogues, and therapeutic drumming.
  - **Collective Healing Ceremonies:** After key events, large-scale "Story Salons" held in coded digital spaces—anonymized voices sharing lived experiences, building cross-community empathy.

# XII. Managing Secondary Trauma & Compassion Fatigue

## A. Rotating Caregiver Roles

- **Mechanism:** Establish formal schedules where peer supporters rotate between active duty (facilitation, check-ins) and respite phases (self-care, micro-rituals), preventing overexposure.

## B. Self-Compassion Micro-Rituals

- **Examples:** Five-second self-hugs, mirror affirmations focusing on "I did what I could today," solo embodied breathing circles—mini-safety valves against burnout.

### C. Professional Referrals

- **Protocol:** Clear pathways to mental health professionals for friends exhibiting signs of complex trauma—ensuring friendship rituals augment but do not replace clinical care.

---

# XIII. Hybrid Ritual Prototypes for Future Crisis Scenarios

### A. AI-Facilitated Mass Micro-Check-Ins

- **Blueprint:** AI chatbots conduct tens of thousands of "How are you?" micro-conversations across populations, flagging high-need individuals for human follow-up.

### B. Drone-Delivered Ritual Kits

- **Concept:** In inaccessible zones, drones drop small "Ritual Boxes" containing scented sachets, tactile tokens, and folded ritual scripts—enabling solitary or small-group enactments.

### C. Immersive Crisis VR Simulations

- **Use Case:** Pre-crisis training in VR—friend groups practice reconnection rituals in simulated disaster environments, building muscle memory for real-world application.

---

# XIV. Guidelines for Research, Training, and Policy Integration

### A. Research Agenda

- **Longitudinal Studies:** Track friendship health and mental well-being across crises, comparing ritual-adopting vs. control groups.
- **Neuroscientific Collaborations:** Investigate neural correlates of crisis ritual efficacy via portable EEG and fNIRS.

### B. Training Frameworks

- **Modular Curriculum:**
    - **Module 1:** Crisis ReconneXion Theory & Ethics
    - **Module 2:** Rapid-Response Micro-Rituals
    - **Module 3:** Chronic Crisis Support & Resilience Rituals
    - **Module 4:** Embodied & Multisensory Techniques
    - **Module 5:** Technology & Hybrid Innovations
- **Certification Levels:** Basic (peer facilitator), Advanced (council member), Specialist (trauma-informed reconnection leader).

### C. Policy Recommendations

- **Institutional Mandates:** Governments and NGOs include ReconneXion protocols in disaster readiness plans, ensuring funding for community-level ritual infrastructure.
- **Cross-Sector Coalitions:** Establish partnerships between tech firms, mental health providers, and civil society to co-develop crisis reconnection platforms.

# XV. Conclusion: From Survival to Emergence

Crisis need not irrevocably sever the ties that bind us. Through **purposefully adapted rituals**, grounded in trauma-informed care, powered by interdisciplinary insights, and buoyed by technological innovation, ReconneXion can transform moments of fear and fragmentation into **catalysts for deeper solidarity, shared meaning, and collective transformation.**

As we navigate an increasingly volatile world—marked by environmental upheavals, social fractures, and rapid change—our ability to **reimagine connection** under strain will determine whether we simply survive or collectively **emerge** stronger, more empathetic, and ever more entwined in the living web of friendship.

**Chapter 18**, titled **"Regenerative ReconneXion: Cultivating Sustained Community Well-Being and Ecosystemic Friendship,"** will explore how ReconneXion principles apply to ecological interdependence, social justice movements, and the quest for a more regenerative society—demonstrating that the bonds of friendship, when extended to all living systems, can become a blueprint for global harmony.

**Chapter 18**
**Regenerative ReconneXion: Cultivating Sustained Community Well-Being and Ecosystemic Friendship**

> "When friendship extends its roots into the living world, it blossoms into regenerative change—for people, communities, and the planet alike."

---

# I. Introduction: From Connection to Regeneration

Friendship rituals traditionally focus on human-to-human bonds, but the **next frontier of ReconneXion** recognizes that **our well-being is inseparable from the health of our ecosystems**. Chapter 18 explores how we can **weave regenerative principles**—borrowed from permaculture, indigenous wisdom, and systems thinking—into friendship practices, creating **ecosystemic bonds** that nurture both human communities and the living earth. In doing so, we transcend merely sustaining relationships and co-create **regenerative cycles of care** that restore soils, rebuild social fabrics, and renew hope.

This exhaustive chapter—surpassing the length of even Chapter 17—unpacks:

1. **Defining Regenerative ReconneXion:** Key principles and mindsets.

2. **Ecological Interdependence & Friendship:** Theory and lived practice.

3. **Bio-Integrated Ritual Spaces:** Designing environments that serve human and non-human life.

4. **Permaculture™ Principles Applied to Social Systems:** Ethics and design methodologies.

5. **Living Rituals:** Gardens, seed-ball ceremonies, mycelial mapping.

6. **Circular Economies of Care:** Mutual aid, time banks, and resource sharing.

7. **Social Justice & Equity in Regeneration:** Ensuring inclusive, anti-oppressive practices.

8. **Institutional Embedding:** Policy, education, and organizational strategies for regenerative friendship.

9. **Technological Synergies:** Bio-sensors, blockchain for provenance, AI for ecosystem monitoring.

10. **Measurement & Participatory Feedback:** Mixed-methods metrics for ecological and relational health.

11. **Case Vignettes:** Eco-village reconnections, urban agriculture collectives, indigenous community protocols.

12. **Challenges, Pitfalls & Ethics:** Greenwashing, extractivism, technofix illusions, cultural appropriation.

13. **Future Visions:** Planetary friendship networks, digital-biotic symbiosis, Gaia hackathons.

14. **Conclusion & Call to Action:** From local seeds to global solidarity.

By chapter's end, you will hold a **comprehensive blueprint** for **regenerative friendship**—practices that honor the **reciprocity of all living systems**, ensuring that our connections leave **the world better than we found it**.

---

# II. Defining Regenerative ReconneXion

## A. Core Principles

1. **Reciprocity with Nature:** Seeing ecosystems not as mere backdrops but as active partners in friendship rituals.

2. **Holism & Systems Thinking:** Recognizing feedback loops between social bonds and ecological health—what affects one reverberates through both.

3. **Resilience through Diversity:** Encouraging biodiverse environments and polyphonic communities—multiple voices, species, and perspectives strengthen the whole.

4. **Care as Currency:** Valuing care work—tending soils, listening circles, cardiovascular co-regulation—as fundamental contributions.

5. **Regeneration over Sustainability:** Moving beyond "maintaining" systems to actively **revitalize** depleted landscapes and frayed relationships.

## B. Contrasting Models

| Sustainability ("Do No Harm") | Regeneration ("Give Back More Than You Take") |
|---|---|
| Minimizes negative impacts | Creates positive, net-restorative effects |
| Maintains status quo | Seeks continual improvement and evolution |
| Often reactive | Proactive and anticipatory |
| Linear resource use | Circular, cyclical resource flows |

Regenerative ReconneXion insists that our friendship rituals not only **preserve** bonds but **enrich** the social-ecological webs we inhabit.

# III. Friendship and Ecological Interdependence

## A. Theoretical Foundations

- **Biophilia Hypothesis (E.O. Wilson):** Humans possess an innate affinity for life; connecting with nature deepens empathy and well-being.

- **Social-Ecological Resilience (Elinor Ostrom, Fikret Berkes):** Community solidarity correlates with robust resource stewardship and adaptive capacity.

- **Relational Ecology (Robin Wall Kimmerer):** Reciprocity, gratitude, and reciprocity ceremonies nurture both human and more-than-human kin.

## B. Mapping Interdependencies

1. **Relational Webs Diagrams:** Visual tools mapping friendships onto food networks, pollination routes, water flows—revealing how our gatherings intersect with ecological processes.

2. **Place-Based Autobiographies:** Friends co-author narratives tying personal histories to local lands—rivers, forests, soils—reinforcing shared stewardship responsibilities.

## IV. Designing Bio-Integrated Ritual Spaces

### A. Principles of Regenerative Architecture

1. **Restorative Biophilic Design:** Incorporate natural light, living walls, rainwater gardens, and native plantings into gathering spaces.

2. **Permeable Boundaries:** Blurring indoors and outdoors through sliding walls, canopy walkways, and microhabitat corridors.

3. **Circular Materials:** Use reclaimed wood, recycled glass, earthen plasters for low-impact, high-story value.

### B. Examples of Ritual Spaces

- **Symbiotic Friendship Hubs:** Community centers where meeting rooms open onto healing gardens; beehives on rooftops provide honey for communal tea ceremonies.

- **Edible Landscapes:** Group-tended orchards integrated into walking labyrinths—ritual harvests coincide with reflection prompts.

- **Mycelium Mortars:** Mycelial network-infused benches that foster fungal health while offering seating for micro-ritual circles.

## V. Permaculture™ Principles in Social Systems

### A. Ethics Extended

1. **Earth Care:** Rituals that tend soil, water, and biodiversity—e.g., seed ball ceremonies before friendship story circles.

2. **People Care:** Ensuring every ritual supports relational health, cultural belonging, and equitable participation.

3. **Fair Share:** Rotating hosting duties, sharing surplus harvests, and redistributing resources among friends.

## B. Design Principles Adapted

1. **Observe & Interact:** Friends engage in joint ecological observation walks, noting seasonal changes to inform ritual timing (e.g., rainwater meditation at first monsoon drizzle).

2. **Catch & Store Energy:** Collect solar data during outdoor walks; share journals about personal energy cycles to schedule rituals when vitality peaks.

3. **Obtain a Yield:** Link rituals to tangible yields—harvested herbs, crafted art pieces, seed packets—to reinforce cycles of give-and-take.

4. **Apply Self-Regulation & Feedback:** Use community audits to adjust ecological impact and relational depth—e.g., scaling back gatherings during drought.

5. **Use & Value Diversity:** Cultivate multi-cultural ritual banks, ecological seed libraries, and intergenerational story exchanges.

6. **Use Small & Slow Solutions:** Start with micro-patch gardens or weekly seed exchanges rather than attempting large monoculture planting.

7. **Use Edges & Value Marginal:** Hold rituals at ecotones—shorelines, field-forest boundaries—and include introverts or marginalized voices in leadership roles.

8. **Creatively Use & Respond to Change:** Embrace unpredictable weather or species migration as ritual elements—celebrate first frost as a candlelit story-sharing prompt.

# VI. Living Rituals: Gardens, Seed-Ball Ceremonies, Mycelial Mapping

## A. Community Friendship Gardens

1. **Design & Planting Ritual:** Friends co-design garden beds according to personal strengths—herbalist friends sow medicinal plants; artistic friends decorate signage.

2. **Monthly "Garden Gratitude" Ceremonies:** Circle rituals among blossoms, offering thanks to pollinators and water keepers—blessing water with song before irrigation.

3. **Harvest-Share Celebrations:** Collective cooking sessions transform produce into shared meals—paired with memory-mapping reflection prompts.

## B. Seed-Ball Friendship Exchanges

- **Process:** Friends roll clay, compost, and native seeds into balls; exchange in pairs or leave in public meadows. Performing a brief vow—"May this seed carry our friendship into the earth."

- **Follow-Up:** Over weeks, friends photograph germination progress, post updates in an AD "Regeneration Thread," sparking ongoing connection.

## C. Mycelial Mapping Workshops

1. **Spore Swab Co-Creation:** In small groups, participants swab local logs or soil to cultivate beneficial fungal cultures in petri dishes—symbolizing group interconnectivity.

2. **Network Weaving Rituals:** Connecting fungal-inoculated tiles in spirals on the ground, friends narrate shared history as they place each tile—physical manifestation of hidden networks.

---

# VII. Circular Economies of Care

## A. Time Banks & Skill-Share Circles

1. **Friendship Time Credits:** Every hour spent in a presence ritual or co-gardening session earns credits friends can redeem for support—meal prep, tutoring, eldercare.

2. **Skill-Share Markets:** Periodic bartering fairs where friends offer workshops—sunprint art, herbal first aid—in exchange for services or goods.

## B. Material Sharing Protocols

- **Regeneration Libraries:** Lending tools—pruners, seed presses, fermentation crocks—across friend networks, reducing consumption and fostering mutual dependence.
- **Repair-Together Cafés:** Regular meetups to fix clothes, electronics, or furniture; combining SA collaboration with AD scheduling and AA repair logs.

---

# VIII. Social Justice & Equity Integration

## A. Anti-Oppression Frameworks

1. **Power Mapping Workshops:** Friends collaboratively chart social power dynamics—race, class, gender—within their networks and design rituals to redistribute leadership.
2. **Accessibility Audits:** Ensuring embodied and ecological rituals are wheelchair-accessible, language-inclusive, and culturally respectful.

## B. Reparative Friendship Ceremonies

- **Land Acknowledgment & Reciprocity:** Before gathering on dispossessed lands, friends perform acknowledgments, followed by AA donations or labor pledges to indigenous stewards.
- **Solidarity Seed Funds:** Friends collectively fund seed grants for marginalized farmers, embedding social justice into regeneration.

---

# IX. Institutional Embedding for Regeneration

## A. Educational Curricula

- **Regenerative ReconneXion Courses:** K–12 and university modules combining friendship rituals with ecological design—project-based learning through school gardens and peer facilitation training.
- **Outdoor Classrooms:** Weekly SA "Living Ritual Labs" integrated into science and social studies, reinforcing embodied connection and ecological literacy.

### B. Workplace Integration

- **Corporate Food Forests:** Office compounds planted as edible ecosystems; employee ritual time "in the forest" to de-stress and co-create.
- **Green Reconnection Councils:** Task forces bridging HR, facilities, and ReconneXion ambassadors to ensure environmental and social healing practices are co-owned.

### C. Municipal Policy

- **Regenerative Zoning Incentives:** City laws requiring communal green spaces in new developments, with mandates for "Friendship Circles" as part of public park designs.
- **Civic Ritual Grants:** Public funding streams for community groups to pilot regenerative friendship projects, from urban orchards to river restoration ceremonies.

---

## X. Technological Synergies: Bio-Sensors & Regenerative Metrics

### A. Eco-Friendship Dashboards

- **Integrated Data Streams:** Combine IoT sensor data (soil moisture, air quality) with AD friendship engagement metrics, visualized in shared dashboards informing ritual timing (e.g., watering meditations after rainfall).
- **Gamified Regeneration:** Digital badges awarded for collective biodiversity improvements—"Pollinator Protector," "Fungal Network Weaver."

### B. Blockchain for Provenance & Trust

- **Seed Lineage Tracking:** Each seed-ball tagged with a unique NFT, recording its origin and distribution history—friends trace how their seed exchanges contribute to community greening.
- **Circulation of Care Credits:** Time-bank transactions recorded on transparent ledgers, ensuring equitable recognition and preventing credit hoarding.

## C. AI-Enhanced Design Assistance

- **Ritual Ecology Simulators:** Generative AI models predict how planting schemes and ritual frequencies affect both social cohesion and ecosystem health over time—allowing friends to co-author living maps.

- **Voice-Activated Ritual Guides:** Smart speakers deliver voice-guided permaculture prompts—"It's time for our seed-ball ceremony; please gather clay and seeds."

---

# XI. Measurement & Participatory Feedback for Community Well-Being

## A. Regenerative ReconneXion Index (RRI)

1. **Components:**
   - **Social Resilience Score:** Ritual participation, mutual aid flows, relational diversity.
   - **Ecological Health Score:** Species richness, soil carbon levels, water retention metrics.
   - **Care Economy Score:** Time-bank balances, skill-share hours, material reuse rates.

2. **Data Collection:** Citizen science apps, qualitative surveys, periodic ecological surveys.

## B. Participatory Action Research

- **Friendship-Ecology Co-Researchers:** Community members trained to collect data, conduct interviews, and present findings—ensuring research is action-oriented and locally grounded.

## C. Adaptive Ritual Design

- **Feedback Cycles:** Quarterly council reviews of RRI data; co-creation sprints to refine rituals, redistribute resources, and address emerging inequities or ecological stress.

## XII. Case Vignettes

### Vignette 1: The Regenerative Eco-Village in Andalusia

- **Overview:** A community of 60 friends and neighbors transforms arid land into a thriving food forest using SA planting circles, weekly AD "Regeneration Reports," and monthly VR-assisted water flow planning sessions. Over five years, soil organic carbon doubled, and relational trust scores soared by 80%.

### Vignette 2: Urban Rooftop Orchards in Tokyo

- **Context:** Apartment residents convert flat roofs into layered orchards. SA "Harvest Rituals" coincide with AD recipe exchanges; bio-sensor networks optimize microclimates. Participants report reduced stress levels, stronger neighborly bonds, and improved air quality metrics.

### Vignette 3: Indigenous-Led Coastal Restoration in British Columbia

- **Protocol:** A First Nations friendship circle integrates traditional clam garden protocols with friendship seed-ball exchanges inland. Joint SA beachwork sessions, supplemented by SD storytelling gatherings during winter, rebuild intergenerational ties and coastal ecosystems.

## XIII. Challenges, Pitfalls & Ethical Considerations

1. **Greenwashing Friendships:** Superficial adoption of ecological language without meaningful practice—use of "eco-friendly" buzzwords to mask extractive behaviors.
    - **Mitigation:** Insist on transparent metrics (RRI), third-party audits, and participatory governance.

2. **Extractivist Tendencies:** Friend circles sourcing materials (plants, water) without replenishment—reproducing the very harm they seek to resolve.

- **Mitigation:** Permaculture ethics: observe impact, design for regeneration, harvest only surplus.

3. **Cultural Appropriation:** Co-optation of indigenous rituals without consent or benefit to origin communities.

    - **Mitigation:** Partner with cultural stewards, share governance, and direct resources to traditional knowledge keepers.

4. **Accessibility & Inclusivity:** Ecological rituals demanding physical labor or mobility can exclude disabled or time-poor friends.

    - **Mitigation:** Provide adaptive roles, remote participation options, and honor diverse contributions.

# XIV. Planetary Friendship Futures: Visionary Prototypes

## A. Gaia Hackathons

- **Concept:** Global, month-long online/offline sprints where friendship networks co-design regenerative solutions—mycelial routing algorithms, community solar grids, ocean cleanup flotillas—culminating in embodied launch rituals.

## B. Digital-Biotic Twin Cities

- **Vision:** Cities digitally mirrored by living models—eco-botanically accurate simulations where friendship circles can test regenerative urban rituals (pop-up bramble hedges, ephemeral wetlands) before real-world deployment.

## C. Sympoietic Friendship Networks

- **Speculative Model:** Web3-enabled platforms where friendship tokens circulate not just among humans but with symbiotic non-human agents—pollinator drones, microbial assistants—blurring lines between social and ecological agency.

# XV. Conclusion: Seeding a Regenerative Legacy

Regenerative ReconneXion is a **radical expansion** of friendship—one that dissolves boundaries between humans and their more-than-human kin, embeds care into ecological cycles, and co-creates **thriving social-ecological systems**. This chapter has offered an **encyclopedic toolkit**: from bio-integrated spaces and permaculture-inspired social designs, to circular economies of care, tech-nature synergies, and participatory metrics.

The **call to action** is clear: let every friendship become a **seedbed of regeneration**, every ritual an **offer to the earth**, and every gathering a **promise of healing**. As we confront climate crises, social upheavals, and fractures in our communal lives, let us lean into the **power of regenerative friendship**—knowing that when we care for each other and the living world with equal devotion, we become architects of a future where **both people and planet flourish together**.

Chapter 19
Transcendent ReconneXion: Friendship, Spirituality, and Collective Consciousness

> "When hearts and minds converge beyond the ordinary, friendship becomes a sacred journey into shared transcendence."

# I. Introduction: Toward a Spiritual Ecology of Friendship

Across the preceding eighteen chapters, we have charted rituals—digital and analog, embodied and virtual, crisis-tested and regenerative—that cultivate presence, empathy, vulnerability, and intentionality. In **Chapter 19**, we ascend to a terrain where friendship evolves into a **spiritual practice**, a collective pilgrimage into depths of meaning, awe, and interconnectedness. **Transcendent ReconneXion** honors that friends can become guides and witnesses on one another's journeys toward expanded consciousness, where personal bonds interweave with the cosmos. We will explore:

1. **Conceptual Foundations:** Defining spiritual dimensions of friendship.

2. **Cosmic Presence Rituals:** Practices that dissolve boundaries between self, friend, and universe.

3. **Artistic Alchemy:** Collaborative art, music, and theater as portals to collective transcendence.

4. **Dreamwork and Symbolic Sharing:** Navigating the unconscious together.

5. **Shared Flow States:** Movement, creativity, and inquiry that produce group ecstasy.

6. **Psychedelic-Assisted Friendship Ceremonies:** Ethical, therapeutic microdosing and sacramental frameworks.

7. **Integration & Aftercare:** Grounding transcendent experiences into everyday life.

8. **Measuring the Ineffable:** Phenomenological and neurobiological approaches.

9. **Community Models:** Ashrams, monasteries, artist communes, and digital zendo networks.

10. **Ethical and Cultural Considerations:** Avoiding appropriation, ensuring consent, honoring diversity.

11. **Emerging Frontiers:** AI-mediated spiritual guides, virtual group transcendence pods, and telepathic interface experiments.

12. **Conclusion:** Friendship as the heart of collective awakening.

This chapter, longer than any before, offers step-by-step designs, adaptation variants, research insights, and visionary prototypes—inviting every reader to co-create ceremonies that uplift both individual souls and collective consciousness.

---

# II. Conceptual Foundations: Friendship as Spiritual Practice

### A. Friendship Beyond the Social: The Sacred Other

- **Theophany of the Friend:** Across traditions (Sufi "beloved," Christian "fellow traveler," Buddhist "kalyāṇa-mitta"), the friend becomes a mirror of the divine, a living icon through whom deeper truths are revealed.

- **Nondual Relationality:** Drawing on Advaita and Dzogchen, genuine friendship can transcend subject-object duality—two beings share a nondual space of awareness.

## B. Stages of Spiritual Friendship

1. **Companionship (Mitāphilya):** Mutual support and trust, laying the groundwork for deeper exploration.
2. **Inquiry Partnership (Sangha-Inquiry):** Joint questioning of assumptions, beliefs, and narratives.
3. **Witnessing Presence:** Silent bearing of each other's meditative or emotional states.
4. **Transcendence Catalysts:** Rituals and practices that actively induce shifts in perception, allowing glimpses of interconnected whole.

## C. Integrating Spiritual Traditions

- **Syncretic Openness:** Transcendent ReconneXion draws upon indigenous ceremonies, monastic disciplines, and modern contemplative modalities—synthesizing without appropriation.
- **Ethical Guardrails:** Ensuring cultural stewards lead foundational practices and that all participants maintain informed consent, especially when entering altered states.

---

# III. Cosmic Presence Rituals

## A. Star Gazing Circles (SA + AD Hybrid)

1. **Preparation:** Friends gather in a natural dark-sky site at dusk. Each brings a small lantern and a personal intention written on biodegradable paper.
2. **Opening Invocation:** A designated "Star Witness" reads an ancient invocation (e.g., from the Dogon or Polynesian star lore) honoring ancestors and cosmic guides.
3. **Silent Contemplation (20 min):** In circles of four, pairs sit back-to-back, breathing in unison as they gaze up. At 5-minute intervals, a soft bell sound cues role swap.

4. **Spoken Reflections (10 min):** After silence, each friend shares a cosmic insight or metaphor arising from the night sky—"I felt my worries shrink beneath Orion's belt."

5. **Digital Memory Capsule:** Photographs of constellations overlaid with reflections are posted in a private AD "Celestial Archive," annotated with coordinates and dates for future star communion.

## B. Sun Salutation Synchrony (SA)

- **Ritual Flow:** At summer solstice dawn, a group of friends performs an extended yoga sun salutation sequence (Sūrya Namaskāra) in perfect unison, each breath and posture aligned.

- **Depth Continuum:** Moves from Surface-Level (external alignment) in early repetitions to Deep-Level (interior awareness) as the practice proceeds—culminating in silent savasana as the sun rises fully.

## C. Breath of the Cosmos Meditation (SD + AA)

1. **Guided Audio:** A 30-minute online meditation mapping inhalations to the expansion of galaxies and exhalations to stellar collapse, narrated by a friend-facilitator.

2. **Personal Journal Prompts (AA):** After the session, participants receive prompts: "What inner horizons did you witness?" and "How does this cosmic breath inform our friendship?"

3. **Follow-Up SD Sharing:** A 60-minute video call where each reads a 2-3 minute excerpt from their journal, with active empathic listening protocols.

---

# IV. Artistic Alchemy: Collaborative Creation as Portal

## A. Mandala of Friendship Ritual

1. **Materials:** Colored sands, flower petals, small stones.

2. **Process (SA):**

- In concentric rings drawn on the ground, friends take turns depositing material while naming qualities they wish to cultivate (compassion, courage, joy).
- A silent circle walk around the emerging mandala allows witnessing of each contribution.

3. **Dissolution Ceremony:** After several hours, the mandala is dismantled in reverse order—friends scatter the sands into a river or garden bed, symbolizing impermanence and the flow of shared intentions.

## B. Group Improvisational Music (SA + SD)

- **Instruments:** Frame drums, tongue drums, chimes, soft bells.
- **Structure:**
    1. **Grounding Pulse (5 min):** A single drum sets a heartbeat.
    2. **Layering Voices (10 min):** One by one, friends add rhythmic or melodic phrases, building a living tapestry.
    3. **Free Expression (15 min):** Collective improvisation with no fixed structure—emergent harmony arises.
- **Integration:** A recording is sent AD to absent friends, inviting them to practice "listening presence" and contribute a digital track for a translocal symphony.

## C. Collective Theater of the Self

- **Mask-Making Workshop (AA + SA):** Friends craft masks representing their shadow selves—fear, longing, untapped potential.
- **Performance Circle (SA):** In a safe, dimly lit space, each friend dons their mask and enacts a 2-minute monologue in the third person ("The Fear struts in on shaky legs…"), witnessed by the group practicing nonjudgmental presence.
- **Group Reflection (SD):** A subsequent video debrief invites deeper vulnerability about aspects each found hardest to embody.

## V. Dreamwork and Symbolic Sharing

### A. Co-Dream Laboratory (AA + SD)

1. **Dream Journaling:** Each friend maintains a nightly dream log.

2. **Monthly Dream Salon (SD):** Participants share one dream (unfolded SL details, then DL imagery and emotion) while others engage in active imagination—asking open-ended questions ("What might the door symbolize for you?").

3. **Collaborative Dream Map (AA):** Key symbols and themes are plotted on a shared digital canvas, illustrating interlocking psyches.

### B. Vision Quest Circuits (SA)

- **Indigenous-Informed Structure:** With cultural consultation, friends embark on a guided 24-hour solo stay in nature with minimal provisions, returning to a communal circle to share visions, challenges, and newfound meanings.

- **Safety Integration:** Pair participants with "Guide Friends" who remain in proximate oversight, ensuring both ecstatic insight and physical safety.

## VI. Shared Flow States: Collective Ecstasy and Mastery

### A. Group Athletic Synchrony

- **Drum-Underwater Synchrony:** In a heated pool, friends practice synchronized treading and arm movements, accompanied by underwater music, culminating in breath-holding meditation circles—melding physical challenge with communal support.

### B. Creative Hackathons as Flow Rituals

- **"Innovation Jam" Format:** 48-hour co-creation sprints where friends solve a shared problem (social, ecological, artistic) using design sprint structures. Ritual elements include sunrise welcome ceremonies, midday embodied breaks, and dawn final presentations as ritual offerings.

## VII. Psychedelic-Assisted Friendship Ceremonies

*Note: All protocols must adhere to local laws, clinical guidelines, and informed consent.*

### A. Microdosing Circles (AD + AA)

1. **Preparation:** Friends agree on a shared dosing schedule (e.g., two days on, two days off) using microquantities (5–10 μg LSD or 0.1 g psilocybin).

2. **Daily Intentions (AA):** Morning journaling of intentions—"Today, I seek deeper empathy with Maya."

3. **Evening Reflective Circles (SD):** 30-minute video calls where each shares observations—changes in sensory perception, emotional openness.

### B. Sacramental Retreats (SA)

- **Structure (3-7 days):**

    1. **Set & Setting:** Held in nature sanctuaries, guided by trained facilitators and cultural stewards.

    2. **Group Ceremony:** Opening Invocations, individual journey spaces, mid-retreat sharing circles with deep empathy protocols.

    3. **Integration:** Post-ceremony integration circles over subsequent weeks (SD and SA), embedding insights into everyday rituals.

### C. Ethical Containers

- **Consent Circuits:** Rituals begin with explicit orientation on consent, trauma-informed facilitation, safe words, and aftercare plans.

- **Elder-Led Guidance:** Engage experienced mentors—indigenous elders, clinical psychologists—to hold ceremonial space and ensure cultural integrity.

# VIII. Integration & Aftercare: Grounding the Transcendent

## A. Twelve-Week Integration Programs

1. **Weekly SD Debriefs:** 60-minute calls for sharing struggles, synchronicities, and action steps inspired by transcendent rituals.

2. **AA Action Journals:** Structured prompts linking cosmic insights to concrete life changes—career pivots, relational shifts, creative projects.

## B. Ritual Anchor Objects

- **Sacred Tokens:** Friends receive small crystals, talismans, or seed packets blessed during ceremonies to serve as daily presence triggers.

## C. Community Check-Ins

- **Monthly "Transcendent ReconneXion" Newsletters:** Curated reflections, testimonials, and mini-ritual suggestions, fostering ongoing group cohesion.

---

# IX. Measuring the Ineffable: Phenomenological & Neurobiological Approaches

## A. Qualitative Phenomenology

- **Interview Protocols:** Deep-narrative interviews exploring shifts in identity, existential meaning, and relational depth post-ritual.

- **Thematic Analysis:** Coding transcripts for core themes—"expanded compassion," "cosmic belonging," "transcendent awe."

## B. Neuroimaging & Biometrics

1. **Portable EEG Studies:** Tracking frontal alpha coherence among friends during shared cosmic presence meditations.

2. **Endocrine Markers:** Salivary cortisol and oxytocin assays before and after rituals to quantify stress reduction and bonding.
3. **Heart-Brain Synchrony:** Simultaneous HRV and EEG measures to detect group entrainment in flow or meditative states.

### C. Mixed-Methods Synthesis

- **Integrated Reports:** Visual dashboards overlay subjective well-being scales with physiological markers, guiding future ritual refinements.

# X. Community Models: Ashrams, Artist Communes, and Digital Zendo Networks

## A. Friendship Ashrams

- **Structure:** Residential centers where friends live together part-time, engaging in daily spiritual practices (chanting, meditation, seva) and hosting Transcendent ReconneXion ceremonies.

## B. Creative Sanctuaries

- **Artist Fellowship Residencies:** Communal studios where artistic friendship rituals—sound mandalas, collective writing marathons—catalyze cross-disciplinary transcendence.

## C. Digital Zendo Networks

- **Global Vipassana Groups:** Online platforms offering daily 30-minute silent sits via livestream, followed by group check-ins—friends across time zones co-cultivate presence.

# XI. Ethical and Cultural Considerations

1. **Avoiding Cultural Appropriation:** Always partner with origin communities when adopting indigenous ceremonies; share benefits and leadership.

2. **Ensuring Informed Consent:** Especially for psychedelic and depth-level rituals—clear orientation, ongoing check-ins, opt-out options.

3. **Equity of Access:** Sliding-scale fees, scholarship seats, remote participation pathways to prevent exclusivity.

4. **Power Dynamics:** Rotate facilitation roles; transparent governance to prevent guru-cult dynamics.

# XII. Emerging Frontiers: AI-Mediated Spiritual Guides & Telepathy Interfaces

## A. AI Chaplains

- **Design:** LLMs trained on sacred texts and relational empathy protocols become 24/7 companionship bots—offering guided presence, personalized mantra generation, and reflective prompts.

## B. Virtual Group Transcendence Pods

- **Prototype:** Haptic-VR chambers where participants' biometric data converges to modulate shared environmental stimuli—wind, temperature, gravity shifts—crafting immersive ceremonial landscapes.

## C. Brain-to-Brain Interfaces

- **Speculative Horizon:** Noninvasive neural interfaces enabling direct sharing of emotional states or images—deepening witness presence and reducing ineffability barriers in friendship.

# XIII. Conclusion: Friendship as the Path to Collective Awakening

In this extended odyssey through the sacred dimensions of ReconneXion, we have seen that **true friendship** can become a **vehicle for spiritual evolution**, a canvas for collective art, a laboratory for consciousness, and a sanctuary for cosmic remembrance. As we chart these practices—rooted in ancient lineages and reimagined through cutting-edge research—we witness friendship's extraordinary power to dissolve isolation, cultivate compassion, and weave individuals into a **living tapestry of shared awakening**.

Now, equipped with this comprehensive, deeply detailed, and longer-than-ever chapter, practitioners may pioneer **Transcendent ReconneXion** rituals—tailored to local cultures, ecological contexts, and technological frontiers—ensuring that friendship not only thrives but becomes the very heartbeat of collective transformation. May these pages serve as both **guidebook and inspiration**, calling us onward to friendships that **touch the stars, heal the earth, and awaken the divine in all of us**.


Chapter 20
Integration and the Living Legacy of ReconneXion

> "The end of a journey is but the threshold of a new path—one we walk together, weaving connection into every moment of our shared lives."

---

# I. Introduction: From Completion to Continuation

Having traversed twenty chapters of theory, practice, and visionary design—from the foundations of modality and depth, through embodied, crisis-tested, regenerative, and transcendent rituals—we arrive at the final waypoint: **Integration**. This chapter is neither epilogue nor farewell, but a **launchpad** for the living, evolving practice of ReconneXion. Here we chart how individuals, friendship networks, organizations, and global communities can:

- **Synthesize** the full tapestry of ReconneXion insights.
- **Institutionalize** rituals into sustainable cultures and systems.
- **Innovate** continuously, adapting to new challenges and emerging technologies.

- **Share** and co-create an open commons of rituals, research, and resources.
- **Commit** personally and collectively to a lifelong path of deep connection.

In **Chapter 20**, we offer an exhaustive guide to ensuring that ReconneXion is not a static doctrine but a **living legacy**, ever-renewing itself through practice, reflection, and partnership. Let us begin the integration.

---

## II. Synthesizing Core Themes: A Meta-Ritual Mapping

### A. Revisiting the Four Pillars and Modalities

1. **Presence:**
   - From five-minute morning calls to "Circle of Presence" ceremonies, presence is the bedrock—anchoring attention in each modality.

2. **Intentionality:**
   - Manifested in scheduled "friend dates," curated emails, and vision-quest commitments, intentionality transforms connection from happenstance into purpose.

3. **Empathy:**
   - Found in micro-breaks, collective breathing, and empathy micro-audit dashboards, empathy fuels trust and mutual understanding.

4. **Vulnerability:**
   - In letter exchanges, Soul Mandalas, and dream-work, vulnerability opens the heart's fullest bandwidth to true reconciliation.

### B. Modalities & Depth in Concert

- **Synchronous Analog (SA):** Richest in nonverbal cues and embodiment—walking conversations, drum circles.

- **Synchronous Digital (SD):** Enables global salons, VR pilgrimages, AI-assisted presence bots.

- **Asynchronous Analog (AA):** Handwritten letters, seed-ball ceremonies, craft-based co-creation.

- **Asynchronous Digital (AD):** Voice-note chains, gratitude forums, AI-driven reflection prompts.

Every ritual is a **point** in this multidimensional space; integration requires mapping existing practices onto the matrix, identifying gaps, and designing new rituals to maintain balance.

---

## III. Meta-Rituals: Ritualizing Ritual Creation and Evolution

### A. The Ritual Incubator Process

1. **Scan & Sense:** Quarterly gatherings where reconnection councils survey emerging needs—burnout hotspots, modality drift, ecological stress.

2. **Prototype & Pilot:** Small "Tiny Ritual Labs" test new ideas over four-week sprints.

3. **Reflect & Refine:** Mixed-methods evaluation—participant narratives, biometric snapshots, engagement analytics.

4. **Scale & Share:** Successful prototypes are published to the communal ritual library, complete with facilitation guides and adaptation notes.

### B. Ritual Audit Rhythms

- **Daily Micro-Checks:** Quick yes/no prompts: "Did I practice presence today?"

- **Weekly Focused Surveys:** 5-question forms evaluating depth, diversity of modalities, and emotional bank balance.

- **Monthly Council Reviews:** Data-driven dialogues generating a "Ritual Renewal Charter."

- **Annual Re-Enchantment Festivals:** Festivals where communities collectively retire, refresh, or reinvent core rituals.

# IV. Institutionalizing ReconneXion

## A. Education & Curriculum Integration

1. **K–12 Frameworks:**

   - **Daily Morning Circles:** Adapted versions of "Feeling Ball" check-ins for classrooms.

   - **Permaculture Friendship Projects:** Science classes integrate community gardens and friendship time banks into learning outcomes.

2. **Higher Education:**

   - **Living-Lab Residencies:** Students co-design campus reconnection spaces and lead embodied micro-rituals as part of coursework.

   - **Accredited Courses:** Certificates in ReconneXion Facilitation co-offered by departments of psychology, design, and sustainability.

## B. Corporate & Nonprofit Adoption

1. **ReconneXion Governance Charter:**

   - Every organization ratifies a charter codifying the Four Pillars, Ritual Calendars, and Ethical Guidelines.

2. **Dedicated Roles:**

   - **Chief Reconnection Officer**, ReconneXion Ambassadors, and Ritual Councils ensure ongoing stewardship.

3. **Well-Being Metrics:**

   - Integrate ReconneXion KPIs (connection satisfaction, ritual participation, empathy contributions) into performance dashboards alongside financial and operational indicators.

## C. Public Policy & Urban Design

1. **Regenerative Zoning:**
   - Planning codes mandating public Friendship Gardens, communal hearths, and reconnection corridors in new developments.

2. **Civic Ritual Funding:**
   - Municipal grants for community-initiated ReconneXion projects—could include seed-ball days, Story Salons in public libraries, or solar-powered ritual kiosks.

# V. Research and Innovation Roadmap

## A. Interdisciplinary Collaborations

1. **Social Neuroscience & Ritual Efficacy:**
   - Joint labs measuring neural synchrony, HRV, and oxytocin levels during varied rituals.

2. **AI Ethics & Facilitation Tools:**
   - Workshops with ethicists guiding the design of AI empathy bots, consent protocols, and bias audits.

3. **Anthropology & Cultural Adaptations:**
   - Fieldwork with indigenous communities to co-design context-specific reconnection rituals, respecting sovereignty and traditional knowledge.

## B. Longitudinal Studies

- **Friendship Cohort Tracking:** Studies following friend groups over a decade to correlate ritual engagement with well-being, career progression, and social capital.
- **Ecological Impact Research:** Measuring how regenerative friendship gardens affect local biodiversity, soil health, and community cohesion.

## C. Open-Source Ritual Library

- **Digital Commons:** A wiki-style platform where practitioners share facilitation guides, multimedia tutorials, and translation modules.
- **Creative Commons Licensing:** Ensuring rituals remain freely available, with attribution requirements to honor originators.

# VI. Training the Next Generation: Curriculum, Certifications, Apprenticeships

## A. Modular Learning Pathways

1. **Foundational Modules:**
    - **Module 1:** ReconneXion Principles & Pillars.
    - **Module 2:** Ritual Design & Facilitation Skills.
    - **Module 3:** Embodied and Sensory Practices.

2. **Specialization Tracks:**
    - **Crisis ReconneXion Leadership, Regenerative Ecology Facilitation, Transcendent & Psychedelic Integration, AI-Augmented Reconnection.**

## B. Apprenticeship & Mentorship

- **Peer Pairings:** New facilitators apprentice under veterans for six months, co-leading rituals and receiving reflective coaching.
- **Capstone Projects:** Each candidate designs and implements a novel ritual series, documented with impact data and participant testimonials.

## C. Professional Credentials

- Levels:
    - **Certified ReconneXion Practitioner** (CRP).

- **Advanced Reconnection Facilitator** (ARF).
- **Master Ritual Architect** (MRA)—reserved for those with sustained impact and original contributions to the ritual commons.

# VII. Global Movements: Networks, Alliances, and Cross-Cultural Confluences

## A. International ReconneXion Federation

- **Structure:** A decentralized alliance of national and regional chapters, each curating localized ritual banks and coordinating international festivals.
- **Annual Convergence:** Rotating host cities hold multi-day gatherings—featuring cross-cultural Story Salons, permaculture-friendship workshops, and tech-nature hackathons.

## B. Digital Diaspora Networks

- **Global Friendship Pods:** Small, transnational micro-communities connected through AD apps and periodic SD micro-retreats—fostering diaspora solidarity and cultural exchange.
- **Cultural Translation Guilds:** Volunteers translate ritual scripts and guides into dozens of languages, adapting symbols and metaphors for local fidelity.

## C. Meta-Ritual Collaboratories

- **Online Platforms:** Virtual labs where designers, researchers, and practitioners collaborate on next-gen rituals—co-authoring interactive digital-analog hybrid experiences.
- **Open Calls & Ritual Jams:** Periodic thematic hackathon events (e.g., "Rituals for Climate Hope," "Rituals of Social Justice") inviting global participants to prototype and share.

## VIII. Digital Commons and Open-Source Rituals

### A. Ritual Libraries & Repositories

- **Structure:** Hierarchical indexing by modality, depth level, context, cultural origin, and resource requirements.
- **User Contributions:** Submission workflows for new rituals, complete with step-by-step facilitation notes, adaptation variants, and participant feedback summaries.

### B. Licensing & Attribution

- **Creative Commons – Attribution-ShareAlike (CC BY-SA):** Rituals can be freely adapted and shared, provided originators are credited and derivatives use the same license.
- **Cultural License Addenda:** For indigenous or marginalized communities, additional protocols ensure benefit-sharing and custodial authority.

### C. Collaborative Authoring Tools

- **Interactive Editors:** WYSIWYG ritual-design platforms enabling co-creation of multimedia facilitation guides.
- **Version Control:** Git-style tracks of ritual evolution, enabling practitioners to branch, merge, and iterate on collective designs.

---

## IX. Sustaining Momentum: Avoiding Atrophy, Curating Novelty, Periodic Audits

### A. Ritual Lifecycle Management

1. **Innovation Phase:** Ideation, piloting, and prototyping new rituals.
2. **Expansion Phase:** Scaling to broader networks, training facilitators.
3. **Maturity Phase:** Rituals become cultural habits—risking mechanization.

4. **Renewal Phase:** Intentional retirement, reinvention, or transformation into new forms.

## B. Curiosity-Driven Variations

- **Ritual Remix Workshops:** Quarterly gatherings where friends remix core rituals—shuffling sequences, substituting modalities, integrating topical themes.
- **Elemental Rotations:** Each month, rituals emphasize a different element—earth, water, fire, air—ensuring symbolic diversity and sensory freshness.

## C. Meta-Audits

- **Balance Scorecards:** Tracking modality distribution, depth diversity, and demographic inclusion.
- **Sentinel Indicators:** Early warnings of ritual fatigue—drop in participation rates, increased drop-off after digital micro-rituals, qualitative feedback of "staleness."

---

# X. Personal Commitment: Lifelong Ritual Practice

## A. Daily Ritual Portfolio

1. **Micro-Presence:** Three-second pauses or friend-facing glances.
2. **Micro-Breaths:** Two synchronized breaths with a partner or distant friend.
3. **Micro-Gratitudes:** One-sentence voice note or text.

## B. Weekly & Monthly Anchors

- **Weekly:** One DL–SA conversation, one DL–SD salon, one AA craft exchange.
- **Monthly:** Story Salon, embodied ritual (dance or nature immersion), regeneration ceremony (seed-ball or garden share).

## C. Personal Journal Templates

- **Quarterly Reflection Framework:** Adapt from Chapter 13's self-assessment: modality tallies, depth scores, emotional bank account deposits/withdrawals, one "sacred vow" for next quarter.
- **Legacy Log:** A living document tracing ritual evolution in one's life—capturing key breakthroughs, co-facilitator learnings, and cross-cultural insights.

## XI. Reflection and Next Steps: Invitation to Co-Creation

1. **Share Your Story:** Submit your ReconneXion journey to the global archive—your triumphs, stumbles, and emergent rituals.
2. **Mentor Others:** Pair as ritual mentors for newcomers, sustaining the cycle of apprentice→practitioner→master.
3. **Collaborate Across Boundaries:** Seek out partnerships beyond your usual circles—environmental groups, spiritual centers, tech hubs—to pilot hybrid rituals.
4. **Contribute to Research:** Participate in open-science studies, grant access to anonymized practice data, co-author publications.
5. **Advocate for Policy Change:** Engage local governments to adopt reconnection metrics in well-being indices and urban planning.

## XII. Conclusion: Friendship as the Fabric of a New World

In closing this twentieth and final chapter, we stand on the shoulders of eighteen prior explorations—each a step toward a vision of **friendship that is dynamic, regenerative, transcendent, and woven into every facet of life**. ReconneXion is not an end state but a **perpetual practice**, calling us to show up, to listen, to feel, to co-create, and to leave the world richer for our presence.

As you move forward, may you carry:

- **The Four Pillars** in your heart.

- **The Modalities** at your fingertips.

- **The Depth Continuum** as your compass.

- **The Ritual Banks** as your toolkit.

- **The Global Commons** as your community.

Our collective calling: to transform separate moments of connection into a continuous **tapestry of belonging**, stretching across continents, generations, and the living earth itself. May ReconneXion inspire every handshake, every shared breath, every ritual circle, and every story told beneath the stars—knowing that when we choose connection, we shape a future of profound shared well-being for all.

Made in the USA
Columbia, SC
20 June 2025